Unconquerable Nation

Knowing Our Enemy
Strengthening Ourselves

Brian Michael Jenkins

This book results from the RAND Corporation's continuing program of self-initiated research. Support for such research is provided, in part, by the generosity of RAND's donors and by the fees earned on client-funded research. RAND is a nonprofit institution that helps improve policy and decisionmaking through research and analysis. Opinions expressed in this book are those of the author and do not reflect positions taken by RAND, its board, or its clients.

Library of Congress Cataloging-in-Publication Data

Jenkins, Brian Michael.
Unconquerable nation : knowing our enemy, strengthening ourselves / Brian Michael Jenkins.
p. cm.
Includes bibliographical references.
ISBN-13: 978-0-8330-3891-3 (pbk. : alk. paper)
ISBN-13: 978-0-8330-3893-7 (hardcover : alk. paper)
1. Terrorism—United States. 2. Terrorism—United States—Prevention. I. Title.

HV6432.J46 2006
363.325'1560973—dc22

2006017631

The RAND Corporation is a nonprofit research organization providing objective analysis and effective solutions that address the challenges facing the public and private sectors around the world. RAND's publications do not necessarily reflect the opinions of its research clients and sponsors.

RAND® is a registered trademark.

Published 2006 by the RAND Corporation
1776 Main Street, P.O. Box 2138, Santa Monica, CA 90407-2138
1200 South Hayes Street, Arlington, VA 22202-5050
4570 Fifth Avenue, Suite 600, Pittsburgh, PA 15213-2665
RAND URL: http://www.rand.org/
To order RAND documents or to obtain additional information, contact
Distribution Services: Telephone: (310) 451-7002;
Fax: (310) 451-6915; Email: order@rand.org

"Being unconquerable lies with yourself."

Sun Tzu
Fifth century B.C.

Foreword

In this book, Brian Michael Jenkins draws on 40 years of research on terrorism, most of it conducted at the RAND Corporation. He has played numerous leadership roles at RAND over those years and is today my senior advisor. But his most enduring contributions have been the fruits of his research efforts.

In Brian's early days at RAND in the 1960s, he focused on the insurgencies in Vietnam and Cambodia, on Vietnamese military institutions, and on the styles and techniques of conflict.

In the late 1960s, Brian began drawing parallels between the rise of urbanization in the war in Vietnam and trends taking place in other parts of Asia and Latin America. The theory of guerrilla warfare as a strictly rural activity was being challenged as the guerrillas were taking their struggles to the cities. By outlining a five-stage process by which urban guerrillas could take over a city, he was able to make recommendations for government countermeasures.

In 1972, in the wake of the murder of Olympic athletes in Munich and the random carnage at Tel Aviv's Lod Airport, Brian circulated an internal note at RAND setting forth an agenda for the study of international terrorism. In that document, Brian cited terrorism as being a new element in international relations that to date had had little systematic examination. He recommended that RAND undertake a study of international terrorism as a potential nonmilitary threat to national security and suggested the following as possibly useful studies: the nature of the threat itself, probable future trends, the feasible limits of providing protection beyond national borders for one's own citizens, the diplomacy of terror, and the technology of terrorism and counterterrorism.

To begin the systematic examination he prescribed, Brian spearheaded the development of a number of datasets and archives at RAND charting terrorist activity since 1968, the year regarded as marking the advent of modern international terrorism. This quickly evolved into the classification of terrorist incidents by tactic, target, country of occurrence, perpetrator, and other categories. The terrorism chronology begun by Brian in 1972 is still regarded as central to RAND's terrorism research activities, providing a peerless ability to combine contemporary awareness with historical trend analysis. Meanwhile, Brian and others at RAND began to use heuristic modeling to help analysts articulate the assumptions that lay behind "intuitive" judgments.

One of the immediate challenges handed to RAND was assisting the U.S. Department of State to develop a policy and set of tactics for dealing with situations where terrorists were holding hostages—how does one bargain for a human life? This assignment also led to an examination of the experiences of those who had been held hostage and ultimately to a training program given to U.S. diplomats and others being sent to high-risk areas.

In the mid-1970s, Brian was studying the impact of new technology on low-level violence. He reported that violence for dramatic effect was flourishing. By the late 1970s, he was exploring the terrorist mindset and terrorist decisionmaking. More than 20 years before 9/11, Brian testified before the U.S. Senate Governmental Affairs Committee, suggesting establishment of a permanent small staff to support the proposed Council to Combat Terrorism, detailing the advantages of such a staff, and concluding that the fight against terrorism would remain a continuing task.

Throughout the 1980s, Brian's research on terrorism continued to be relevant. He explored the psychological implications of media-transmitted terrorism, developed frameworks for studying terrorist groups, summarized the intelligence constraints in the investigation of terrorism, examined the terrorist threat to commercial aviation as well as to the maritime community, and cautioned his listeners to be prudent but not paranoid.

Brian's study of terrorism continued through the 1990s, although for the early part of that decade he was not on staff at RAND. By the late 1990s, he was back at RAND and working with RAND staff on a seminal piece, *Countering the New Terrorism.*

Countering the jihadist enterprise has been his focus since 9/11, and his work on deterrence and influence in counterterrorism offers a multifaceted strategy that includes attempting to influence those elements of terrorist systems that may be deterrable, while preserving core American values.

It might be tempting to call this book the capstone of Brian's research career, but this is almost certainly not the case. Brian's energy, intellectual curiosity, and deep commitment to the United States and its principles ensure that we will all benefit from his work well into the future. Let's call this an interim report, based on the first 40 years of Brian's work.

I want to acknowledge the role of RAND's many clients over those years in making possible RAND's research on terrorism and the role of RAND's donors in helping make this book a reality.

James A. Thomson
President and Chief Executive Officer
RAND Corporation

June 2006

Contents

Acknowledgments

Although I alone am responsible for the ideas related in this volume, many people helped me to refine my thinking and express myself more clearly. I am especially indebted to David Cohen and Greg Treverton for their thoughtful and thorough reviews. I have benefited no less from the many informative conversations we have had over the years.

Secretary of State George Shultz, Governor James Gilmore, and Ambassador L. Paul Bremer also read the manuscript and offered me the benefit of their vast firsthand experience in addressing these issues. I also want to thank my RAND colleagues, in particular, David Aaron, Paul Davis, Michael Rich, Brent Bradley, and Alan Hoffman, who readily exposed any evidence of sloppy thinking or exposition. Larry Sanchez and Sam Rascoff of the New York Police Department, LTC (retired) James MacNamara, and James Fallows provided additional written commentaries.

John Godges, David Egner, and especially Janet DeLand, with whom I have worked for many years, made the writing better and also provided continued encouragement when paragraphs became stubborn thickets that blocked forward progress.

My thanks also to the able publications team, Jane Ryan, Paul Murphy, Ron Miller, John Warren, Todd Duft, Kelly Schwartz, Pamela Van Huss, and Peter Soriano.

To all of RAND's librarians, and especially Roberta Shanman, Barbara Neff, and Kristin McCool, I am indebted for their assistance in tracking down often arcane information.

The public erroneously assumes that RAND research can always depend on generous and farsighted government funding. The fact is, creative research projects outside of the mainstream of current government concerns often find little support. While it may seem odd given the nation's current attention to terrorism, RAND's research on terrorism for many years subsisted in a wilderness where government attention was episodic and support was minimal. I am indebted to RAND's two presidents since 1972, Don Rice and Jim Thomson, both of whom invested RAND's own precious resources to sustain the research program when formal government interest in analysis of terrorism and counterterrorism waned.

Finally, my very special thanks to Terry, who with astonishing patience and good nature, typed and retyped endless revisions, demanded explanations on behalf of future readers, and told me when it was time to put my pen down and work out my irritability at the gym.

Unconquerable Nation

Historic American Engineering Record/Jack E. Boucher

Instead of surrendering our liberties
in the name of security, we must embrace liberty
as the source and sustenance of our security.

CHAPTER ONE

How We Prevail

Secret Service agents gunned down the first team of assassins before they got to the President, but it was a close call. A second team of gunmen managed to get into the House of Representatives, where they wounded five congressmen. A terrorist bomb caused damage but no casualties at the Senate. Troops took up positions at the Capitol and the White House, both of which had been set ablaze. By sundown, Washington was sliding out of control; columns of black smoke could be seen for miles. Authorities were unable to save the White House, which was completely destroyed by fire.

In New York City, a huge vehicle bomb exploded on Wall Street, killing 33 people and wounding more than 400. Another bomb exploded in downtown Los Angeles, killing at least 20. Yet another bomb killed and maimed hundreds in the heartland. An explosion leveled a Texas town, while fires destroyed most of Chicago and San Francisco.

That was not as bad, however, as an inexplicable deadly epidemic that hit the nation's capital in the summer. By autumn, one-tenth of the city's population had died. Similar deadly outbreaks swept across the country. Nationwide, 1 in 200 Americans died. Cities announced their own blockades against those fleeing the stricken areas. The fabric of society was unraveling with riots and looting.

Following riots, the Army patrolled the streets in Washington, Detroit, and Los Angeles; 120,000 people were interned as potential subversives. The worst crisis, however, was the receipt of a credible nuclear threat.

All this is not some hypothetical future terrorist scenario invented by the U.S. Department of Homeland Security to test preparedness, the screenplay for a new Hollywood disaster thriller, or a survivalist fantasy. All of the events listed above, in fact, occurred during the course of America's history.

In 1950, assassins tried to rush Blair House, where President Truman was staying while renovations were under way at the White House. In 1954, terrorists opened fire on the House of Representatives. A bomb caused heavy damage to the Senate in 1983. And British troops burned down the White House and part of the newly constructed Capitol building in 1814, when only a rainstorm saved the rest of Washington.

A horse-drawn cart filled with explosives (an early vehicle bomb) blew up on Wall Street in 1920, and suspected members of the Dynamite Conspiracy set off a huge bomb in Los Angeles in 1910. Timothy McVeigh's bomb killed 168 people in Oklahoma City in 1995.

In 1947, a ship loaded with nitrate fertilizer blew up, leveling Texas City. The city of Chicago was destroyed by fire in 1871. San Francisco was destroyed by fire following the 1906 earthquake.

In 1793, yellow fever killed 5,000 people, one-tenth of the total population of Philadelphia, which at the time was the nation's capital. Subsequent yellow fever and cholera outbreaks killed thousands in American cities during the nineteenth century, but none of these outbreaks compared with the Spanish flu epidemic of 1918–1919, which killed approximately 600,000 people in the United States and between 25 and 50 million worldwide.

Race riots required calling out the National Guard and federal troops in a number of cities in the second half of the twentieth century. I personally watched the columns of smoke through a train window as the train pulled out of Union Station in Washington, DC, on April 14, 1968, at the beginning of the widespread race riots following the assassination of Rev. Martin Luther King, Jr. During World War II, 120,000 Japanese-Americans were interned.

The most terrifying incident of the Cold War, the Cuban missile crisis, occurred in 1962, when the two superpowers stood nose to nose, armed forces on high alert on both sides, nuclear weapons at the ready.

America's Dark Moments

There have been many dark moments in America's history. Almost everyone's short list includes the destruction of the World Trade Center towers on September 11, 2001; the December 7, 1941, attack on Pearl Harbor and World War II; the Civil War; the 1929 stock market crash and the Great Depression; the assassination of President John F. Kennedy. Most Americans would also include the burning of the nation's capital by British troops in 1814, the Chicago fire, the Johnstown flood, the San Francisco earthquake, and the Spanish flu and other epidemics.

Loss of life is the common element in all these crises. For a nation seen by many in the world as bellicose, Americans themselves see the casualties of war as disaster. The Civil War, in which 558,000 died, tops the list, followed by World War II with 407,000 Americans dead, World War I with 117,000 U.S. deaths, the Vietnam War with 58,000 Americans dead, and the Korean War with 37,000 Americans dead. And whatever criticism we may heap upon our presidents while they are in office, we are angered and dismayed when they are physically attacked.

We also include poverty and suffering among our darkest historical moments. Noteworthy are the events that represent the lack or loss of values: slavery and continuing racial discrimination, the annihilation and dispossession of native Americans, the ruthless suppression of striking workers in the nineteenth century, the internment of Japanese-Americans during World War II, the "witch hunts" for communists in the 1950s, the Watergate scandal in the 1970s. The singling out of these events as America's dark moments reflects the values Americans hold dear: life, the inalienable rights of all people, equal justice for all, security in its broadest sense, fair play, political morality.

Just as noteworthy are the omissions. Americans do not dwell much on abstract issues such as past humiliations (including those in Vietnam and Iran), perceived insults to national honor, challenges to the nation's rightful place in the world, assaults upon our religious beliefs and moral values. These are the types of concerns voiced by our terrorist adversaries.

It is also noteworthy that Americans view the nation's dark moments as summons to courage, opportunities to reflect and to do what is right. Each dark moment is seen as a challenge, awful at the time, but ultimately met—not a descent into darkness.

As the United States faces a new array of threats that arose at the end of the Cold War and were so stunningly clarified on September 11, 2001, Americans are again summoned to demonstrate courage, to draw upon deep traditions of determination in the face of risk, to show self-reliance and resiliency. There has been too much fear-mongering since 9/11. We are not a nation of victims cowering under the kitchen table. We cannot expect protection against all risk. Too many Americans have died defending liberty for us to easily surrender it now to terror.

We should heed the admonition that President Franklin Delano Roosevelt delivered in his 1933 inaugural address: "Let me assert my firm belief that the only thing we have to fear is fear itself—nameless, unreasoning, unjustified terror which paralyzes needed efforts to convert retreat into advance."

It should not be fear that propels us, but confidence that we will ultimately prevail. We have never been driven forward by fear. At our best, we have been defined by our visions.

Strategy for an Unconquerable Nation

The title of this book is *Unconquerable Nation.* The phrase derives from a quote by the ancient Chinese strategist Sun Tzu, who 25 centuries ago wrote, "Being unconquerable lies with yourself."[1] The choice of this title does not signal an attempt to apply the principles of Sun Tzu's ancient treatise on the art of war to the current war on terrorism. Sun Tzu's passages tend to be abstract, cryptic, sometimes opaque, and therefore subject to continuous interpretation, which may, in part, explain their enduring appeal.

Sun Tzu offers inspiration, not precise instructions. His philosophy of war is straightforward. Warfare, which had by the 5th century B.C. become a large-scale enterprise, requires popular support and proper strategy. That strategy must be based on a thorough understanding of the enemy and of one's own strengths and weaknesses. "Being unconquerable" means knowing oneself, but as understood by the ancient strategists, "knowing" means much more than the mere acquisition of knowledge. "Knowing oneself" means preserving one's spirit, a broad term. "Being unconquerable" includes not only disciplined troops and strong walls, but also confidence, courage, commitment—the opposite of terror and fear.

One can easily see the appeal of this construct in the context of current circumstances. This philosophy alters Americans' mental model of today's conflict. It elevates the necessity of knowing the enemy, something we have not made sufficient effort to do. It moves us from relying almost exclusively on the projection of military power and viewing homeland security as physical protection to mobilizing our spirit, courage, and commitment. While we strive to destroy our terrorist enemies by reducing their capabilities, thwarting their plans, frustrating their strategy, and crushing their spirit, we must also rely on our own psychological strength to defeat the terror they would create. Instead of issuing constant warnings and alarms, we must project stoicism and resolve. Instead of surrendering our liberties in the name of security, we must embrace liberty as the source and sustenance of our security.

Looking Back

This book is based in part on objective research, particularly as it applies to knowing the enemy, and it also includes the personal reflections of someone who has thought about terrorism for a long time. I initiated RAND's research on terrorism in 1972 with a simple memorandum, which observed that this phenomenon was likely to spread and increase and could create serious problems for the United States and its allies; I proposed that we should therefore take a serious look at it.

It required little prescience to make that statement in 1972. By then, Palestinian extremists had already begun to sabotage and hijack airliners; urban guerrillas in Latin America were regularly kidnapping foreign diplomats and demanding the release of their imprisoned comrades, a tactic that quickly spread to Europe and the Middle East; the first terrorist groups had appeared in Europe and Japan; and terrorist bombings had become increasingly common. One had only to take a few small steps beyond the headlines of the day to see these disparate tactics merging to form a new mode of conflict.

Certainly, I was not able to foresee the remarkable trajectory of terrorism over the next three and one-half decades. I did not forecast terrorists holding hostage Olympic athletes, OPEC oil ministers, hundreds of passengers aboard a cruise ship, guests at an embassy party in Lima, or hundreds of theatergoers in Moscow; bombs on trains and subways in Paris, Moscow, Madrid, Manila, and London; nerve gas on Tokyo's subways; the Senate Office Building contaminated with anthrax; huge truck bombs exploding in the center of London and the middle of Oklahoma; suicide bombers strapped with explosives walking into restaurants, shopping malls, buses, and hotel lobbies or driving trucks into embassies, synagogues, and mosques; jumbo jets blown out of the sky; hijacked planes flown into skyscrapers. Any predictions of these terrible events would have been dismissed in 1972 as the stuff of fantasy and hysteria.

Longevity in a particular subject matter does not guarantee wisdom or insight, but it does permit perspective. It provides a firsthand opportunity not only to recall events, but to recall what else was going on during each event—a difficult war in Vietnam, a crisis in the Middle East, another Cold War confrontation—providing a context that newcomers to a subject sometimes miss.

It is wrong, for example, to view the history of America's previous efforts to counter terrorism through the dust and debris of the 9/11 terrorist attacks, as some government officials have done. The scale of those attacks completely altered the context in which subsequent decisions were made. Responses that were unimaginable before 9/11 became mandatory afterwards. The world changed. Yet we had also learned valuable lessons during the three decades of counterterrorist efforts prior to 9/11. While 9/11 demanded new responses, all that we had done beforehand was not mistaken or futile.

At the same time, longevity imposes humility. Thirty years ago, I thought I knew more about terrorism and knew it with far greater certainty than I do today. Beneath the patina of authority that comes with time, a long perspective obliges one to review and revise one's own earlier forecasts and conclusions.

The Growth of Terrorism Research

Terrorist tactics have a long history, but contemporary international terrorism is a relatively recent phenomenon. The first airline hijacking for political ends occurred in 1968, and the first successful kidnapping of a diplomat by urban guerrillas in modern times took place in 1969. The two events that galvanized worldwide concern and led, in the United States, to the creation of the Cabinet Committee to Combat Terrorism—the Lod Airport massacre in Israel and the murder of athletes at the Munich Olympics—occurred in 1972. These events mark the beginning of terrorism as a new mode of conflict.

The term "international terrorism" was not created by its practitioners; it was an artificial term invented by analysts. In the early 1970s, participants in ongoing wars sometimes employed terrorist tactics; indeed, the entire repertoire of some small urban guerrilla groups fell into the category of terrorism. Some terrorist events spilled over into the international domain in the form of hijackings, attacks on foreign targets, or terrorists themselves going abroad to pursue their campaigns. All these events were aggregated into a separate field of political violence.

The initial concern of Americans was not the conflicts themselves; rather, we were concerned with preventing the conflicts from spilling over into the international domain. Uruguayans kidnapping other Uruguayans in Uruguay was unfortunate, but it was a matter for the local authorities. Uruguayans kidnapping foreign diplomats, on the other hand, became an international matter. I mention this as a caution to those who may reach too far in attempts to correlate the incidence of terrorism with social, economic, or other attributes of society. Terrorism, particularly international terrorism, which is our main concern, is a small, artificially defined segment of political violence. Moreover, it represents the actions of very small groups. We must keep that in mind when looking for root causes.

Looking back, it seems now that the analysts of terrorism not only defined the issue, but also may have given terrorism greater coherence than the terrorists did themselves. Carlos Marighella, the leader of an urban guerrilla group in Brazil, wrote the *Mini-Manual of the Urban Guerrilla*, and a few other early veterans offered advice, but the first generation of terrorist practitioners seldom viewed their own employment of terrorist tactics as a distinct mode of armed conflict or thought of it in terms of a coherent strategy.[2] It was the analysts who put terrorist tactics into a broader context and, in so doing, contributed to a theory of terrorism.

How Terrorism Has Changed

Terrorism has changed dramatically since the events of the late 1960s. There appear to be fewer conflicts and fewer terrorist organizations today. Traditional political ideology, the engine of conflict in the 1970s and 1980s, has declined as a motivating force, while the force of ideologies drawing upon religion has increased.

The most dramatic change has been the escalation of terrorism. More than 30 years ago, I wrote that "terrorists want a lot of people watching, not a lot of people dead." The phrase became an aphorism. It meant that terrorist concerns about self-image, group cohesion, not alienating perceived constituents, or provoking public backlash imposed constraints on their actions.

These self-imposed constraints were not universal or immutable, and by the mid-1980s, it was clear that they were eroding. As I noted in a paper I delivered at a conference in 1985, "the number of incidents with fatalities and multiple fatalities has increased." More alarming was "the growing number of incidents of large-scale, indiscriminate violence." Terrorists were detonating huge car bombs on city streets and planting bombs aboard trains and airliners, in airline terminals, at railroad stations, and in hotel lobbies, "all calculated to kill in quantity."[3]

There are several explanations for the escalation. Terrorists themselves had become increasingly brutalized and more proficient. As terrorism became more commonplace, maintaining public attention and coercive power required escalation. Internal dynamics were at work, too. Fainthearted terrorists were being shoved aside by more-ruthless elements, while political fanatics were giving way to religious fanatics who claimed God's mandate, allowing them to ignore ordinary moral constraints. These tendencies culminated in the attacks of September 11, 2001.

Today, many (although not all) terrorists want a lot of people watching *and* a lot of people dead. The most recent terrorist attacks have had as their paramount goal the highest body count possible. We see this in recent jihadist operations around the world. Only the lack of means has prevented greater carnage.

Killing in quantity is difficult, although there is still room for escalation beyond the 9/11 benchmark. Since 9/11, about 40 people, on average, have died in each major jihadist terrorist attack. Return on investment per bomb runs between 12 and 20 fatalities. Achieving more fatalities requires multiple coordinated attacks—ten bombs in Madrid, four in London, three in Amman. Chemical and biological agents have already been used, although with limited results. Not surprisingly, the most significant attacks have been carried out by cult members or religious fanatics.

Yet our worst fears about what terrorists might do have not been realized. Chemical and biological terrorism have been of concern for decades. According to a survey taken more than 20 years ago, most terrorism experts had thought that terrorists would attack with chemical weapons by the end of the century, a forecast confirmed in 1995 with the release of nerve gas on Tokyo's subways, but with less lethal consequences than we had imagined. The experts were less persuaded in 1985 that by the end of the century we would see terrorists waging biological warfare.[4] Then 2001 brought the anthrax letters, although the attack was small in scale. Analysts have long worried about cities being held hostage by terrorists armed with weapons of mass destruction, but while letters have been received from lunatics claiming to have nuclear weapons, such an event has not happened yet.

The possibility of nuclear black markets, terrorists with nuclear weapons, and the dispersal of radioactive material was the stuff of novels in the 1960s, and of growing official concern certainly by the early 1970s.[5] Official anxiety was heightened by the collapse of the Soviet Union and the exposure of its vast nuclear arsenal to corruption and organized crime. Indeed, nuclear terrorism remains a major concern. Graham Allison, in his 2004 book *Nuclear Terrorism: The Ultimate Preventable Catastrophe*, concluded that "a nuclear terrorist attack on America in the decade ahead is more likely than not."[6]

Although precision-guided surface-to-air missiles are widely available on the black market and are believed to have been in some terrorists' arsenals for years, there is only one example of such missiles being used against commercial aircraft outside of a conflict zone; that was in Kenya in 2002, when al Qaeda operatives fired two missiles at a commercial plane. Terrorists have not attempted to seize or sabotage operating nuclear reactors. Terrorists have not attacked agriculture.

Nor has terrorism escalated horizontally. There are no more terrorist organizations in the field today than there were 10 or 20 years ago. And there is even less organization today than there was before, as those employing terrorist tactics have moved away from formal military structures.

As we have learned, counting the total number of terrorist incidents can be tricky. Much depends on the definition of a terrorist incident. For many years, RAND's own database at least provided consistency. It showed a dramatic increase in the total number of incidents in the 1970s and early 1980s, reaching a high point in the latter half of the decade, then tailing off in the 1990s. The annual totals were in the hundreds. Since 9/11, the U.S. government's annual reports first showed a surprising decline in the number of incidents, which turned out to be false, and then showed dramatic increases into the thousands owing to changes in accounting methods and the insurgency in Iraq. Merely counting terrorist incidents does not capture the qualitative change in terrorism toward increasingly indiscriminate violence.

The incidence of international terrorist attacks with 25 or more fatalities, however, shows a different trajectory. There were 11 such attacks in the 1970s, jumping to 19 in the 1980s, then dropping back to 12 in the 1990s, but the total has gone back up to 19 between 2000 and the first part of 2006.

Nevertheless, terrorists have not fulfilled our (or their) darkest fantasies. Despite the appearance of mass-destruction scenarios in books, broadcasts, and screenplays for 30 years, terrorists have not tried to implement most of those scenarios. Why? It could be that such operations are far more difficult to execute than we imagine, or that they are harder to control, or that they are not as attractive to terrorists as we think they would be. We still don't adequately understand the terrorist mindset.

What did change beyond question on 9/11 were our perceptions. The 9/11 attacks redefined plausibility. Scenarios previously dismissed as far-fetched became operative presumptions. In the 1970s, analysts extrapolating from terrorist seizures of hostages thought that large-scale threats would be used to hold cities hostage in order to make political demands. Today, the scenarios are extrapolations of 9/11: devastating attacks carried out without warning and intended to kill rather than to coerce.

Another significant development in terrorism involves communications. I confess to being the author of another aphorism: "Terrorism is aimed at the people watching—terrorism is theater." By choreographing dramatic acts of violence, terrorists attract attention to themselves and their causes. But while authorities have complained about the role of the media in broadcasting terror, the terrorists have also complained about media coverage.

The media focus on the human drama—the victims, the pathos, the very elements that terrorists exploit to get attention. But the media seldom convey the terrorists' messages. Part of the problem is that terrorists have historically tended to be poor communicators, which may be one reason for their resorting to dramatic violence to attract an audience. When kidnapping, murder, and masked press conferences were insufficient to persuade people to read their manifestos, terrorists sometimes demanded publication or broadcasts as part of their price for returning or releasing hostages.

More recently, terrorists have improved their communications skills and have exploited new technology—video cameras and especially the Internet—to reach their audience directly. Their production values have gotten better. Their marketing is more sophisticated. One terrorist organization has even started its own television network.

The Internet is especially important, since it allows rapid, unmediated access to a global audience. Many terrorist organizations now have their own web sites. Osama bin Laden began communicating regularly to followers via taped video recordings. Well-done terrorist videos and DVDs are circulated on the Internet, and today's jihadists are even using videogames for recruiting. Online magazines provide instruction in bomb-making and terrorist tactics. Actual terrorist attacks, pleas by those held hostage, and gruesome beheadings are fed directly into the Internet, engaging the audience in a virtual jihad.

Counterterrorism also has evolved over the past 30 years, from combating terrorism, a narrowly defined problem, to the multidimensional "global war on terror." Not surprisingly, the 9/11 attacks attracted the attention of a new generation of scholars. Some of the many books that have filled the terrorism bookshelf since 9/11 are diatribes of shrill polemics and fear-mongering, and some are journalistic quickies to exploit the market, but there has also been a lot of excellent analysis.

Amid the noise, we need to remember that history does not march single file. There is no single historical thread, no inexorable sequence of events from the hijackings of the early 1970s to the 1980 Iran hostage crisis to the 1983 bombing of American Marines in

Beirut to the 1988 sabotage of Pan Am 103 to al Qaeda's actions in the 1990s to 9/11. Assertions that prior U.S. policy failures led to 9/11 flatten history and bend the facts.

This is especially true in examining the use of military power. Since the 1970s, I have argued that the employment of military force has to be an option to rescue hostages held by terrorists or to respond to terrorist campaigns and attacks. And almost 30 years ago, I asserted that it should be a well-understood principle of American policy that in order to prevent the acquisition or use of weapons of mass destruction by terrorists, the United States will do whatever it deems necessary, including using unilateral, preemptive, military force. (At that time, I had in mind attacking terrorists in countries whose governments were unable or unwilling to take action themselves and where time did not permit other solutions.)

However, I also recognized the difference between policy options and actual decisions. Circumstances might not permit the use of military force or might indicate that it was not the wisest course of action. At some times, military force has been employed; at other times, it has been considered but rejected; and at still others, it has been used ineffectually. Nonetheless, although the use of military force in specific circumstances short of war gradually became an accepted component of America's counterterrorist arsenal, going to war over terrorism remained as unimaginable prior to 9/11 as not using military force was unimaginable after 9/11.

In my view, if the Taliban regime in Afghanistan was not going to cooperate quickly by shutting down al Qaeda and bringing its leaders to justice, the regime had to be removed, and al Qaeda's training camps in Afghanistan had to be dispersed. These actions should be, I argued in September 2001, only the first salvos in an unrelenting campaign to destroy al Qaeda's terrorist enterprise. I saw these actions as being concurrent with the ongoing efforts to combat terrorism worldwide. They would inevitably draw the United States into some contests beyond its immediate areas of interest, but I did not envision a U.S.-led global war to eliminate all terrorist groups. I believed that each case would require a different mix of policy instruments.

Basic Beliefs

This book began as a project to compile the briefings, memoranda, and essays that I have written over the past six years into a single coherent volume. Reviewing my own work, I find that certain basic themes recur:

The enemies we face have changed fundamentally. There is no single military power that can match that of the United States, but the diverse adversaries of today pose an array of security challenges. Each one is unique, requiring great adaptability on our part. Today's foes do not threaten the global devastation that would have resulted from an all-out nuclear exchange—the paramount concern during the Cold War—but their capabilities could nonetheless produce disastrous levels of death and destruction. Dissuading or preventing terrorists from acquiring and using weapons of mass destruction will require new ways of thinking about deterrence, preemption, and retaliation.

Patterns of armed conflict have also changed. While precision-guided weapons have greatly reduced collateral casualties and damage, guerrilla wars and terrorist campaigns have paradoxically moved in the opposite direction, becoming more destructive, less discriminate, focusing the violence on civilian populations rather than military targets. In conflicts driven by ethnic or tribal antagonisms or by religious fanaticism rather than secular political goals, noncombatants seldom find any of the protections theoretically accorded to them. Massacres, ethnic cleansing, kidnapping, amputation and rape as strategic weapons, assaults on religious centers, the systematic murder of teachers and health workers, the destruction of crops, and starvation are frequent features of today's conflicts. To finance themselves, guerrilla groups and terrorist organizations have increasingly turned to criminal activities, providing profit motives for perpetual conflict. Where conflict has degenerated into warfare among competing warlords, rival armies avoid debilitating battles with each other while terrorizing civilian populations. The border between conflict and crime is blurring.

Unrelenting pressure on the al Qaeda organization and its terrorist allies has forced the jihadists to operate at a lower, but still lethal, level. However, the United States has neglected the political war. A wanted-poster approach condemns us to a strategy of stepping on cockroaches one at a time. What we must also do is shatter the appeal of the jihadist ideology. Even as we keep al Qaeda's leaders on the run, pursue and kill or capture terrorist operatives, and foil terrorist plots, we must, at the same time, defeat their missionary enterprise. This means pursuing a campaign against jihadist recruitment, encouraging defections, turning around those in captivity.

Although President George W. Bush warns Americans that "the war on terrorism will take a while," it is not clear that either those in the administration or average citizens at home fully comprehend what that means—or the great challenge it presents, especially to an impatient society. We need to stop looking for "high noons" in a hundred-years war. One of the most common complaints from allied intelligence services is that the United States is determined to make visible scores in the short term, even at the expense of long-term intelligence gains. We are hampered in Iraq by the consequences of continuing pressure in the military to go for knockout blows, repeated and premature assertions that the enemy is on the ropes, and growing political pressure for a timetable to pull out.

Much of our impatience derives from an inability to foresee the end. What does "victory" mean? Campaigns against terrorists seldom end with victory in any traditional sense of that term. Terrorist groups are rarely destroyed. Instead, as circumstances change, they eventually become irrelevant.

Americans must be ferociously pragmatic for the long term. As a matter of principle, the United States opposes terrorism in all forms. However, that does not mean we should immediately attempt to take down every identified terrorist organization.

The invasion of Iraq was a dangerous distraction. Even if Saddam Hussein had been hiding weapons of mass destruction, he was boxed in once the weapons inspectors had returned, which had been accomplished only as a consequence of the threat of invasion. To invade was to risk great costs in return for marginal gains, costs that inevitably would fall mostly on Americans. But we cannot erase the war in Iraq, and withdrawal poses new dangers. We are there now, and whatever we do from now on should be calibrated to cause no further harm to us or the Iraqis.

In the longer struggle against the jihadists and future terrorist foes, we will ultimately prevail. We will contain them, reduce their appeal, outlast them. This is not to say that there won't be further costly terrorist attacks against Americans abroad or on U.S. soil. The greater danger is the reaction the attacks may provoke. Terror, not terrorists, is the principal threat.

America's courage is its ultimate source of security. We cannot expect a risk-free society. While we must try to prevent terrorist attacks because of the impact they have on society as a whole, we should be realistic about risk: The danger to individual Americans is not great. We have in our history faced worse.

Homeland security begins at home. To empower the nation against fear, every citizen should have a role; all Americans should know what they can do to take care of themselves, their families, their neighbors, their community.

Whatever we do, American values must be preserved. The right response to terrorism is not unlimited surveillance and unchecked powers of arrest. There must be rules about what we can do with those who are in our custody. Torture can never be legal. American values are not luxuries. They are strategic resources that will sustain us through a long war.

Straight Talk

The reader will find strong personal opinions on these pages. There is much concerning the conduct of the war on terror[7] that I agree with: the muscular initial response to 9/11, the removal of the Taliban government in Afghanistan, the relentless pursuit of al Qaeda's leaders and planners, the increasingly sophisticated approach to homeland security, and, although I have deep reservations about the invasion of

Iraq, President Bush's determination to avoid an arbitrary timetable for withdrawal.

The list of things with which I do not agree is longer. As explained in this book, these aspects of the war on terror have, if anything, undermined our campaign: the needless bravado, the arrogant attitude toward essential allies, the exploitation of fear, the exaggerated claims of progress, the persistence of a wanted-poster approach while the broader ideological struggle is ignored, the rush to invade Iraq, the failure to deploy sufficient troops there despite the advice of senior military leaders and the head of the Coalition Provisional Authority, the cavalier dismissal of treaties governing the conduct of war, the mistreatment of prisoners, the unimaginable public defense of torture, the use of homeland security funding for political pork barrel spending, and the failure to educate and involve citizens.

This book is not intended to serve any political agenda. Its sole objective is to reckon how America can defeat its terrorist foes while preserving its own liberty. Throughout the Cold War, Americans maintained a rough consensus on defense matters, despite substantive disagreements. Unity did not require the suspension of honest differences or of civilized political debate. But today's fierce partisanship has reduced national politics to a gang war. The constant maneuvering for narrow political advantage, the rejection of criticism as disloyalty, the pursuit by interest groups of their own exclusive agendas, and the radio, television, newspaper, and Internet debates that thrive on provocation and partisan zeal provide a poor platform for the difficult and sustained effort that America faces. All of these trends imperil the sense of community required to withstand the struggle ahead. We don't need unanimity. We do need unity. Democracy is our strength. Partisanship is our weakness.

The book is not without uncertainties and even some apparent contradictions. Ideology is easy. Reality is messy. Well into the fifth year of the campaign against al Qaeda and the jihadist enterprise, and in the fourth year of fighting in Iraq, the future trajectories of these contests simply are not yet clear. There may be long lulls that tempt us into dangerous complacency interspersed with spectacular terrorist attacks that cause us to question any claims of progress. It is our foe's doctrine to attack when we are inattentive. As in all long wars, we can expect surprises.

Organization of the Book

Chapter Two provides a sober assessment of the current situation. It concludes that while the United States has made progress in degrading the jihadists' operational capabilities, it has failed to dent their determination or halt their recruiting. Meanwhile, a tenacious armed resistance continues in Iraq. Nothing indicates that it will end soon. Insurgents cannot defeat U.S. forces in open battle, but we cannot stop the violence. The insurgents' strategy is to make our situation untenable, to drain our resolve. Opinions in America differ sharply, with some claiming that military pressure and political progress will eventually reduce the Iraqi insurgency to manageable brigandage and others arguing that the continued U.S. presence further fuels the fighting.

Dismissing terrorists as crazy fanatics and consigning them to the realm of evil have discouraged a deeper understanding of our foes and have restricted discussions of counterterrorist strategy. But understanding how they view the world, warfighting, and operations opens up new ways of thinking about counterterrorist strategy. Chapter Three explores the terrorist camp—the thinking of terrorist leaders, the appeal of their ideology, their indoctrination and recruiting methods, and their operational code. The chapter concludes with a hypothetical briefing that might be given to Osama bin Laden.

Chapter Four offers a new set of strategic principles to guide our conduct. It argues that the recasting of counterterrorism as "war" immediately following 9/11 was a good idea but that the "global war on terror" conflated too many threats and lumped together too many missions. The focus should be on the destruction of the jihadist enterprise, where the United States has made progress but risks losing support and momentum as a consequence of growing complacency and the controversial war in Iraq. American efforts understandably have focused almost exclusively on thwarting operations and capturing terrorists—the visible tip of the iceberg. We now have to expand that strategy to impede recruiting and encourage rehabilitation. Meanwhile, there is no easy solution to Iraq. Staying the course until victory is achieved is not a strategy, but neither is a timetable for withdrawal, and withdrawal itself is dangerous, especially if it leaves behind a failed state in the heart of the Middle East. Continuing American involvement in Iraq while we figure out how to do it better may be our best approach. Whatever the outcome in Iraq, there is no near-term prospect that the fight against the jihadists will end there.

Chapter Five addresses how we can strengthen ourselves. Homeland security should move beyond gates and guards and become the impetus for rebuilding America's decaying infrastructure. We need to adopt a realistic approach to acceptable risk and to get a lot smarter about security. Instead of stoking fear, we need to build upon American traditions of determination and self-reliance and begin firing up citizen participation in preparedness and response.

Above all, we need to preserve our commitment to American values. Counterterrorism is not simply technique. It confronts us with dilemmas that often have a moral dimension. Whatever we do must be consistent with our fundamental values. This is no mere matter of morality, it is a strategic calculation, and here we have at times miscalculated.

Historic American Engineering Record/Jet Lowe

We have been able to degrade al Qaeda's capabilities, eliminate its planners, chase its leaders, and disrupt some of its operations, but we have not yet devised the means to reduce the appeal of its ideology or stop its recruiting.

CHAPTER TWO

An Appreciation of the Situation

In mid-2006, nearly five years after 9/11, how is America doing in the global war on terror? The question itself reflects the typically American desire to keep score, to measure progress. Fighting in World War II provided visible mileposts—the invasion of North Africa, the march through Italy, the return to the Philippines, the landing at Normandy, the liberation of Paris, the fall of Berlin, VE Day, VJ Day. It was a bloodier contest, but one in which we knew where we were going.

The Cold War that followed lasted decades, and the current contest could easily do the same. The Iron Curtain came down in 1946, and the Berlin Wall remained in place until 1989. The intervening 43 years saw many ups and downs, with the ultimate outcome uncertain to the very end. It is against the anticipation of decades of conflict that we review the progress of the past five years in the global war on terror.

Although the war on terror has become the second longest war fought by the United States, there have been few decisive battles or turning points to mark its course. This is the nature of insurgencies and terrorist campaigns. Since 9/11, the few mileposts that we can point to include the defeat of the Taliban in late 2001; the resurgence of jihadist terrorism in 2002 and 2003 with the attacks in Bali, Mombasa, Riyadh, and Casa Blanca; the U.S.-led invasion of Iraq and the swift march to Baghdad in the spring of 2003; and the extension of jihadist operations into Europe in 2004 and 2005 with the attacks in Madrid and London, concurrent with the escalation of the insurgency in Iraq.

However, this list suggests more order than actually existed. The reality was one of uncertain beginnings, unconnected opportunistic terrorist attacks rather than terrorist campaigns, a U.S. invasion that many considered to be a dangerous distraction from the more critical task of destroying al Qaeda, a ferocious but diffuse armed resistance in Iraq rather than a centrally directed insurgency, and much-trumpeted American military offensives that had inspiring names but little permanent effect.

Deaths of American soldiers in Iraq have occurred at much lower levels than in previous wars, but the lack of unarguable results in the U.S.-led campaign has been especially frustrating to a nation of pragmatists. In 2003, Secretary of Defense Donald Rumsfeld himself lamented the difficulty of measuring progress when he said, "Today we lack metrics to know if we are winning or losing the global war on terror. Are we capturing, killing or deterring and dissuading more terrorists every day than the madrassas and the radical clerics are recruiting, training, and deploying against us?"[8] Three years later, questions are still on the table. Are we winning or losing? Should we get out of Iraq as soon as we can, or should we stay the course? Are we any safer today than we were on that fateful day in September 2001? Or are we in even greater danger?

The absence of clear indicators leads Americans to look for things to count, regardless of their relevancy. Some measure the country's own inputs—for example, how much it is spending on security—and label increases as progress. Public officials rely on spin to convey progress. For different reasons, our political leaders and military commanders continuously claim that we are making progress, that we are winning, that the enemy is desperate and on the run, that the insurgency is in its death throes, that our victory is inevitable. And inevitably, official credibility is eroded as the bloodshed continues. Only since late 2005 have more sober expressions of the uncertainties we face, admissions of setbacks, and warnings of more deaths to come surfaced in the public remarks of those in charge.

Assessments of progress depend on how this new war is defined. According to one definition, it is a campaign to destroy the jihadist terrorist enterprise led by al Qaeda and its affiliates. Yet it has become inextricably intertwined with the struggle to suppress an insurgency in Iraq and a resurgent armed resistance in Afghanistan. The war on terror is also described as an effort to defeat other terrorist organizations that have American blood on their hands or that might threaten the United States or its allies. It is a decades-old effort to combat terrorism as a mode of conflict. It has become conflated with efforts to prevent the proliferation of weapons of mass destruction, on the presumption that their development by states such as Iraq, Iran, or North Korea will lead inevitably to their acquisition by terrorists. And, finally, the war is described by some as an effort to secure the American homeland itself.

Measuring progress in each of these endeavors is difficult enough, let alone assessing progress in the aggregate. This is hardly a new situation. The four decades of the Cold War were marked by dramatic events, setbacks and triumphs, confrontations and détente, worries about widening missile gaps and windows of vulnerability, deployments of new weapons and wars fought by proxies. But could we at any moment say where we were in the struggle, whether we were safer or less secure, or how much longer it would continue?

Only three months after September 11, 2001, I was asked in a Senate hearing whether "it was over," since no further terrorist attacks had occurred. The question was premature. It is still premature, but now, nearly five years after the 9/11 attacks, it is possible to attempt what army staff officers once called "an appreciation of the situation." It is still early, the situation is immensely complicated, and the outcome is not yet clear, but through the smoke and fog of war, some things are discernible.

The assessment must start with the jihadists who, inspired by al Qaeda's ideology, remain the principal terrorist threat to the United States. Al Qaeda's brand of jihadism seeks to transform Islam's discontents into a muscular religious offensive that elevates the concept of jihad from a struggle within one's soul to an unlimited war against the West. Jihadism is a radical cult of violence that draws on a rich anthology of religious theory to support its position and has its own operational code, which we will discuss later. Jihadism is not synonymous with Islam, but its rhetoric and actions do appeal to a broader Islamic community. Contemporary jihadism differs from previous jihads. The shared experience of combat in Afghanistan, a vast population of Muslim immigrants, and new means of communication—especially the Internet—have combined to create a global consciousness and produce a truly global enterprise. Al Qaeda has helped to create this, but the jihadist phenomenon transcends al Qaeda.

Early Progress Against al Qaeda

The United States and its allies have made undeniable progress in degrading the operational capabilities of the jihadist terrorist enterprise, most significantly by overthrowing the Taliban and eliminating al Qaeda's readily accessible training camps in Afghanistan. The Taliban were vulnerable. As al Qaeda's number two leader, Ayman al-Zawahiri, wrote four years after their defeat, the Taliban had, by their extreme actions, separated themselves from the people and were isolated, both domestically and internationally.[9]

Overthrow of the Taliban

The swift campaign to take the Taliban down was imaginative and unorthodox. A conventional U.S. invasion of Afghanistan would have required months of buildup and potentially could have condemned American forces to repeat the disastrous Soviet experience. Instead, backed by U.S. airpower and coordinated by Special Forces and intelligence operatives, the Taliban's fiercest Afghan enemies, animated by tribal vendettas and cash, were recruited to fight on the ground. This had a subtle, perhaps unanticipated yet salutary effect. Faced with an American onslaught, Taliban fighters could easily have retreated and gone to ground to wage a protracted guerrilla war; but when confronted by other Afghans, their own warrior traditions and fear that retreat would be interpreted by their peers as the loss of

God's support encouraged them to stand and fight, with devastating consequences. City after city fell.

In contrast to the Taliban fighters, the al Qaeda jihadists could and did run. Doubtless already anticipating a ferocious response to the September 11 attacks, al Qaeda had its escape plans in place, and its cadres cleared out and headed to the mountains.

Destruction of Training Camps

Al Qaeda's training camps in Afghanistan were a critical component of the jihadists' enterprise, although the actual training that went on in them was not their most important function. Instruction in clandestine operations, terrorist tactics, weapons skills, and bomb-making can be provided in almost any cellar or remote farm; basic knowledge can even be imparted on the Internet, although hands-on experience helps enormously. Indoctrination was an especially important function of the camps. Isolated from all other sources of information, recruits consumed an exclusive diet of al Qaeda's ideology.

Training in Afghanistan became a magnet for eager jihadists from all over the world, an international jamboree where one could graduate from words to action. Getting there was in itself many acolytes' first step into the underground, since it required leaving behind family, studies, and jobs. Moreover, it often required traveling under a fake name, with false papers. Making the pilgrimage to Afghanistan tested commitment.

Living together with jihadist recruits from every corner of the world, sharing hardships and danger, provided an important bonding experience. Camps were subdivided along national lines, but even with houses of different flags, the idea of jihad as a global campaign rather than a collection of national efforts was reinforced. Nationalities were mixed in advanced al Qaeda training, and the personal bonds established there created powerful, lasting ties that will survive for decades. Al Qaeda still draws on this human capital of veterans and recruiters, as well as underground networks to move people.

The fighting in Afghanistan also provided an opportunity for actual combat. Seasoned Afghan guerrillas may have thought little of the foreign volunteers, and there are reports that the less-promising students were sent to the front as cannon fodder, but the fighting, although desultory, was real. The result had less to do with battlefield learning than with gaining experience under fire, experiencing the exposure to danger and death, the suppression of sensitivities, the hardening of attitudes—what in a less-squeamish age used to be called "blooding" the troops.

The camps also supported al Qaeda's strategy of building relationships with other groups in the jihadist constellation. Al Qaeda could connect the groups with a worldwide struggle and could raise their technical capabilities. Distant organizations from Southeast Asia to North Africa sent men to train in Afghanistan. Some of them were inducted directly into al Qaeda's fold, giving them a kind of dual citizenship. However, pledging loyalty to bin Laden did not mean giving up membership in one's original organization. It is this dual loyalty to bin Laden and to their home-based organizations that made al Qaeda a truly international organization. Some trainees returned with sets of connections that could provide them with continuing financial aid or technical assistance. These same connections would benefit al Qaeda, by extending its recruiting and operational reach.

The camps provided a continuing flow of volunteers from which al Qaeda's planners could recruit operatives. This global reservoir enabled the planners to assemble specialized combinations of talent, including candidates suitable for pilot training who also were willing to carry out suicide missions. By putting dispersed talent and centralized operational planners together, the camps enabled al Qaeda to operate at a level far above that of previous terrorist organizations.

While destroying the camps imposed some limitations on the jihadist enterprise, it did not end recruitment, training, or the preparation of terrorist operations. These activities continue in dispersed fashion, at local sites and at remote locations in Pakistan and the southern Philippines, but the distant camps are not as easily accessible, the journey is more dangerous, and the entire process is far less efficient. And while the Internet can provide basic instruction in terrorist tactics and bomb-making, it cannot entirely replace hands-on experience, nor can it duplicate the shared sense of cause, hardships, and danger that produce the strong bonds of brotherhood. And yet, the 7/7 London bombers were still able to create a suicide pact built upon local bonding.

Subsequent Indicators of Progress?

Captives and Casualties

The total number of jihadist operatives detained worldwide is not a significant indicator of progress. Published reports indicate that several thousand al Qaeda combatants have been killed or captured, and about 1,000 remain in U.S. custody.[10] These numbers do not include all the Taliban combatants captured in Afghanistan or the insurgents in Iraq, about 14,000 of whom are in U.S. custody. Only a small portion of the Iraqi insurgents are members of al Qaeda.

Whether these losses are significant depends on how many al Qaeda combatants we think there are, and again, much depends on definition. Reports of al Qaeda job application forms, salaries, and benefit packages describe a level of al Qaeda organization that no longer exists—indeed, they imply more organization than there ever was. Recent estimates of al Qaeda's core strength run between 300 and 500. An uncertain figure to begin with, it is even more uncertain now. Estimates of "associate membership," a term that again implies more formality than exists in reality, or some form of looser association run in the low tens of thousands.[11] The total number of recruits that have passed through al Qaeda's training camps at one time or another is estimated to be between 70,000 and 120,000, but not all of these joined al Qaeda, and fewer still remain al Qaeda operatives. In addition, these figures would not include the total membership of all of al Qaeda's allies, those recruited by al Qaeda affiliates since 2001, or autonomous cells that emerged to carry out terrorist attacks such as the 2005 bombings in London but were never identified as al Qaeda members and did not pass through the training camps in Afghanistan. However, some may have received training after 2001 in Pakistan. And beyond these lie vast pools of fired-up young men in radical Islamic organizations, mosques, and madrassas.

The overall picture that emerges is one of thousands of determined individuals with very slender connections. Moreover, this is a dynamic population. Recruiting is constant. At the same time, terrorist losses are continuous. Some of those who went through the training camps claim to have decided right away that al Qaeda's brand of jihad was not for them. Others have undoubtedly dropped out in the years since they attended training. Still others have been killed or captured.

Jihadists also vary in their level of commitment. Some are willing to serve as martyrs, while others choose only to provide passive support. Individual jihadists are constantly calibrating and recalibrating their level of commitment, depending on their perception of events and their personal circumstances.

Access to a global reservoir provided quantity, which al Qaeda translated into quality, but large numbers are not needed to carry out terrorist operations. Al Qaeda is a tiny army. Even the 9/11 attacks were carried out by only 19 men with perhaps an equally small number of supporters outside the country. Major attacks since 9/11 have involved only handfuls of terrorists. This war cannot be won by attrition.

In contrast, al Qaeda's key operational planners are hard to replace. Experience counts. With fewer central planners, there will be less learning, fewer innovations, fewer operational refinements. Continued pressure on the enterprise, keeping its leaders on the run, and impeding internal communications have all degraded al Qaeda's operational capabilities.

Thwarted Attacks

Increased intelligence efforts and unprecedented cooperation among the world's security services have no doubt thwarted some terrorist attacks. British authorities say they have foiled eight to ten plots, and President Bush said in a speech in 2006 that ten terrorist attacks had been prevented, including several in the United States.[12,13]

It is always hard to count things that don't occur. One cannot say exactly how many terrorist attacks would have taken place if authorities had not intervened. Jihadists continually reconnoiter targets on the street and on the Internet. When they are not actually preparing or carrying out operations, terrorists constantly talk about what they could do, what they dream of doing. Plans pile up. Proposals are constantly being pitched. An operation in the planning stages is likely to have several iterations. It may be shelved and later renewed. Much of this is psychologically fulfilling fantasy—a kind of virtual jihad.

In interrogations, captured terrorists may reveal some plans, talk about invented plots to mislead their captors, or boast of grandiose schemes to impress and frighten an eager audience. Does the arrest of a key figure mean that one or ten future attacks were prevented? Does a captured target folder mean that one or multiple operations were thwarted?

Authorities worldwide have adopted a more aggressive posture, moving in earlier to break up potential plots rather than waiting until they mature or, worse, are carried out. Moving in earlier means suspects may be apprehended while their plans are still in the talking stage. In some cases, authorities may make the arrests simply to disrupt suspected preparations for terrorist operations without having precise information on exactly what was being planned. While this may prevent a planned attack, it also makes prosecution difficult, as suspects can claim that they were only talking and never had serious intentions.

As a consequence, the number of prosecutions is small compared with the number of people detained, which reflects a preventive law enforcement approach rather than the traditional reactive approach. It is sufficient to say that the operational capabilities of the jihadists have been degraded and that terrorist operations are being thwarted. Keeping score is difficult and irrelevant.

Disrupted Funding

We also have disrupted al Qaeda's cash flow. The jihadist enterprise is supported by sympathetic contributors identified during the war in Afghanistan, cooperative charities, and, according to some observers, frightened Gulf states seeking immunity from terrorist attack. This funding has in the past enabled al Qaeda to support a global network of paid operatives, finance terrorist operations, and purchase influence through financial aid to other organizations.

But while authorities can estimate how much funding has been blocked—it is in the hundreds of millions of dollars—there is considerable uncertainty about how much money may still be getting through. No doubt it is less, but a downsized al Qaeda core and a more decentralized organization also have reduced al Qaeda's financial needs.

The total amounts of suspected terrorist funding being blocked by the authorities have declined each year since 2001.[14] This could suggest various things: success at drying up the jihadists' revenue streams, more skillful evasion of financial controls by jihadist bankers, or declining needs. Nevertheless, occasional reports do suggest that al Qaeda is short of funds.

Unfortunately, terrorist attacks do not usually require large financial resources. The 9/11 attacks did cost an estimated half million dollars, including expenses for travel, support, and flight training, and involved large bank transfers. However, four truck bombings in Turkey cost $170,000—only $42,000 each.[15] The 2004 Madrid bombings cost no more than $15,000.[16] The 2005 London bombing cost a mere $2,000.[17]

The declining scale of the attacks represents progress. But as large-scale financial transactions have become more dangerous, terrorists have adapted their financing, making use of informal banking networks to transfer smaller sums. Eager jihadists must now provide their own funding, which they do through petty crime or even from their own resources.

Although not an entirely new phenomenon—Ahmed Ressam, the would-be millennium bomber, for example, funded his activity in the 1990s by small robberies in Montreal—this intersection between low-level crime and terrorism has become a signature feature of today's more-decentralized jihadist operations. In 2006, police investigating a series of gas station holdups in Southern California stumbled upon a prison-based jihadist plot to attack religious and military sites.

International Cooperation

Although the United States has led the charge in the war on terror, at times stiff-arming its traditional allies to pursue its own course, embarrassing them with its swaggering rhetoric and high-handed demands, and berating them publicly when they have chosen not to come along, international cooperation has remained strong. Cooperation among intelligence services is unprecedented in terms of the number of countries involved and the speed with which information is exchanged. Allied forces operate alongside American forces in Afghanistan, Iraq, and elsewhere. This has made the operating environment extremely hostile for jihadists worldwide.

Another achievement, accomplished early in the war, was persuading Pakistan to abandon its support for the Taliban and become an ally in the campaign against al Qaeda. Complaints continue about the undemocratic nature of Pakistan's government and the quality of its cooperation, but a hostile government in Islamabad would have seriously complicated efforts against the jihadists.

Other countries, portions of whose populations were sympathetic to al Qaeda and whose governments might have preferred to adopt a more passive stance in the global campaign against the jihadists, were jolted to action by subsequent terrorist attacks on their territory. Attacks in Indonesia, Morocco, Egypt, Jordan, and, above all, Saudi Arabia—a stronghold of jihadist sympathies—demonstrated the jihadists' readiness to kill fellow Muslims and justify the murders by denouncing the victims as apostates or dismissing them as collateral casualties who would be compensated in paradise. The carnage eroded al Qaeda's popularity and galvanized governments that were determined to crush the challenge to their own survival, even if it meant closer cooperation with infidels. Each terrorist attack provoked a massive crackdown that reduced the jihadists' capabilities for further operations.

No Terrorist Attacks in the United States

For Americans, the most important measure of success has been the absence of another major terrorist attack in the United States.

Clearly, al Qaeda remains determined to strike again. Bin Laden has said so. While another attack on the scale of 9/11 cannot be ruled out entirely, there is growing consensus among analysts that such an attack in the United States is not likely. What is more difficult to explain is the absence of smaller-scale attacks in this country.

It is true that al Qaeda's operational capabilities have been reduced, Western intelligence has improved, security in the United States is tighter, and a few local plots have been thwarted in the early stages. But better intelligence and security cannot be the entire explanation. Since 2001, jihadists in other parts of the world have attacked residences, restaurants, hotel lobbies, nightclubs, commuter trains, subways, churches, synagogues, and crowded city streets. The same targets are vulnerable in the United States.

In his January 2006 message, Osama bin Laden stated that America's security measures have not prevented terrorist attacks. Jihadists do not want simply another attack, they want another truly spectacular blow, and they have long time horizons. Planning for the 9/11 attacks began in the mid-1990s. Bin Laden promises that there will be a new attack, but he characteristically offers no time frame.

Other explanations for the absence of attacks in the United States are also possible. Jihadist planners might worry that smaller terrorist attacks will provoke even tighter security, making it more difficult for them to prepare another major assault. Their own operational code tells them to lie in wait, to attack when the enemy is inattentive. Or they might be concerned that a major attack on American soil would only infuriate Americans and harden their resolve at a time when jihadists want to sap the country's determination to remain in Iraq. These explanations suggest central decisionmaking and a continuing measure of influence over local volunteers, or at least a shared understanding of strategy.

It is also possible that local communities are exercising some degree of control, encouraging neighborhood hotheads to fulfill their desire for action abroad, not at home where it would complicate everyone's life. Or it could just be a matter of luck. The absence of attacks in the homeland is a success that we cannot entirely explain.

Organizational Deterioration of al Qaeda

A recent RAND report describes several modes of al Qaeda behavior in the post-9/11 environment.[18] Core al Qaeda members or those with close ties to al Qaeda's historic leadership facilitate the creation of new cells, although these may operate independently to attack Western targets. The terrorist campaign waged in Saudi Arabia by "Al Qaeda in the Arabian Peninsula" and the activities, inside and outside Iraq, of "Al Qaeda in the Land of the Two Rivers," formerly led by Abu Musab al-Zarqawi, would fall into this category.

Al Qaeda also behaves as a collaborator through its relationships with like-minded groups such as those in Indonesia, Pakistan, and Kenya. Finally, al Qaeda may simply inspire attacks. This is where it functions more as an ideology than an organization. Murder in the Netherlands and possibly the 2005 bombings in London would fall into this category, unless external connections are eventually discovered.[19]

Al Qaeda may also be practicing what might be called a sort of "Johnny Appleseed jihad." Like the 19th century American folk hero who planted apple seeds across the American frontier to provide bounty for later pioneers, al Qaeda recruits individuals, trains them, then disperses them to undertake operations with no further contact. These are not the "sleepers" that so many people worry about—undercover agents who remain dormant until "awakened" by a message from headquarters to carry out preplanned acts of sabotage. They are even something less than the "facilitated" cells described in the aforementioned RAND report. Recruitment of other conspirators, planning, and operations are left to local initiative. Some of these seeds of jihad may blow away in the winds of changed circumstances, and the devotion of some recruits may wither with time, but some will create local cells and carry out attacks.

The loosening of its organization puts al Qaeda just one step away from a "leaderless resistance" type of organization. Leaderless resistance, the invention of an American right-wing extremist,[20] envisions a vast movement of individual and small-group actors operating in common cause, unconnected except in their beliefs—a rebellion without a center. The utility of leaderless resistance is that it prevents infiltration by authorities, since there is nothing to infiltrate. It also enables a movement's toothless ideologues to claim credit for every disparate attack that occurs.

Such a model would be completely contrary to al Qaeda's image of itself as the vanguard of jihad. The premise of al Qaeda's operations, which is the premise of almost all terrorism, is that its adherents must be galvanized by action, not left alone. Leaderless resistance would reduce al Qaeda to mere exhortation. It would destroy any possibility of coordination. Of course, al Qaeda's ideology seeks to inspire individuals to initiate their own jihad, and it provokes unconnected acts, some of which its leaders may claim credit for, but al Qaeda must regard these as an adjunct to its global campaign. To rely exclusively on exhortation would be an admission of failure and would defy al Qaeda's powerful organizational imperatives to inspire and to command the global jihad.

There has been dispersal and, with it, organizational decay of al Qaeda, but there is also evidence of a structure that survives. Even operations judged to be purely local hint of tantalizing connections: post-9/11 visits to Pakistan; suspected but unidentified jihadist expediters who energize local cells, provide technical expertise, then disappear; a videotaped testament of a suicide bomber in London that somehow ends up spliced to a message from Osama bin Laden's second-in-command, Ayman al-Zawahiri, who is presumably somewhere in Pakistan. There are also networks that are able to recruit and move local volunteers to dispersed training camps in Pakistan or recruits from surrounding Arab countries and Europe to fight in Iraq.

Overall, however, these changes bring quality-control problems, smaller-scale operations, a diminishing central role, and the ever-present danger of centrifugal forces and the reemergence of divisions that could destroy the unity necessary to sustain the global effort.

Failures in the Campaign

An honest assessment of the situation must include our failures as well. Bin Laden has not been captured, nor have Ayman al-Zawahiri or a number of other top al Qaeda leaders. Boasts that we have eliminated two-thirds or three-quarters of al Qaeda's leadership reflect a statistical illusion. The "eliminated" column is cumulative: As new leaders step up to replace those killed or captured and are in turn killed or captured themselves, their numbers are added to the "eliminated" column. Gradually, those eliminated outnumber the survivors and replacements who remain at large. We have, for example, captured al Qaeda's third-in-command several times. Presumably, only one number three is still in action. And, for all the numbers, there still is one who is third-in-command.

Al Qaeda's Resilience

The jihadist enterprise has proved resilient under pressure. Little remains of the more-centralized bureaucratic al Qaeda of the late 1990s. Ever evolving, al Qaeda has downsized. Although target choices and proposed terrorist operations may still have been pitched to the center as late as early 2004, a ruling council no longer appears to review proposals and approve operations.[21]

Al Qaeda itself has transcended its organizational skin to become more of an ideology, a source of inspiration. Operations are, of necessity, decentralized, with greater local content and fewer of the transactions that intelligence services look for—communications, border crossings, money transfers. Greater clandestinity is a requirement. We are now dealing with many local al Qaedas, rather than one central al Qaeda, although it may be premature to write off the center.

The jihadist enterprise today appears to comprise a small number of surviving leaders in hiding among sympathetic tribesmen on the border between Pakistan and Afghanistan or possibly in Pakistan's cities. These leaders are able to communicate publicly and presumably clandestinely with a small cadre of operatives. Al Qaeda affiliates operate in Afghanistan, Pakistan, Saudi Arabia, and Iraq. Local jihadists in Morocco, Spain, and elsewhere in Europe maintain some level of lateral connections that they can call on for assistance. More-distant jihadist groups in South and Southeast Asia continue their own armed struggles.

Jihadists receive much of their instruction from terrorist manuals on the Internet. Fewer recruits seek training abroad. They join together locally for one-off attacks, avoiding groups that could be identified or penetrated by authorities. Command and control are provided by local converts. Like many global corporations, al Qaeda is increasingly relying on part-time personnel.

We have strained al Qaeda's organization, but we have not put it out of business. Since September 11, 2001, jihadists affiliated with al Qaeda or inspired by al Qaeda's ideology have carried out major terrorist attacks from Bali to London on an average of about one every two months, not counting the continuing violence in Afghanistan, Kashmir, Iraq, Israel, and Russia. The 9/11 assault on America established al Qaeda's credentials. Regardless of whether later attacks are actually connected, every one bears al Qaeda's label. Fortunately, all of the subsequent attacks have been pre-9/11 scenarios, most of them bombings, mostly multiple attacks, and many involving suicide attackers. Body count appears to be the paramount criterion, outweighing any iconic value of a particular target—just about any crowded venue will do. More than a thousand people have died in these attacks, thousands more have been injured. Large-scale attacks are seen as successes to be emulated. The bloodiest attacks in Bali, Madrid, and Iraq now set the global standard for jihadists everywhere. Increasingly, the war in Iraq also has become the major driving issue.

Survival of al Qaeda's Ideology

America's biggest failure is on the political front. The United States has not silenced or blunted the appeal of al Qaeda's ideology. Even as we have degraded its operational capabilities, its message continues to spread. Struggles continue for the control of mosques. Qurans with jihadist footnotes continue to circulate. The number of places where the language of violent jihad is an acceptable conversation is increasing. Al Qaeda continues to communicate and recruit through more channels than it did ten years ago. Before 9/11, only a few web sites were dedicated to al Qaeda's brand of jihad. Today there are thousands.[22]

American officials have begun to admit that the United States is far behind in the information war. "Our enemies have skillfully adapted to fighting wars in today's media age," Secretary of Defense Donald Rumsfeld said in a speech to the Council on Foreign Relations in New York in February 2006, "but for the most part we, our country, our government, has not." He said that while the terrorists "have successfully . . . poisoned the Muslim public's view of the West, we in the government have barely even begun to compete in reaching their audiences."[23] This also was the conclusion of the Djerejian Commission, which noted in its report that "in this time of peril, public diplomacy is absurdly and dangerously underfunded, and simply restoring it to its Cold War status is not enough."[24]

Almost every opinion poll indicates growing antipathy among Muslims toward America. While they may not all support al Qaeda's peculiar interpretation of jihad, significant numbers sympathize with its quest and even its methods, including terrorist attacks. There are ample sources of anger. Some of it predates 9/11. America has inherited the still potent resentment felt against the European imperialists who imposed their rule on most of Africa, the Middle East, and Asia and what many in these regions regard as the continuing exploitative behavior of the West. Those who feel kicked around in history are likely to take some satisfaction in seeing the mighty get hit. But much of the resentment is recent, stemming from the invasion and occupation of Iraq; the abuses at Abu Ghraib and Guantanamo prisons; public defenses of torture (of Muslim detainees); bellicose threats to Muslim nations such as Syria and Iran; overt heavy-handed pressure on other governments, including those in Pakistan and Indonesia, to crack down harder on local militants; perceived new insults to Islam, which are inevitably exploited by radicals. All of these strengthen al Qaeda's call.

We cannot say with any confidence how things will turn out. The current jihadist terrorist campaign is likely to continue for many years. Al Qaeda will not quit—its leaders have no alternatives. It will remain capable of inspiring and facilitating further attacks. Local conflicts in the southern Philippines, Indonesia, Bangladesh, Kashmir, Western China, Central Asia, the Caucasus, and the Palestinian territory will go on with or without al Qaeda connections. Jihadist recruiting will also be fueled by the lack of political and economic opportunities in much of the Middle East, combined with tensions arising from growing immigrant Muslim communities in Europe, the difficulties of integration, economic problems, and sons of immigrants seeking self-identity in extreme expressions of faith and politics. At the same time, there has been no global uprising. The numbers joining jihad remain modest. Al Qaeda's relevance could fade with endless repetition of bombings, with time, and with gradual changes in the social and political environment.

Still, if it can sustain the fight, al Qaeda could get lucky. Afghanistan, where the insurgents are showing new strength, could slide back into chaos. Pakistan could fall apart. The removal of either Afghanistan's President Hamid Karzai or Pakistan's President Pervez Musharaff, both of whom have been targets of repeated assassination attempts, could be destabilizing. Saudi Arabia has successfully dealt with the first cohort of jihadist attackers but could be confronted with a second, larger, and more-experienced wave of Saudi jihadists returning from Iraq. Much now depends on the outcome of that contest.

The Iraq Factor

Historians will debate the wisdom of America's invasion of Iraq, seeing it as either a clever lateral escalation that redefined the war on terror militarily and politically or a dangerous detour from the focused pursuit of al Qaeda. The final judgment will depend very much on the outcome. What will Iraq look like three years, five years, or ten years from now? Despite confident claims and pessimistic predictions, we don't really know at this point. Less debatable are the immediate consequences of the invasion. The initial military campaign was a stunning display of American military capability, but the brilliant execution of the invasion itself was matched by the utter failure to anticipate (or the determination to ignore and not prepare for) a fierce resistance. How successful the United States is in dealing with that resistance will have a significant effect on the future course of the war on terror.

Here again, claims of progress must be interpreted within the limitations of "insurgency math." In the Vietnam War, "progress" was measured by enemy body count and kill ratios, and elaborate systems were developed to evaluate security in the countryside. In the end, none of this mattered.

In the Iraq war, commanders use an array of statistics to measure progress; enemy body count is not among them, although the number of insurgents captured is. The statistics include estimates of enemy strength, the number of enemy-initiated attacks, the number of improvised explosive devices (IEDs)—a leading source of friendly casualties—that are detonated or instead are discovered and disarmed, the number of car bombs, the number of Coalition forces killed and wounded, the strength of Iraq's security forces. These mostly battle-oriented measures do not measure perceptions of security. Military commanders speak of control, but they often use the term in a narrow military sense meaning command of the terrain, which does not always translate into ordinary security. A battalion of infantry may be able to defeat any local insurgents, but can the mayor of the town walk down the street at night? Additional figures are used to assess the quality of life: the employment rate, the number of hours the electricity is on each day, the availability of fresh water.

Such numbers must always be interpreted with care. The absence of enemy attacks may mean progress, or it may mean that the insurgents effectively control a neighborhood or city despite the presence of Coalition or government forces. Or it may mean that no government authorities are there to record enemy activities. Military commanders determined to succeed may wittingly or unwittingly exert pressure on their units' reporting. An aggressive commander demanding more contact with the enemy is likely to get it, at least on paper. Sometimes, the military's own "can do" attitude gets in the way of realistic appraisals. The incentives and opportunities for mischief are many.

Progress (or the lack of it) may occur subtly in ways that are hard to measure. Perceptions, both in Iraq and in America, count more than statistics, although opinion polls that measure attitudes under occupation can be misleading. It is, in sum, hard to tell how we are doing. The lack of metrics pushes us toward a different analytical approach, one in which we try to measure strengths and weaknesses. But in an insurgency, as in counterterrorism, our strengths do not always translate into enemy weaknesses, and vice versa. We may, for example, correctly point out that the armed resistance being confronted in Iraq today does not have the capacity to take over Iraq. This is true, but it is irrelevant, since that is not the insurgents' current strategy. Takeover would be part of a post-American withdrawal struggle. The more appropriate question might be, do Coalition and Iraqi forces have the capacity to significantly reduce the violence? Our assessment must take into account strengths and weaknesses on both sides.

No Imminent Collapse of the Insurgency

We talk about "the insurgency," but in Iraq, the term is misleading. There is no unified insurgency comparable to the Viet Cong or the Irish Republican Army (IRA). Iraq's armed resistance comprises a number of independent groups united only in their determination to drive the American occupiers out of the country. Slender threads link some of the groups, but there is no unified structure and no common political agenda. The mix includes irreconcilable Saddam Hussein loyalists, purged Baathist Party members, displaced and disaffected Sunnis, and local and foreign jihadists.

Some of the groups are bitter rivals. Jihadists under one banner or another appear to be increasingly dominating the mixture. This suggests both isolation and tenacity, along with growing ruthlessness as the insurgents' perceived constituency switches from Iraqis to God. It is most evident in the group formerly led by Abu Musab al-Zarqawi, which claims credit for the bloody attacks on Shi'ite targets.

Shi'ite militias do not actively participate in the insurgency, but they are not entirely under Iraqi government control either. They remain an autonomous force ready to go after the Sunnis or to confront the government or Coalition forces if aroused.

Much of the violence is purely criminal. Made outlaws by the American invasion, some groups find profit in prolonging chaos. These include the Iraqi gangs that kidnap for ransom or sell foreign hostages to the jihadists, extort money from local and foreign businesses, run various rackets under the occupation, and engage in the systematic looting and sale of antiquities from Iraq's now unprotected archeological sites. Even if the insurgency is suppressed, Iraq will still have a serious long-term crime problem.

The things we can measure do not indicate imminent collapse of the insurgency. Estimates of insurgent strength have increased over the past two years. In the early days of the Iraqi insurgency, at the end of 2003 and the beginning of 2004, the estimated insurgent strength nationwide was around 5,000. By May 2004, the estimate increased to 15,000, then in July, to 20,000. Throughout 2005 and into the spring of 2006, despite reports of more than 50,000 insurgents being killed or detained, the estimates of insurgent strength have remained in the range of 15,000 to 20,000. Insurgent recruiting has clearly continued. These are only estimates, to be sure, but the trajectory is clearly upward.[25]

Enemy-initiated incidents continue to occur at the rate of about 75 a day.[26] Multiple-fatality bombings show an upward trend. In the absence of other accessible indicators, easily tracked U.S. casualties have become the sole focus of American public attention. U.S. losses, measured against the much higher levels of most 20th century American wars, are not crippling, but they may prove to be politically unsustainable.

Reconstruction is behind schedule, although vital infrastructure is slowly being improved. An elected Iraqi government is in place, but it is important to avoid the American presumption that political progress means diminished violence. Sophisticated political institutions can coexist with high levels of political violence, as is amply illustrated by the tenacious civil wars in Colombia and Sri Lanka, which have been practicing democracies for decades.

Meanwhile, U.S. intelligence is inadequate, and there are too few American, Coalition, and government troops in Iraq to stamp out the insurgency. Even with ample recruits, Iraqis will need years to take over their own security. Their performance is improving, but Iraq's security forces lack logistics, armor, mobility, airlift, and staff coordination. Coalition forces cannot control Iraq's borders with Iran or Syria, both of which have incentives to make things difficult. Even bringing security up to the level of that on the U.S. border with Mexico, hardly an impenetrable barrier, would require a huge investment and might have little significant impact on the insurgents' operational effectiveness.

"Fighting Them There Instead of Fighting Them Here"

The invasion of Iraq galvanized jihadists worldwide, facilitated new recruiting, provoked new terrorist attacks, and provided a new destination point for jihadist volunteers eager for action. Clandestine networks that once facilitated the transport of recruits to Afghanistan reorganized to deliver recruits to Iraq. Foreign fighters, primarily from Arab countries, make up about 10 to 15 percent of the insurgent strength.[27] These foreign fighters are reportedly the majority of suicide bombers. The same networks also operate in reverse, providing a route out for hardened operatives who depart Iraq and return to the neighboring Middle Eastern or European countries.

Because suicide bombings have been the principal tactic of al Qaeda's cell in Iraq, which was led by Jordanian Abu Musab al-Zarqawi, and because Zarqawi was a frequent communicator to the public and was seen as the mastermind behind efforts to foment a civil war through attacks on Iraq's Shi'ites, there has been a tendency to see the insurgency as an al Qaeda operation. This ignores the fact that Iraqis have constituted 90 percent of the resistance.

The obstinate belief among some American officials that there was a close relationship between Saddam Hussein and al Qaeda, combined with the prominent role of jihadists in the current insurgency, has led to the persistent claim that by fighting terrorists in Iraq, America reduces the likelihood that it will have to fight them in the United States. It is an appealing idea but one that does not stand up to analysis.

To begin with, the argument assumes that there is a fixed number of terrorists in the world. Eliminating one in Iraq subtracts one from the total. In fact, most of the combatants killed or captured by Coalition forces in Iraq are Iraqi insurgents created by opposition to the invasion itself. They were not part of the broader jihadist enterprise, although some were converted to al Qaeda's ideology after joining the resistance.

True, some of the foreign jihadists who have showed up to fight in Iraq might have been candidates for operations in their own countries had there been no war. But their numbers do not appear to be great, and many are from countries adjacent to Iraq. Still, we do not know with any certainty the volume of jihadists going into Iraq or the number going out. At some point, Iraq may become a net exporter rather than a net importer of terrorists.

Nor are we, in the jargon of movie Westerns, heading the outlaws off at the pass. Iraq is not a front line through which terrorists must pass on their way to somewhere else. Moreover, fighting in Iraq is not so distracting to jihadists elsewhere that they are unable to prepare and carry out operations. The pace of terrorist operations has not slowed a bit since the invasion of Iraq.

The "fighting them there, not here" logic does work if one adopts a sort of preemptive line of thinking that runs something like this: If Saddam Hussein had been permitted to develop weapons of mass destruction, he might have been tempted to arm terrorists with them. Removing him, therefore, was a way of preventing al Qaeda from acquiring such weapons, which it most certainly would have used against the United States. But this is scaffolding built on *if, might,* and *would,* not on analysis.

British Prime Minister Tony Blair offered a broader and more nuanced interpretation of the connection between the fighting in Iraq and the fight against terrorism: "If Iraq becomes a stable, democratic country able to defeat terrorism here [in Iraq]—which is the same kind of terrorism that we face the world over—if we can defeat it here, we deal it a blow worldwide."

The fact is, the war in Iraq has now become a critical theater in the broader campaign against the jihadists, and both sides know it. It is not because of the simple-minded notion that fighting them "there" means not fighting them "here." It is in the broader area of perceptions touched upon by Prime Minister Blair. If we can defeat the jihadists in Iraq, we will have dealt them a serious blow. And if instead, the United States is forced to withdraw in failure as Iraq spirals into sectarian chaos, the jihadists will have again proved their ability to defeat a superpower, while Americans descend into partisan finger-pointing.

A Training Academy for Jihadists

Meanwhile, the insurgency in Iraq is providing a training ground for jihadists that is more useful than the experience in Afghanistan. Much of Afghanistan is a sparsely populated, undeveloped mountain wilderness, where guerrilla fighting is unique. But the insurgency in Iraq offers lessons in urban guerrilla warfare in a very hostile environment, techniques of concealment, clandestine communications, roadside ambushes, sniper and counter-sniper tactics, and sabotage of vital infrastructure. These are more-fungible skills.

Learning in a guerrilla group or terrorist organization is a function of frequency of operations. Attacks at the rate of 75 a day offer numerous opportunities for learning and innovation. Both sides get smart fast. The insurgents have been extremely inventive in the construction of explosive devices, using shaped charges that can penetrate armor, remote detonating methods that cannot easily be jammed, creative ways of planting bombs on the fly, and sequenced attacks to penetrate defensive perimeters and increase casualties. Some of these new techniques are being disseminated through insurgent and jihadist web sites, raising terrorist capabilities worldwide. Knowledge gained in Iraq is already showing up in other places.

The insurgency is also producing a new cohort of battle-experienced jihadists to join the now-aging Afghan veterans. Although some of the foreign jihadist volunteers are used for suicide missions, others will survive and will eventually spread their skills, whatever the outcome of the fighting in Iraq. A protracted war in Iraq will continue to provide opportunities for learning, while success in counterinsurgent efforts will send the survivors fleeing to surrounding countries. Jordan, Syria, Yemen, Saudi Arabia, and the other Gulf nations must brace for new waves of more-experienced terrorists, some of them dedicated jihadists and others Iraqi renegades with no other options.

In any long contest, there are inevitably surprises—unpredictable events that can significantly alter the course of the war or how it is perceived. The insurgents in Iraq lack the capacity to launch a nationwide offensive on the scale of the 1968 Tet attacks in Vietnam, but they might carry out a major terrorist attack with heavy U.S. casualties. The insurgents understand this. Osama bin Laden reminds them that the devastating terrorist bombing that killed 244 U.S. Marines in Beirut in 1983 persuaded America to withdraw from Lebanon, and that the deaths of 17 American soldiers in Mogadishu forced the United States out of Somalia in 1993. In March 2006, authorities discovered a plot by insurgents to infiltrate Baghdad's heavily guarded Green Zone and seize hostages at the American and British embassies. This is just the kind of dramatic event that would be seen to puncture official declarations of optimism. Increasingly indiscriminate insurgent violence may provoke a backlash against the insurgents by angry Iraqis, but it could still lead to a full-scale sectarian civil war. A mistake in U.S. targeting leading to a terrible tragedy with heavy Iraqi casualties or revelations of new abuses could further turn U.S. and world opinion against the prolonged conflict.

Mounting Discontent and Competing Views

President Bush has demonstrated himself to be a resolute commander in chief, but he finds himself under growing pressure from two directions. First, public opposition to the war in Iraq is growing. The initial justification proved false—no weapons of mass destruction were found. Saddam Hussein's connection with 9/11 is now discredited—Iraq had nothing to do with the attack. The costs of the war are mounting. Its outcome is increasingly uncertain.

Second, opposition comes from the Pentagon itself. Wars wreck armies. When national survival is at stake, this is not an issue. But in a war of choice, preserving military capability to deal with other contingencies must be reckoned. With the fall of Baghdad, the continued fighting in Iraq ceased to be the Pentagon's preferred war. It has become precisely the kind of messy conflict American commanders hoped to avoid after Vietnam. The insurgency is stretching military manpower, reducing the reenlistment intentions of active-duty personnel,[28] ruining equipment, raising costs, and diverting acquisitions of new weapons. It also risks destroying military morale, along with perceptions of American military competence. Public expressions of confidence conceal private awareness that indefinite involvement increases the risk of ultimate failure.

The lack of clear-cut indicators of the situation in Iraq allows very different assessments, each of which is backed by some evidence, and each of which has different implications for the future. The official U.S. government position is that we are making progress in Iraq and ultimately will prevail if we stay the course. According to an independent assessment by retired General Barry R. McCaffrey, who toured Iraq in April 2006, the situation is "perilous, uncertain, and extreme, but far from hopeless." U.S. strategy is "painfully but gradually succeeding."[29] Proponents of this view can point to a number of positive developments: The insurgency is now concentrated in a few provinces. It offers no political program and has limited political appeal, in contrast to the undeniable political progress that has been made in creating a new Iraqi government. Reconstruction is behind schedule but making progress. The economy is slowly recovering. Iraqi security forces are expanding, and their performance is improving. This will permit a withdrawal of some U.S. forces, although American soldiers could stay in Iraq for years. These claims are true in the dimensions cited. However, the administration's credibility is undercut by premature past declarations of victory, repeated claims that we are winning despite continuing bloodshed, and a tendency to ignore obvious difficulties.

Proponents of a second view agree with the claim that we are making progress, but they argue that it will take too long, kill and wound too many American soldiers, cost too much, oblige us to become hated occupiers, and destroy our armed forces. In this view, staying the course is politically untenable. Unless the level of violence changes significantly, by 2008, five years after the invasion and an election year in the United States, between 3,000 and 4,000 American soldiers will have been killed and 20,000 to 30,000 will have been wounded. Direct U.S. expenditures will have amounted to nearly half a trillion dollars (some would argue as much as $2 trillion if the indirect costs are calculated).[30] Therefore, it is argued, the United States must withdraw before 2008.

A third view argues that we cannot defeat the insurgency without deploying significantly more troops, which is highly unlikely, or making significant changes in strategy, deployment, force structure, and tactics. According to this view, while encouraging the newly elected Iraqi government to be inclusive, to rein in the militias, and, hopefully, to avoid a sectarian civil war, we must reconfigure Coalition forces for pacification. In fact, however, the armed forces are making only modest changes in equipment, tactics, and training in response to their experience, and they are likely to resist fundamental changes in deployment and force structure.

A fourth position argues that the United States is the problem. Our continued military involvement inevitably fuels the insurgency, while our understandable security measures endanger and alienate ordinary Iraqis. Under this view, the Iraqis want us out and we should withdraw.

Common to all four positions is the element of American withdrawal. "Victory," however it may be defined, is no longer a prerequisite to getting out. Military and political realities in Iraq are forcing the United States to recast its objectives. As opposed to "mission creep"—the gradual expansion of military goals once operations begin—we see in Iraq what might be called "mission shrink," which can be defined as the gradual downshifting of objectives to reduce expectations. What began as an easily won war to effect regime change has become an effort to defeat a growing armed resistance. With the failure to attract more contributors to the U.S.-led coalition and the unwillingness to commit more U.S. troops, the objective has been downsized again to simply enabling the Iraqis to take over the war. Slow progress in that effort has led to the recognition that the fighting in Iraq is likely to continue long after U.S. soldiers depart, which in turn decouples American withdrawal from any specific criteria on the ground. This is precisely what officials in Washington want to avoid—a timetable that makes withdrawal the paramount objective.

The Dangers of Withdrawal

Withdrawals are always dangerous. The argument that insurgents will simply stand down until the Americans leave, then renew their attacks, is wrong. Stand-downs are dangerous for insurgents. Inactivity reduces the flow of recruits and risks the departure of those already in the resistance. Moreover, insurgents know that any subsidence in the violence will reduce the pressure on the United States to get out—many Americans want to leave primarily because too many American soldiers are being killed or wounded and the effort is costing too much. In addition, standing down would expose the insurgents to a sudden offensive. The United States is not offering any truces, nor would such offers be trusted. The insurgents have to keep fighting to hold their forces together, to keep pressure on the United States, and to be battle-ready for the crucial post-American-withdrawal struggle, which they anticipate.

Significantly reducing the number of U.S. forces deployed in Iraq and replacing them with newly fielded Iraqi forces would diminish overall strength on the government side. Although the Iraqi forces have the advantages of language and acceptability to the population (unless they are dominated by Shi'ite and Kurdish volunteers), they lack the strength of the American forces they replace, and it will take at least two to five years for them to develop into an effective force.[31] Ambassador L. Paul Bremer, who led the Coalition Provisional Authority and who believed from the beginning of the insurgency that there were too few troops, has warned that American forces should not "stand down" as Iraqi forces "stand up," but the combined total of Iraqi and Coalition forces should increase, confronting the insurgents with overwhelming strength and saturating the territory with military and police forces.[32]

Withdrawals also will reduce the military power of those American soldiers who remain, limiting their ability to respond to new contingencies and exposing them to increased danger. The United States will be sidelined. Withdrawals, once initiated, tend to accelerate.

On the other hand, efforts to remain in Iraq as long as possible in order to ensure a favorable outcome will require reducing American casualties, which means avoiding enemy contact and confinement to garrisons. While constant danger can hardly be called a morale-builder, inaction can be devastating to morale. Once soldiers are convinced the United States is getting out, morale will be a problem anyway. No one wants to be the last soldier killed in a dead project.

Without U.S. protection (or constraint), Iraqi forces increasingly will do things their way. This could mean inaction and accommodation, or it could mean human-rights abuses that will further embarrass the United States. The perception that the United States is getting out will also reduce our ability to influence Iraqi political developments. Gratitude, either for toppling Saddam Hussein or for leaving Iraq, will not be the predominant expression. Even previously friendly Iraqi politicians will find it necessary to brandish their nationalist credentials and to deny their past dependence on the occupiers—if necessary, by becoming resistant to American pressure. The Iraqi street may become even more hostile, producing images that will increase U.S. domestic pressure to accelerate the withdrawal. We will have few friends on the way out.

Preparing for the Long Haul

Guerrilla wars often go on for decades and seldom end neatly. Over a period of years, a guerrilla subculture may emerge in which the entire society is devoted to the fighting. Criminal activities necessary to refill war chests become an end in themselves. Political grievances become secondary to maintaining cash flow. Such operations don't willingly put themselves out of business. Some civil wars end only when both sides collapse in exhaustion.

It seems unlikely that Coalition forces will be able to completely wipe out Iraq's armed resistance in the foreseeable future. Political deals that co-opt some of those in the resistance are possible and could reduce the violence, but other insurgents, especially those motivated by religious zeal, will not easily lay down their weapons. "Victory," in its classic sense, will not be achieved, nor does any scenario envision an insurgent takeover. It seems more likely that some level of fighting will go on in Iraq for years. Within that narrowed spectrum, several outcomes are possible.

At the positive end of the spectrum, a reasonably stable government could face a continuing terrorist campaign. Baghdad could resemble Belfast at the height of the Troubles. Despite the violence, this would be a dramatic improvement over the current situation.

Alternatively, Iraq might come to resemble something like today's Colombia, a democratic and progressive country suffering from a long-term insurgency that kills several thousand people a year (less than one-sixth the current death rate in Iraq). Or perhaps Iraq might look more like Algeria in the decade after 1992, an arena of bloody Islamic violence and brutal government repression. But even this would be a significant improvement over the current level of violence.

At the other end of the spectrum, sectarian violence might escalate further, with Shi'ite militias waging war on Sunni insurgents, a bloody partition of the country, ethnic cleansing, and slaughter in the name of Allah. Baghdad could come to resemble Beirut during Lebanon's civil war, a barricaded capital in a failed state. Some observers have called for an orderly partition to prevent a bloody civil war.[33]

Whatever the outcome, the jihadists will never recover in Iraq the same sanctuary they enjoyed in Afghanistan. They will still find themselves surrounded by hostile forces—Shi'ite and Kurdish militias; Iraq's own army, presumably still backed by the United States; and on Iraq's frontiers, Syria, Jordan, Saudi Arabia, and the other Gulf states, all determined to contain the ideological and terrorist threat to their own regimes.

Where does that leave our overall assessment? The United States has not been able to crush al Qaeda. We have been able to degrade its capabilities, eliminate its planners, chase its leaders, and disrupt some of its operations, but we have not yet devised the means to reduce the appeal of its ideology or stop its recruiting.

A bold gamble to deliver a strategic blow, eliminate a potential threat in Iraq, and fundamentally change the politics of the Middle East has instead generated a new conflict that is now important to both sides. American efforts have yet to succeed. It seems increasingly unlikely that the United States can deliver an Iraq free of continuing violence. But neither will continued fighting in Iraq result in the caliphate from which al Qaeda's jihadists can conquer the Middle East. Jihadists may fantasize that U.S. retreat from Iraq will lead to America's collapse, as they believe the Soviet retreat from Afghanistan led to the collapse of the Soviet Union, and that Middle Eastern governments will fall one after another, but neither event is likely. Whatever the outcome, the war will not end in Iraq.

It is evident that this conflict will not be decided in the near future but will persist, as did the Cold War, possibly for decades, during which setbacks will be obvious and progress will be hard to measure. Beyond al Qaeda, we confront a protracted ideological conflict, of which the terrorist campaign waged by disconnected jihadists is a symptom. This wider war will include periodic terrorist attacks, as the jihadists exploit issues that anger the Muslim world, seek ways to sabotage local and Western economies, and intimidate Muslim states into passivity or passive support. Jihadists will also seek to expand their media campaigns, infiltrate non-jihadist Islamic missions, take control of existing congregations, and increase their recruiting opportunities. For galvanizing issues, the jihadists will be able to rely upon the periodic manifestations of racism, Islamophobia, and the heavy-handed actions of a security-obsessed West. Jihadists will incorporate local grievances in their agendas, while local dissidents will use the jihadist campaigns to advance their own political ends.

At the same time, radical Islamists will fund new missions, seek to establish hegemony over the interpretation of faith, push for separate status and autonomy in societies where Muslims are a minority—separate schools, separate courts—and, in Muslim countries, demand a stricter application of Sharia, or Quranic law. In their international campaign, the jihadists will seek common grounds with leftist, anti-American, and anti-globalization forces, who will in turn see, in radical Islam, comrades against a mutual foe. Unchecked, the continued terrorist campaign and continuing insidious pressures toward radicalization and extremism could produce a string of Taliban- and Tehran-like regimes. Preparing for this long war will require a deeper understanding of the challenge we confront and the formulation of a set of strategic principles to guide our actions.

Historic American Engineering Record/Jet Lowe

If you want to know what enemy leaders are thinking about, listen to what they have to say.

CHAPTER THREE

Knowing Our Enemy

Action films rarely inquire into the mindsets or motives of villains. The villains are simply presented as bad guys, foils for superheroes. Cyclops is always a monster. Dragons breathe fire. Witches are wicked. One need not ask why.

We are likewise inclined to see terrorists as fiends, wild-eyed expressions of evil, diabolical but two-dimensional, somehow alien—in a word, inhuman. Government officials routinely denounce terrorists as mindless fanatics, savage barbarians, or, more recently, "evil-doers"—words that dismiss any intellectual content. The angry rhetoric may resonate with apprehensive homeland audiences, but it impedes efforts to understand the enemy. We cannot formulate multidimensional responses to terrorism that combine physical destruction with political warfare if we do not see our adversaries as anything other than comic-book villains.

This was not the case during the Cold War. Although few Americans inquired deeply into Marxist doctrine, battalions of Kremlinologists devoted decades of scholarship to understanding how Soviet leadership viewed the world, thought about strategy, calculated the balance of terror that prevented nuclear war. When confronted with the challenge of guerrilla warfare in the early 1960s, young Special Forces officers pored over the writings of Mao Zedong, Che Guevara, Regis Debray, and Carlos Marighella in order to better understand this new breed of adversaries.

Sometimes, such analysis can be done best outside of government, where analysts are freed from the immediate demands of operational intelligence as well as from the institutional and bureaucratic harnesses that may constrain thinking. This is not to ignore the recent and highly original work on terrorists done in the intelligence community or by individuals who have pursued the subject on their own, often with little official encouragement.[34] More than 50 years ago, Nathan Leites of RAND wrote the pathbreaking book *The Operational Code of the Politburo.*[35] Understanding the enemy has continued to be a feature of RAND's research over the past half-century. During the Vietnam War, RAND conducted in-depth (and sometimes controversial) studies of the structure, motivation, and morale of the Viet Cong, and in the 1970s, I and other RAND researchers began to explore terrorist mindsets and decisionmaking.

There are numerous obstacles to trying to think like the enemy, not the least of which has been America's pragmatic approach to terrorism. In an effort to push beyond the futile polemics that impeded (and still impede) efforts to define terrorism and to concentrate on building international consensus on the need for measures to deal with it, the United States has generally defined terrorism according to the quality of the act, not the identity of the perpetrators or the nature of their cause. Terrorist tactics are usually presented as ordinary crimes—murder, kidnapping, hijacking—that fall into the realm of terrorism because they are calculated to create fear and alarm for political ends. In this strict constructionist approach, the act defines the terrorist, not the other way around. Any deviation from it, even inquiries into terrorists' mindsets—or worse, into their motives—has risked sliding into the philosophical swamp in which one man's terrorist was another man's freedom fighter.

This narrow approach was partially successful in producing a corpus of international conventions that reflected agreement on the need to prohibit certain tactics or attacks on certain categories of targets—for example, taking hostages, airline hijackings, or attacks on diplomats. Little by little, the conventions eventually covered most of what terrorists do, but they did not define terrorism itself.

Almost anyone who employed the prohibited tactics for political ends could be called a terrorist. The term then became promiscuously applied to a broad spectrum of entities, from individuals like the so-called Unabomber, Theodore Kaczynski—whose pretentious political rant only partially masked serious mental disorder—to secret police and other government entities that routinely resorted to terrorist tactics in order to discourage domestic foes or that employed terrorism as a means of surrogate warfare against enemy states. This large and diverse population makes it extremely difficult to talk about commonalities.

The Desire to See Terrorists as Mentally Disturbed

One corridor of inquiry welcomed in the early 1970s was psychopathology. Researchers looked for a terrorist or terrorist-prone personality. This put terrorism in the realm of aberrant behavior, comfortably outside the domain of politics and strategy: Because terrorists did crazy things, they must be mentally disturbed. Some investigators went further, seeking physiological explanations for terrorism. One psychiatrist advanced the theory that in addition to serious psychological problems, terrorists might suffer from vestibular malfunctions—inner-ear disorders that upset their balance and made them defiant of authority. The hijackers this psychiatrist interviewed, he said, not only had abusive fathers and highly religious mothers, but were late walkers who in adulthood substituted a struggle against authority for their earlier struggle against gravity. According to his theory, hijacking an airliner was simply their creative way of overcoming both gravity and authority. This is Freudian psychodynamics, always interesting, highly speculative, difficult to confirm.[36]

A corollary of this theory claimed that zinc, then becoming a popular vitamin supplement, was critical to the proper formation of the inner-ear structure and that the Middle East was a zinc-deficient region. Although bordering on the bizarre, these tantalizing theories found a welcome audience among those who wished to see terrorism as an illness. Their politically conservative advocates sometimes slyly slipped in asides like, "Lenin [or perhaps they said Stalin] was also a late walker," thereby suggesting that both terrorism and communism were behavioral disorders.

While psychiatrists and psychologists have had little luck in defining a terrorist personality, terrorists do seem to share some common personality attributes. They tend to be true believers who see the world in black and white, us versus them. They are action-prone risk-seekers, determined to demonstrate the fervency of their beliefs through violent means. They have an unusual fascination with firearms and explosives, finding magazines about guns and ammunition more appealing reading than ideological material. Those held hostage by terrorists have reported that their captors spent an inordinate amount of time cleaning and oiling their weapons, far more than necessary for maintenance, suggesting a fetish quality. The guards of one hostage introduced him to the submachine gun that had killed an ambassador as if it were an autonomous actor.[37] A Freudian analyst would find fascinating the cartoons drawn by one terrorist in prison, which show a connection between an exploding bomb and sexual orgasm. One is tempted to see repressed sexual rage in recurring jihadist fantasies about knocking down tall buildings. "I picked up a Kalashnikov," says one jihadist leader, "and after feeling the weapon in my hands, found that it was ready to talk to the enemy. The bullet was in the chamber and it was ready to fire and I felt ecstatic . . . my joy knew no bounds."[38] But do these tendencies turn certain individuals into terrorists, or are they merely the reflections of their participation in terrorist operations, which, after all, are about violence?

Undoubtedly, the ranks of terrorists have included sociopaths and psychopaths, thugs attracted by the prospect of violent action or who exploit political pretensions to cloak violent tendencies. But there have been few genuinely psychotic terrorists, individuals crazy in any clinical sense. Terrorism does not appear in the manual of mental disorders. Nonetheless, since terrorism is seen as bizarre behavior, the perception that terrorists must themselves be mentally disturbed remains, and this has discouraged inquiry into terrorist mindsets, worldviews, and strategies. At the same time, the fact that the earlier psychological inquiries proved fruitless has also discouraged such efforts.[39]

Behavioral studies that place terrorists in the framework of a self-isolating group or subculture offer a more promising line of inquiry. Here, terrorism is seen not as individual aberrant behavior, but rather as the product of the beliefs, mindsets, traditions, and operational code of a group. If an individual can be persuaded to adopt the code of the gang or group, individual behavior becomes more understandable.

But if terrorists could not be dismissed as crazies, they could instead be elevated to the realm of evil. Evil is a powerful concept. It resonates with those who have a Manichaean view of the world and is popular with those who see the devil not as a theological abstraction but as a real-world operator. This view also discourages research: Evil people are just evil. No further explanation is required, no deeper inquiry is necessary. To explore the mindset or the decisionmaking of evildoers is to try to fathom evil itself—it is futile and unnecessary. In this view, any inquiry that suggests taking terrorists out of the evil-incarnate category also undermines the inquirer's claim on good.

The understanding of terrorism itself can arouse suspicions. "Understanding" simply connotes comprehension, but "to be understanding" suggests something less judgmental, a softening of attitude toward punishment and retribution, substandard zeal in pursuing dangerous evildoers. Terrorists are not to be understood but to be eradicated.

American Discomfort with Questioning Beliefs, Impatience with Debating Motives

Some obstacles to knowing the enemy are peculiar to Americans. Although they are capable of ferocious partisan politics, Americans tend to be uncomfortable countering ideology. During the long Cold War against the Soviet Union, Americans firmly believed the notions of liberty, democracy, and capitalism to be superior. But most Americans saw the Soviet-American contest in secular geopolitical terms, even as American political leaders referred to "Godless communism" and called the Soviet Union the "evil empire." These were rhetorical devices. Citizens of an overtly religious nation, diverse in its religions and religious doctrines, Americans are nonetheless reluctant to inquire into the nature of anyone's individual faith. Tolerance dictates that beliefs, as opposed to overt manifestations of piety, be kept private, although this view has been changing in recent years.

This tolerant sentiment imposes constraints on inquiries that are seen as trespassing on religious beliefs. Most Americans are absolutely sincere in saying they have no quarrel with Islam, although ethnic prejudices against Arabs and other Middle Eastern–looking Muslims, especially since 9/11, are manifest. Unwittingly, this posture gives up a lot of ground to al Qaeda–inspired jihadists who have laced their revolutionary ideology with fundamentalist religious themes. They do so to gain adherents, but it also deters religiously tolerant opponents from challenging their beliefs and assertions.

Somewhat different obstacles prevail inside government circles. Communication of information becomes more economical at the higher levels in the hierarchy of officialdom. As time to communicate gets shorter, complexities are concentrated into brief talking points. Months of analysis are squashed into minutes. Caveats are discarded. The process does not permit providing much more than conclusions and action items. There is little time to discuss motives.

Prior to 9/11, briefings on terrorism always faced the additional problem of keeping the audience's attention. During the Cold War, Cabinet secretaries might spend considerable time examining the implications of political changes in Moscow or Soviet military research and development. After all, the survival of civilization hung in the balance. But terrorists were hardly considered superpower foes. They were nuisances, tiny handfuls of men with bombs and machine guns who created distracting crises. Should the commanders of the world's mightiest military power be obliged to listen to the political pretensions and Byzantine clan connections of some obscure little band in the back alleys of Beirut? There was one marked exception to this prevailing attitude: Long before 9/11, Secretary of State George

Shultz convened informal weekend meetings, invited outside advice, and personally participated in sometimes combative debate aimed at understanding the new terrorist adversaries.

That, of course, changed with 9/11, but al Qaeda and its affiliates, in American eyes, remained unworthy foes—dangerous certainly, and to be destroyed, but not to be dignified with detailed analyses of how they hoped to take over the world. Furthermore, terrorists did not mirror our military capabilities or match U.S. government organization. Government institutions are seldom eager for analyses that render themselves irrelevant. This is changing as a consequence of the campaign against al Qaeda and the continuing conflicts in Afghanistan and Iraq, but systematic efforts to raise awareness of the current enemy's way of thinking and methods still run into skepticism from senior military officers.

All of these factors have combined to impede the lines of inquiry that are prerequisite to formulating a strategy for what will probably be a very long struggle. Apart from some offices scattered throughout the intelligence community and islands of inquiry in the military services, the United States still lacks the institutional structure that will drive the investigation, assemble results from all sources, and identify new lines of attack.

The Jihadist Mindset

An inquiry into the mindset, motivations, and operational thinking of the jihadists connected with al Qaeda or inspired by its ideology would begin by asking about the worldview of jihadists, their view of war, their concept of fighting. It would ask not only what their strategy might be, but how they think about strategy. How do they view operations? Can we discern an operational code? By that we mean, what might make their hearts race? Are there things they would not do? What criteria guide their selection of targets, and how do they plan operations? Given their mindset, how might they assess their own situation? What is their vision of the future?

This is not a psychological study. It does, however, require that the analyst adopt the mental perspective of the subject. Switching sides analytically, which is not always easy, opens up entire new vistas. It suggests new analytical frameworks for intelligence. It challenges our presumptions. It points toward new counterterrorist strategies.

The terrorist attacks of September 11, 2001, and the events that followed have prompted an avalanche of books about terrorism, jihad, and al Qaeda. Today there are more than 200 post-9/11 titles. Some are superficial offerings hastily produced to exploit the market, and some are highly polemical, but many reflect solid scholarship that informs us about the nature of the terrorist foes we face. The analysis presented here has been augmented by excellent historical studies that put contemporary jihadist ideology into a historical context. Original jihadist documents are also becoming increasingly available.

Very little material that derives from interrogations of detained terrorists is in the public domain, although some material has emerged through official commission reports and testimony at terrorist trials. However, the jihadists who remain at large are not quiet. They communicate regularly in video and audiotapes and on numerous web sites. These communications reflect ambitions, assertions, exhortations, and fantasies, the stuff of propaganda, all mixed together, but they are nonetheless revealing.[40]

Today's news media also represent a powerful investigative machine that quickly provides detailed accounts of events and, more relevant to our focus here, information about the people involved. Published interviews with relatives and acquaintances of terrorists, coupled with official accounts and trial testimonies, contribute to a group portrait. There are no less than eight books in English about bin Laden himself. To be sure, the reporters sometimes get it wrong, just as intelligence collected through clandestine sources is sometimes wrong, but overall, there is a lot of useful material.

The portrait that emerges from that material differs from the popular view. The jihadist terrorists we confront are neither extraterrestrial nor satanic. They are hard, determined men, but men still. They disagree. They argue. Their mindsets and their concepts of fighting are foreign to us, but they make sense in the context of their own beliefs and circumstances. The terrorists can be deconstructed and understood.

Listening to the Enemy

I start with a simple proposition: If you want to know what enemy leaders are thinking about, listen to what they have to say. Terrorists traditionally have been poor communicators. One might suppose that if they had been effective communicators, they might not have become terrorists. One reason for carrying out dramatic acts of violence is to make people pay attention to the perpetrators' words. Technological developments in the late 20th century—television, communications satellites, video cameras—provided terrorists with access to an audience of global proportions. But while violent incidents attracted the attention of the news media, the coverage focused on the human drama, the burnt flesh and raw emotion of the event; the terrorists' message was lost in the sobs and shouting.

The librettos never matched the action anyway. Terrorists offered unwieldy slogans, incomprehensible rants, mind-numbing strategic directives filled with impenetrable prose. Even when terrorists were granted airtime or front-page space in return for the release of hostages and the audience was willing to make a determined effort to listen or read, it was never easy to figure out what the terrorists were talking about. From their tiny closed universes, they spoke an alien language. Without guns and bombs, terrorists could bore you to death.

Not so with al Qaeda. The 9/11 attacks established the brand. They gave al Qaeda global stature and a degree of credibility that its leaders still trade on. Technology also benefited bin Laden. From the top down, the jihadist enterprise is about communications. Its leaders are, above all, talking heads. No previous terrorist chieftains have ever communicated so prolifically or effectively; nor have they ever had the extended reach provided by modern communications technology, continuous news coverage, sympathetic television outlets, and the Internet.

Charismatic communicators have always effectively exploited the media available to them to spread their message. For centuries, books, broadsheets, pamphlets, newspapers, and speeches to assembled audiences were the only available tools. Later, both Franklin Roosevelt and Adolf Hitler used live radio to talk directly to their people. The Nazis added filmed spectacles to reinforce their message. Fidel Castro still delivers marathon speeches on television. Tape cassettes with messages from the Ayatollah Khomeini circulated in Tehran before the Iranian revolution. But none of these vehicles could compare with the Internet in its ability to carry a message quickly and directly to millions of people around the world.

The Polemics of Osama bin Laden

Our best source of information about al Qaeda is Osama bin Laden himself. Delivering a message of endless holy war against a demonized enemy, bin Laden is a frequent and fervent communicator. Before September 11, he made bellicose pronouncements, issued declarations of war, and conducted interviews with reporters in which he listed the grievances of those he appointed himself to represent and outlined the course of action that he claimed God commanded. Between September 11, 2001, and April 2006, despite being the world's most hunted man, bin Laden broadcast 24 statements. His rants are dismissed as propaganda, which, of course, they are. But his words also provide a window into the thinking of al Qaeda's leadership.

Bin Laden's personal messages are augmented by those of his principal lieutenant, Sheikh Ayman al-Zawahiri. Until his death, the commander of al Qaeda's forces in Iraq, Abu Musab al-Zarqawi, also augmented these messages. Leaders of al Qaeda affiliates elsewhere have made additional statements and have even launched online magazines, while hundreds of web sites carry official communiqués and claims from various fronts in the jihad, discuss targets and tactics, and offer instruction on how to make bombs. Suicide attackers leave taped messages to be played after their deaths. Jihadists talk a lot.

Satellite television stations based in the Middle East play excerpts from bin Laden's and Zawahiri's latest commentaries. Broadcasting the other side's voice brings these new news outlets political credibility and advertises their own presence. But even al Jazeera rarely broadcasts bin Laden's speeches in their entirety, whereas the Internet offers direct, unmediated access. Material that news outlets might choose not to present is soon available through other channels. The original texts are in Arabic, a language spoken by about 200 million people, but translated excerpts are quickly distributed, enough to send the hordes of reporters and terrorism experts swarming.

The Origins of the Ethos

The successful campaign of the mujahedin against the Soviet occupation of Afghanistan imparted to its participants, and especially to the volunteers from abroad, a strong sense of identity. Considered inferior fighters by their Afghan allies—those fierce bearded men, unconquered and uncorrupted by alien culture—the foreign volunteers had to develop their own equally fierce ethos. It was grafted onto a selective rendition of militant Islam expressed through the concept of jihad, which was interpreted exclusively as physical combat—tribal warrior traditions that were seen as the ultimate expression of manhood and virtue. With superior religious devotion, the foreign volunteers would be more ruthless, more ready to die.

Like all exclusive identities, the jihadist identity offered self-confidence, self-esteem, a strong sense of belonging. It turned determined recruits into men who considered themselves to be, and were expected to act as, heroes. That is the secret of all military elites: men who, beyond grueling training and physical endurance, have dug deep into reserves of inner spiritual strength to pass the trials and proofs of admittance.

Victory in the face of long odds granted a mythical status to the Afghan veterans but set them adrift, craving new enemies. Eternal warriors require eternal war. The new war was Osama bin Laden's invention. He created and communicated a new narrative of never-ending conflict with the infidel aggressor and its Western avatar, the United States. From the Crusades to the Persian Gulf War, he assembled a perpetual foe. From the military campaigns of the Prophet Muhammed himself, bin Laden distilled a doctrine that would assure ultimate victory.

Every major terrorist attack directed or inspired by al Qaeda has been intended to preserve and propagate the sense of heroic identity and mission that first developed in Afghanistan. Attacks would inevitably provoke counterattacks, thereby confirming bin Laden's allegation of continuing aggression, ensuring the isolation of the jihadists from all rival influences, and making bin Laden their exclusive interlocutor.

A band of outlaw believers pursued by enemies of their own invention—conceptually, it is little different from what Jim Jones did when he led his Christian tribe to Guyana in 1978, although in that case the violence turned inward and the believers all perished in a mass homicide/suicide. Conceptually, it also differs little from the mindset that Shoko Asahara inculcated in his murderous cult in Japan in the 1990s.

A Powerful Polemic

Wartime communications are aimed primarily at the home front. In the case of al Qaeda, the home front consists of those who already subscribe to the jihadist ideology or who may be persuaded to subscribe to it. Osama bin Laden clearly states to his minions his overall purpose: "My message to you concerns inciting and continuing to urge for jihad, . . . so lend me your ears and open up your hearts to me."[41] Lest anyone misunderstand the purpose of jihad and consider it a form of spiritual calisthenics, bin Laden is explicit: "It is a religious-economic war," he says. "There can be no dialogue with the occupiers except through arms."

Bin Laden excoriates those of substandard zeal. He denounces the American aggressors as infidel conquerors, interested only in stealing Arab oil, or as war profiteers seeking corporate dividends in bloody conflict. He argues that the United States can be brought down by destroying its economy. He extols those who die for the cause as heroes and asks God to accept them as martyrs.

Bin Laden's themes are hardly new: "The situation is desperate . . . we are the victims . . . surrounded by enemies . . . our backs to the wall . . . our people persecuted . . . entitled to revenge . . . war is the only alternative to annihilation . . . Providence commands us . . . history propels us . . . heroism is demanded . . . sacrifices are necessary." This was Hitler's message too.

It is a powerful polemic, a rallying cry filled with references to humiliation, shame, God, heroism, and honor, and like all such messages, it has a certain appeal to the young and restless who are filled with natural rage. It also evokes sympathy among broader audiences, even if few sympathizers actually join al Qaeda's jihad.

To counteract the popular view that al Qaeda's top leadership is on the run, isolated, and out of touch, the dissemination of bin Laden's messages is intended to show that despite the intense high-tech manhunt, he remains at large and in touch. He is still able to observe events, and he remains able to communicate publicly with growing frequency, confident that his communications will not compromise his own security. He demonstrates his continued relevance by provoking reactions—public commentary, threat alerts, and statements from world leaders, including President Bush himself. Bin Laden's followers see proof of his survival as evidence of divine protection.

His messages also serve to confirm his leadership. He does not merely communicate, he hands down judgments, he summons, he lays out strategy, he asserts his authority even over attacks in which al Qaeda plays no role, he congratulates, he hands out promotions. He claims that he is busy preparing further operations.

Like any politician on the campaign trail, bin Laden presents several personas—warrior, statesman, missionary. A skilled propagandist, he segments his audience into fighters, potential recruits, sympathetic Muslims, and the broader Arab and Muslim communities. He occasionally reaches out further to proselytize among those of any faith opposed to American policy and others dismayed by the continued fighting in Iraq. These tend to be politically more-sophisticated messages, with less emphasis on warrior themes, although bin Laden is always aware of his base.

For each group, bin Laden offers specific messages: Violence is justified because Muslims are persecuted everywhere and must defend themselves. Corrupt Muslim tyrants allied with the infidels are apostate and must be overthrown. The "Zionist-Crusader chain of evil" (bin Laden's answer to President Bush's "axis of evil") must be broken. Muslims must not wait until the infidels' inexorable aggression destroys their faith; now is the time to join jihad. If Muslims fail to take action, the American-led infidel assault will not end until Islam is wiped out. Muslims must mobilize "to repulse the grand plots that have been hatched against our nation."

Sometimes, bin Laden's tone is gloomy. He warns that "the situation is serious and the misfortune is momentous." These are "pitch-black misfortunes," he repeats. His litany continues with references to "adversities and calamities," "hard times," "hypocrites" who have "submitted and succumbed to U.S. pressure," "sell-outs," resulting in "a great deterioration in all walks of life"—in sum, "a miserable situation." Hyperbole frequently figures in political rhetoric, but bin Laden's repetition, intensification, and exaggeration are both poetic and typical of Arabic style.

Some analysts have interpreted bin Laden's sometimes dark language as evidence of growing disillusionment and depression, inferring that he foresees defeat and doom. Indeed, one suspects that he, like all terrorists, is probably prone to disillusionment and depression, and his own martyrdom can never be far from his mind. But another interpretation is also possible: If he truly thought his side was losing, would he deliberately paint such a bleak picture? If we read carefully, we see that it is not al Qaeda that suffers "pitch-black" misfortunes, it is Islam. And the message is not one of despair; it is a call to arms.

Invoking the Divine

Bin Laden's speeches often have the quality of sermons. Like any fire-and-brimstone preacher, he warns his audience that the world is full of sin and going to hell, that the congregation is guilty of substandard zeal, that the end is nigh, that God's judgment awaits. The only way people can redeem themselves is through faith in God, expressed not merely by "performing some acts of worship," but by embracing armed struggle.

He frequently invokes God: "jihad in the cause of God," "God will judge them," "the rules set by God," "God suffices us . . . he is the best supporter." "By God, I am keen on safeguarding your religion and your worldly life!" he thunders.

Bin Laden also invokes the divine in more subtle ways. He refers to the battle of Badr, where the Prophet Muhammed defeated vastly superior enemy forces through the intervention of God. Speaking shortly after 9/11, bin Laden, still reveling in the glow of his triumph, admitted that even the calculations made by the operation's planners did not predict that the towers would fall. Yet the towers did come down, resulting in death and destruction far greater than what al Qaeda had expected. Was this truly an admission, or was it a sly way of suggesting that divine intervention rewarded the attackers with greater success than anyone had imagined? Was it not clear proof that Allah was on al Qaeda's side? Jihadists elsewhere have similarly pointed to natural disasters, including Hurricane Katrina, as evidence of God's wrath on the infidels.

A talented storyteller, bin Laden weaves parables from the Prophet's life with contemporary events, conflating centuries of history with today's headlines to illustrate a never-ending story of conflict. Although Americans regard the war on terrorism as a finite undertaking, with a beginning—9/11—and an end, bin Laden regards the war as a perpetual condition: "The struggle between us and them, the confrontation and clashing, began centuries ago, and will continue . . . until Judgment Day." The perpetual enemy merely changes costume. American leaders, according to bin Laden, are the pharaohs of the age (the same epithet that jihadists had applied to assassinated Egyptian President Anwar Sadat). Sometimes Americans are the new Romans, aggressively expanding their empire. Americans are later reincarnated as the Crusaders attempting to impose their colonies in the Holy Land.

Months before the invasion of Iraq, bin Laden said that American leaders were worse than the Mongol hordes led by the infidel

Hulagu Khan, who in the 13th century invaded the caliphate and sacked Baghdad, slaughtering tens of thousands of men, women, and children. Hulagu, the grandson of Genghis Khan, went on to take the city of Damascus, then swung south to crush the troublesome cities of Gaza and Nablus. For a while, Muslims feared that he would march on the holy cities of Mecca and Medina, wiping out Islam at its spiritual core. Bin Laden's historical reference, seemingly obscure to us, was to his audience a clever analogy which suggested that American armies, once in Iraq, would threaten Iraq's neighbors and expand their mission to occupy the entire Middle East. Of the American-led "raids," bin Laden says, "No one knows where they will end."[42]

In bin Laden's pronouncements, terrorist attackers are hailed as heroes. Further attacks are threatened, although bin Laden is never specific about the targets. Plans must be kept secret, and target selection is secondary anyway, for reasons we will come to later. But he warns that the war will again be brought to the United States: "You will see them in your homes the minute they [the preparations] are through." It is a message intended to give hope to those eager to see action, without commitment to a timetable, which no leader likes.

Bin Laden is a fatalist. What will happen? "No one knows," he says, except that God's support assures ultimate victory. To fulfill the obligation to keep fighting, to wage jihad as God commands, to inflict further blows on the enemies of God, to prove that one is worthy of God's support are the immediate requirements. Offering a specific plan of victory is politically risky and theologically presumptuous. Only God will decide when and how. The fight will continue until Judgment Day.

Offers of a Truce

Despite this eternal animosity and his own admonition that there can be no dialogue except through arms, bin Laden has on two occasions offered a truce to his foes. In 2004, he promised at least temporary immunity from terrorist attack to European nations that pulled their troops out of Afghanistan and Iraq. And in 2006, he offered the United States a truce in order to get on with the reconstruction of Afghanistan and Iraq.[43] What are we to make of these offers?

One unlikely explanation is that the offers were evidence of a war-weary leader who wants to give peace a chance. Government officials in both Europe and the United States promptly rejected the offers—there would be no "peace in our time" with the likes of bin Laden. American officials repeated the long-standing policy that we do not negotiate with terrorists. The assumption in both rejections was that the governments were the intended recipients of the offers. They were not. Bin Laden was again posturing in front of his jihadist audience, who would recall that in the tradition of jihad, a truce is a tactical maneuver, not a sign of weakness.

By offering Europeans a truce, bin Laden was hoping to exploit widespread sentiments in Europe against the American-led war in Iraq and fears of more attacks like the one in Madrid. He altered his language for the occasion. Religious references were reduced, and he spoke of "bloodsuckers" and "merchants of war" and "the billions of dollars in profit [the Iraq war brings] to the major companies . . . such as . . . Halliburton."[44] He railed against the "Zionist lobby," the "White House gang," and those "who are steering the world policy from behind a curtain." These are expressions more commonly found in the literature of the far left, suggesting that bin Laden might also be fishing for recruits in new waters, beyond the bounds of Islam.

His offer of a truce to the United States was in a similar vein. Intended to further erode the authority of a president whom bin Laden saw as weakened, this message, too, was loaded with language of the far left, implying that the fighting persists only because the billions spent are going to "those with influence" and "merchants of war." Talking about the reconstruction of Afghanistan and Iraq is also bin Laden's way of reminding his jihadist listeners that both countries need reconstruction because the United States invaded them, thereby reconfirming the U.S. role as the aggressor.

Consistent with al Qaeda's worldview, the jihadists believe they are fighting a defensive war that enables them to employ any and all means. If the infidels reject bin Laden's generous offers of truce and persist in their aggression, they must bear the responsibility for the punishment they will receive. Osama bin Laden has given fair warning, a traditional requirement in the Islamic rules of war. Like all terrorists, bin Laden thereby displaces culpability. If further violence happens, "Do not blame us," he says. "Blame yourselves."

Do bin Laden's public statements contain coded instructions to his followers to carry out attacks, as the coded BBC broadcasts of World War II did? The White House warned news media that it was dangerous to repeat bin Laden's messages, because they might contain coded messages to operators or incite people to kill Americans. Bin Laden himself dismissed the notion as farcical.

Some observers think that his tapes invariably presage attacks, but the evidence is not convincing. Since September 11, 2001, al Qaeda has released an audiotape or videotape containing bin Laden's voice every couple of months. Zawahiri's communications further crowd the calendar.

During the same period, al Qaeda's affiliates or jihadists inspired by the organization have carried out more than 30 major terrorist attacks. This does not include those in Russia—Chechen terrorists deny taking instructions from bin Laden—or in Iraq, where the violence has been continuous, or in Afghanistan. A major terrorist attack has occurred, on average, every eight weeks.

This means that there is often an attack shortly after a speech, but the lags between speeches and subsequent attacks vary from a few days to several months, hardly a reliable indicator or evidence of a coded connection. Moreover, security concerns make delivery of any tape from wherever bin Laden may be hiding to al Jazeera television a complicated and uncertain process for delivering operational instructions. In addition, we must assume that if bin Laden can get tapes to al Jazeera, however circuitous the route, he can also privately communicate with at least some of his commanders in the field. Concealing coded instructions in a public message requires separate communication in order for the intended recipient to understand the code. We leave code-cracking to the espionage buffs.

References to Carnelian Idols and Falling Towers

When talking about the destruction of the World Trade Center's twin towers, bin Laden refers to Hubal, a powerful pagan idol of red carnelian and gold that was worshipped by the Arabs of Mecca before Muhammed captured the city and destroyed the statues of Hubal along with hundreds of other idols. This is a powerful visual metaphor—Muhammed tearing down the idols, al Qaeda's men bringing down the towers in the name of God.

The architect of Hitler's cult reported that in the final days of World War II, Hitler himself became obsessed with the destruction of New York, seeing its skyscrapers burning like huge torches in the sky. As is evident from the Taliban's demolition of the Bamiyan Buddhas in Afghanistan to the videotaped beheadings of hostages in Iraq, the jihadists are iconoclasts, destroying with fire and sword the icons and symbols of their foes.

Bin Laden deliberately uses antique language to underscore warrior traditions. He appears with a Kalashnikov, but he speaks of steeds and swords. Jihadists do not speak of operations; they use the word "raid," a principal tactic of traditional tribal warfare. Captured al Qaeda training films about kidnappings and assassinations show jihadists leaping from trucks as they skid to a stop in a cloud of dust or leaping onto the backs of motorcycles as they speed off in the getaway—displays of horsemanship in a motorized age.

Jihadists are urged to pay no attention to their own losses, focusing instead on the losses they inflict on the enemy. Bin Laden is most graphic when describing the atrocities inflicted upon innocent Muslims or the punishment inflicted upon demoralized enemy soldiers. Bloody passages describing enemies with "torn limbs," "ripped apart," "eaten by demons of mines" and finding no escape "except for suicide" offer vicarious victories to wavering warriors.

Carefully crafted images accompany bin Laden's continuing call to arms. He exchanged wealth and comfort for hardship and danger.

Scenes of him descending a mountain path underscore his Spartan life. His clothes are simple, although always remarkably clean given the conditions in which he lives, suggesting stage management rather than frontline footage. His face is gaunt, his beard long, scraggly, and streaked with gray, in contrast to the exquisitely trimmed goatees of Arab potentates. This man would be out of place at a baccarat table in Monte Carlo. He looks like a prophet. His rifle is almost always visible, a reminder that he is a warrior.

It is the gun that ultimately gives his words relevance. Without 9/11, without further threats and continuing terrorist attacks to give him credibility, Osama bin Laden would be a minor eccentric. It was 9/11 that established his voice, that now commands a global audience for his communications. That was its purpose.

How Criticisms of bin Laden Miss the Point

It is easy to dismiss bin Laden's polemics as patent and often crude propaganda, which, of course, they are. We parse and criticize the content of his messages. His religious scholarship is deficient. He twists Islamic texts. He chooses selectively from the Quran to support his positions, ignoring all contrary teachings.

He exaggerates the independent role of the jihadists in defeating Soviet forces in Afghanistan. He fails to credit America's distribution of Stinger missiles that enabled outgunned insurgents to bring down Soviet helicopters. His explanation of the Soviet Union's subsequent collapse as a consequence of its defeat in Afghanistan is simplistic.

He fails to credit the United States for rescuing persecuted Muslims in Bosnia and Kosovo, for ensuring the independence of the Muslim republics after the Soviet collapse, for denouncing the excesses of the Russian forces in Chechnya. He falsely portrays America as determined to occupy the entire Middle East, steal its oil, subjugate its people, destroy its religion.

He contradicts himself, denouncing democracy, yet hailing the victory of Hamas in democratic elections. He offers no concrete political program, little hint of how things will be governed in the reestablished caliphate.

He inflates his own role as leader of a global movement. He claims responsibility for terrorist attacks that, insofar as we know, have no operational connection with al Qaeda's central leadership.

But to argue the content of bin Laden's communications is to miss the message. It is an American conceit that he is engaged in a debate with us. We are merely foils to enhance his arguments. His narrative rests upon themes of faith and history that resonate throughout the Arab world. His hyperbole hardly exceeds that of much political rhetoric.

It is not possible to defeat him by pointing out his distortions of the Quran. He does quote selectively. However, his most ardent listeners are not sophisticated religious scholars; they are angry and impatient young men already stirred up by radical imams, men who probably have seen circulating versions of the Quran that elevate jihad and define it in purely military terms.

While he overstates America's hostility toward Muslims, his complaints about the plight of the Palestinians or the suffering of Iraqis under the sanctions that were in effect before the war or in the chaos that followed the American invasion ring true with many Muslims.

Bin Laden does not offer a political platform. Prophets seldom do. He is summoning men to arms, not seeking votes. Were the Christian Crusaders led by men with political pamphlets? What appeals to his audience is not a political program but adventure, a chance to fight back, to carry out heroic deeds, to avenge centuries of humiliation, to restore lost honor. He offers self-improvement, redemption, salvation, martyrdom, paradise.[45]

It is true that bin Laden asserts his authority over attacks that, insofar as we know, were planned locally, not directed by al Qaeda central. But this is the way Americans view the struggle; we look for actual connections—instructions, agents, money transfers. If these don't exist, there is no connection. Bin Laden sees things differently. In his view, the jihadist enterprise is a single global struggle ordered by God. The existence or absence of the hard wiring sought by Western intelligence analysts has little meaning. Bin Laden, in his own eyes, is a warrior implementing God's will, a leader tallying his victories. This is, of course, an assertion that elevates his own authority, but it is one that is consistent with his beliefs.

Osama bin Laden is but a single man. Lacking a standing army at his command and spending his life in hiding make him militarily insignificant, but he still has the awesome power of ideas and words at his command. He is a motivator, not a field commander. He does not lead men in battle; he inspires them to fight.

The Jihadist Ideology

The genius of al Qaeda lies in its ability to articulate an inspiring ideology, revolutionary in its aim to overturn the current global order as thoroughly as its adherents destroyed the World Trade Center. This ideology is distilled from religious writings, historical narratives, and warrior traditions from the deserts of Arabia to the mountains of Afghanistan. Al Qaeda's ideology appears to still have traction even as the operational capabilities of the original organization are being degraded. Although it is impossible to count the number of jihadists in the world, we can say with confidence that jihadist views have become a powerful current within the discourse of the Muslim world and politics beyond.

What do we call the adherents of this ideology? Some have used the terms "Islamicists" or "Islamic extremists," but these miss the ideology's political component, and they offend the Muslim community, which rightly rejects the equation of al Qaeda's terrorism with the Islamic faith. Al Qaeda now means many things—a group of individuals who have sworn loyalty to Osama bin Laden, a constellation of groups affiliated with al Qaeda, individual militants fired up by its message. "Jihadists" may be the most appropriate term for the adherents of the ideology. These are individuals for whom jihad has become the sole reason for existence.

Jihadists agree with bin Laden that Islam is in mortal danger from a hostile West led by the United States. As they look at the map, they see that although larger American military units have deployed elsewhere in recent years, U.S. forces remain on holy ground in Saudi Arabia, and they lie just over the horizon in Kuwait, the United Arab Emirates, Bahrain, Qatar, and Oman. The United States has toppled the Taliban and continues to operate in Afghanistan, where foreign forces are increasing.

From the jihadist perspective, America supports the Zionists who occupy Palestine and subjugate the Palestinian people. In the eyes of jihadists, apostate regimes in many countries have become American puppets joining in the oppression of true Muslims. And jihadists believe that Saudi Arabia is corrupt, Iraq's government is a quisling regime propped up by American tanks, and Pakistan's government is a puppet that has abandoned the true path of Islam.

The West in general and the United States in particular are also responsible for condoning, if not perpetrating, the massacres and other atrocities inflicted upon Muslims in Bosnia, Chechnya, and the southern Philippines, as well as other places where jihadists believe Muslims continue to be persecuted.

America's threat is seen by the jihadists not solely as external. Jihad is, at root, a spiritual struggle. The jihadists view America as the leading source of the corruption that threatens Muslim souls. Pervasive American culture affronts morality. America's notions of a secular society, individual liberty, and gender equality—along with its materialistic ideology and its concepts of free trade—represent a poison that can destroy Muslims, seduce them, lead them from the true path. In the eyes of the jihadists, America must be fought on a moral and spiritual level as well as a political level.

The antidote to this poison is jihad, not merely as an internal spiritual quest, but as a war. Joining jihad provides the means for striking back at the infidels, halting the territorial encroachments of the aggressors, ending the massacres of the devout. Jihad is an elixir that will empower the jihadists themselves, give vent to their rage, end their humiliation, restore their masculinity, cleanse their souls, and demonstrate their worthiness before God to ensure their passage to paradise. "If the jihad does not need us," thunders one message, "we need the jihad, for it is a purification for the soul."

The United States thus also presents an opportunity for the jihadists. While the United States is seen as the greatest threat to Islam, it provides a common enemy and thereby a basis for building unity among Islam's diverse national, ethnic, and tribal groups. Disunity is the cause of Islam's weakness, according to the jihadists. Disunity prevented a unified response to the Crusades. Disunity allowed external foes to conquer and occupy Muslim territory piecemeal. Disunity dissipates the ability of Muslims to repulse the infidel occupiers today. But, according to the jihadist ideology, jihadists united against a common foe, mobilized from around the world, can—with God's help—defeat a superpower, just as they defeated the Soviet Union in Afghanistan. The United States, the leader of disbelief, provides that unifying foe.

The jihadists believe that through highly visual violent action, jihad will awaken the Muslim community, demonstrate the power of jihad, inspire the faithful, and foster spiritual revival. To the individual, jihad offers an opportunity for revenge, an opportunity to restore honor and ultimately Islam's lost greatness. It is a powerful message with an appeal that thrives on the failure of previous ideologies to bring Arabs and Muslims worldwide respect and influence.

The jihadists define their struggle through action. Islam is to be defended through action. Believers will be awakened, inspired, recruited, and instructed through action. Action will propagate jihadist ideology, expand its following. Action will unify the global struggle. Action will shield believers from corruption. While eloquent words can inspire, the eloquence of action is the ultimate expression of true belief.

Jihadists realize that they are no match for America's military might in open battle. Instead, they believe that their superior spirituality will defeat America's superior technology. While they are ready to die for their convictions, they see America's sensitivity to casualties and its materialism as vulnerabilities. They know they will not defeat America militarily; they want instead to impose unacceptable costs in blood and treasure that will force the United States to withdraw from the Middle East. Both concepts of warfare—spiritual and economic—seek to defend or recover territory lost to foreign invaders.

Although both use violence to proselytize, jihad guerrilla warfare differs from Maoist doctrine in that there is no direct contact between the jihadists and the population to be persuaded. Jihadists engage their audience only through claims of responsibility or posthumous statements issued on web sites and through the news media. They are avatars in a virtual world.

Moreover, jihadists don't see their power coming from the masses. Jihadists lament injustices, but they are not interested in merely improving anyone's material well-being. They harbor no pretense of popular will being expressed through formal political structures. Jihadists seek to arouse, not organize, the people. In fact, jihad offers little in the way of a practical political program at all. True believers say that legitimate authority derives only from God, whose will is to be imposed from above. Jihad simply brings the word of God, to which one submits.

Mao did not see guerrilla warfare as an independent form of warfare, he did not believe guerrilla warfare alone could achieve victory, and he rejected unorganized guerrilla warfare. Mao was very much an organization man, not a romantic anarchist. The jihadists carefully organize individual raids, but beyond galvanizing Muslims worldwide to action, they offer no theory about how this vast army of fighters, if they showed up, would be organized: An unstoppable horde led by a thousand sheikhs galloping across the plains in the name of God? Thousands of autonomous little al Qaedas answering directly to bin Laden?

A Political Strategy or a Religious War?

Is there a strategy beyond the narrative? Analysts debate this. Some see al Qaeda as a political insurgency, driven by specific grievances—oppression by corrupt local leaders, Israel's subjugation of the Palestinians, the presence of U.S. forces, the theft of Arab wealth. According to this view, al Qaeda's violence is a response to specific policies. It expresses itself in religious language because this provides it with a set of symbols and references that resonate throughout the Muslim world and give its political rebellion legitimacy. In other words, its war aims are political—jihad is mere propaganda. As a political insurgency, it seeks concrete goals—above all, control of a state as it had in Afghanistan, or a piece of a state as a safe base from which it can continue its campaign.

Other analysts see the jihadist enterprise as a global mission. While it has certain political aims, such as driving the Americans out of the Middle East, toppling the House of Saud, or controlling contiguous territory, its religious expression cannot be discounted. The jihadists seek to achieve these secular goals in order to attain what ultimately are religious ends. Religion is not a propaganda ploy but, rather, is inseparable from the jihadists' political goals. There is no difference between the spiritual and the political realm.

If anything, the jihadists' stated grievances—either under previous sanctions or under American occupation—while sincerely felt, are in fact political propaganda to attract religious recruits and foment unity. Those who are recruited into the jihad enter it via religion, often intensified by righteous anger. The jihadists are inspired by religion, aroused by evidence of persecution of Muslims, and exhorted to take action in its defense. This is not to say that al Qaeda's brand of jihadism is synonymous with Islam or a component of it. Islam is a religion; al Qaeda's brand of jihadism is a cult of violence. Like any cult of violence, it sanctifies killing as a holy act.

If the political issues raised by the jihadists were addressed, assuming for a moment that doing this were possible—that is, if the United States were to withdraw all of its forces from Afghanistan, Iraq, and the rest of the Middle East; if American support for Israel were to end; if the government of Saudi Arabia were to fall—would the jihad then end, its adherents content with control of the Holy Land? Or would jihad continue to expand across the Maghreb and into Central, South, and Southeast Asia? Do we see jihadist rhetoric as mere propaganda to attract distant recruits or as a declaration of war aims?

Neither the rhetoric nor the actions of the jihadists give clear indication of whether theirs is a secular revolution wrapped in religious robes or a religious war exploiting political grievances. At times, Osama bin Laden seems narrowly focused on Saudi Arabia; at other times, he describes a broad religious struggle. Ayman al-Zawahiri, an

Egyptian, tends to speak in more political language. Both men claim broad authority, and both make broad appeals.

Attacks in Afghanistan, Saudi Arabia, and Iraq make sense in a strategy of seeking a safe base. Other attacks suggest more global aims. The jihad has attracted many tribes whose local aims must be added to the list. Jihadist leaders, recruiting worldwide, have little interest in narrowing their appeal.

It is unlikely that the secular goals of the jihadists will be met. Whatever happens in Iraq, the United States is unlikely to withdraw from the Middle East or to abandon Israel, while the West will continue to depend on oil from the Middle East at something less than the $100 a barrel bin Laden thinks is the right price, and therefore will not be indifferent to events in the Saudi kingdom. While we may suspect that the jihad would continue even if the first of the jihadists' demands (withdrawal) were met, we are unlikely to run the test.

Jihadist strategy is notional and opportunistic. Its objectives are broad: to drive out the infidels from Muslim lands, topple "apostate regimes" like the House of Saud and the Egyptian government, foster religious revival, expand the Islamic community. Ultimately, the jihadists seek to reestablish the caliphate, which stretched from the Himalayas to the Pyrenees at its height 600 years ago. Jihadist strategic scenarios—narratives of the future rather than strategies—vary in detail, but the ultimate goal remains building a following, not taking ground in the military sense. The time horizon for success is distant, and in any event, success will be determined by God. The jihadists' strategy, therefore, is neither linear nor sequential. There is no jihadist "road map" to victory. Strategic objectives do not dictate action—action *is* the objective. Allah is the strategist.

That may be changing with time. Below bin Laden, mid-level jihadists have initiated a strategic discussion. Scattered thinkers, communicating primarily on the Internet, with no central direction or hierarchy, are autonomously collaborating, exchanging documents on strategy, offering targeting suggestions and information. Whether this talk will influence future operations remains to be seen, although the February 2006 attack on the world's largest oil facility, in Saudi Arabia, may be a response to these discussions.

Operations Are Imperative

Operations are imperative for al Qaeda. Without attacks as recruiting posters, potential recruits will go elsewhere. Contributors will not support an inactive organization. Continued operations ensure "branding"—making clear that al Qaeda is the vanguard.

Military objectives do not determine specific operations. Operations are the objective. Therefore, we don't see a sequence of related attacks but, rather, disconnected attacks. There is no link between attacks on residential compounds in Riyadh, attacks on nightclubs in Bali, and attacks on subways in London. There is still no link between al Qaeda's continuing flow of words and the terrorist attacks that occur. While all are within the broad framework of al Qaeda's jihad, each is a separate project.

Only in the Iraq insurgency can one discern sustained campaigns to discourage recruits from joining the Iraqi security forces, or to disrupt oil production, or to exacerbate sectarian tensions by attacking Shi'ite mosques.

Another exception to the unconnected opportunistic operations might be al Qaeda's continuing emphasis on targeting the enemy's economy. All large-scale terrorist attacks, of course, have economic effects. The 9/11 attacks caused billions of dollars in direct damage, tens of billions in indirect costs, hundreds of billions in cascading effects. And if one includes the costs of the wars in Afghanistan and Iraq, plus increased security costs, the figure may surpass a trillion dollars. Attacks on nightclubs and hotels discourage tourism, which directly hits the economy of the nation attacked. The February 2006 attack on the oil-processing facility in Saudi Arabia increased the price of oil. Going after oil production has been a recurring theme in the jihadist discourse for more than two years. But even these fragments of campaigns are exceptions. Most of the attacks are one-off displays.

As displays, jihadist attacks must offer good visuals, demonstrate organizational reach and skills, cause heavy casualties, create terror, and provide opportunities for individual heroism and sacrifice. Iconic targets are desirable—the World Trade Center, the Pentagon, landmark properties.

Attacks Demonstrate Prowess

Showmanship in carrying out spectacular attacks demonstrates prowess. Operations therefore must be successful. It is not necessary that the attackers survive—martyrdom demonstrates their commitment and adds to the enemy's alarm—but the operation must not be seen to fail. Ambitious operations must be weighed against risks of failure, since failure brings humiliation to the attackers and embarrasses the enterprise. Even more seriously, jihadists believe that God's will is expressed in success and failure. To succeed is to have God's support. Failure signals God's disapproval. As a consequence, jihadist planners are conservative.

Typical of terrorist planning, the suitability of the operation comes first, feasibility second. Considerations for operational feasibility include access to relevant information, the accessibility of the target, the level of security, the availability of reliable people, physical requirements, complexity, and costs.

Old playbooks predominate. Catastrophic attacks with unconventional weapons remain jihadist ambitions, but determined fighters with conventional explosives remain the most reliable weapons. Multiple attacks increase death and destruction, but operations with too many moving parts risk failure. Jihadist planners continue to think big but execute conservatively.

Often, schemes start big and are then scaled back. For example, when jihadists who wanted to attack the American embassy in Pakistan found that it was too well defended, they were instructed to reconnoiter other Western embassies, but these, too, were difficult targets. Finally, the leaders ordered an attack on the vulnerable Egyptian embassy. This illustrates that it is not the target that draws the attack, but the attack that ultimately determines the target. We see this again and again, and the post-9/11 attacks underscore the point. Although some attacks occur at venues that have symbolic value, in most, the attackers settle for a high body count as the sole criterion of success.

There is a steep descent from bin Laden's grandiose claims to actual terrorist attacks. He has said that it is the duty of Muslims to acquire weapons of mass destruction.[46] By al Qaeda's reckoning of deaths inflicted upon Muslims by American aggression, Muslims are entitled to kill 4 million Americans, 2 million of whom may be children.[47]

Material found at al Qaeda's training camps in Afghanistan and intelligence reports confirm al Qaeda's interest in chemical and biological weapons and suggest that al Qaeda was trying to develop the capability for at least a low-level attack involving the dispersal of radioactive material. There was also a crude sketch of a nuclear bomb. These were frightening indications of intentions, but al Qaeda was not close to having an arsenal of weapons of mass destruction.

Jihadist plans, including those that were foiled by authorities or that were attempted and failed, reflect ambitions for large-scale, spectacular attacks but at a lower level of technical sophistication. In addition to the more than 30 attacks carried out since 9/11 by al Qaeda or those inspired by its ideology, there have been many more that failed or were foiled by authorities (see Appendix B). The plans that did not succeed show greater imagination and ambition. A number of them involve lethal chemicals, botulinum toxin, and ricin, but none would have caused mass casualties. Nuclear power plants came up as a target, but the idea was shelved because planners also feared losing control—a fascinating insight. The dispersal of radioactive materials also crossed their minds. So did acquiring or fabricating a nuclear weapon, although these ideas never got very far. Left unmolested, the jihadists could be expected to pursue these ambitions.

Most of their plans, however, appear to be simply more-spectacular versions of what we have seen already—increasing body count where they can, through more multiple attacks and bigger bombs. Their chemical schemes, if carried out, would have produced neither mass destruction nor mass casualties. A lot of the foiled plots consist of exactly what terrorists do now—detonation of car bombs and smaller devices amid crowds.

Comparing the list of foiled plots with the list of actual attacks in Appendix A, we see terrorists shifting downward from their fantasies toward simpler attack scenarios and softer targets. This reflects not only the reduced operational capabilities of the jihadists after 9/11, but also the planning process itself, which moves planners away from complexities and uncertainties toward simpler, more-reliable attack modes that provide greater assurance of tactical success.

The same thing happens in "Red Team" exercises, in which analysts who actually plan terrorist operations put terrorists (or their "Red Team" surrogates) back in the main role. Often, the analysts initially prove more diabolical than actual terrorists, but interestingly, they start to narrow the scenarios once operational planning begins. From the terrorists' perspective, some operations appear less attractive than we imagine or more challenging when it gets down to detailed planning.

The actual attacks that jihadists have carried out illustrate the continued diminution from bin Laden's ambitions to assured success. For the most part, the terrorists have attacked easy, undefended targets. They have limited their tactics to armed assaults and conventional explosives. They have relied on the personal conviction of the attackers—their willingness to sacrifice their lives—not technology.

Decentralization of the jihad may have caused a change in the planning dynamics. Prior to 9/11, the still entrepreneurial but more-centralized planning process of al Qaeda meant that several terrorist projects were in various stages of preparation at any one time. In 1998, for example, al Qaeda's planners were working on preparations to bomb the American embassies in Africa, the millennium attacks in Jordan and the United States, the idea of attacking a U.S. warship in Yemen, and the attacks on the World Trade Center and Washington. These were bold, high-risk operations. In fact, even though the millennium attacks were discovered by authorities and the first attempt to sink a ship in Aden harbor failed, no one but the attackers knew about the plans at the time. The other attacks succeeded, as did a second attempt in Yemen. Failures provided opportunities to learn and perfect.

The dispersal of al Qaeda's leadership shifted operational planning to the operatives themselves. When planners are operatives, their calculations change, especially in the case of suicide missions. What had been an ongoing enterprise under al Qaeda's central leadership becomes a single chance, which, therefore, absolutely must not fail. Suicide attackers are willing to sacrifice their lives, but not to waste their sacrifice. That pushes planners toward safe bets—easy targets and low-tech operations aimed at killing as many people as possible.

The jihadist idea of warfare emphasizes process and prowess—not progress. Warfare is not a terrible phenomenon for the jihadist; peace is not the natural state of society. While Americans see warfare as a finite undertaking, the jihadists view war as a perpetual condition. Jihadists see man as inherently a warrior. If they are not fighting an external foe, men will fight among themselves. Confronting an outside enemy will bring unity and will unleash the great strength latent in the Islamic community.

Still, there are debates among jihadists. Even the most fanatic, those who believe that God mandates the slaughter of all infidels, debate the acceptability of collateral Muslim casualties. They argue about whether Shia Muslims are potential allies or apostates and, if the latter, whether they are legitimate targets of violence. They wonder aloud whether tactics such as kidnapping or taking children hostage, as was done in Russia, are counterproductive.

Objections in such debates appear to be based on political pragmatism or maintaining warrior values, not on theology or morality. Critics inside the jihad argue that the masses won't understand deliberate attacks on Muslims whose support is needed or that some tactics create a negative image that enemies can exploit. Some attacks have been criticized within the movement as being cowardly or unmanly.

Building an Army of Believers

The jihad must be seen as a missionary enterprise, not merely as a military contest. Jihadists consider recruiting not simply as a requirement to serve operational needs, but as an end in itself, a way to build an army of believers. Yet al Qaeda never created a centralized recruiting structure. Its recruiting is a diffused, mostly informal effort, localized but connected.

Before 9/11, some individuals directly connected with al Qaeda were instructed to establish themselves in various countries to engage in recruiting. They continued to take orders from al Qaeda's leadership even after 9/11, but they have since gradually gained autonomy. Others who share al Qaeda's jihadist ideology recruit on their own initiative. It works like a true underground: Everyone knows someone, but no one knows everyone.

Despite the lack of a central structure, the recruiting techniques employed by the various jihadist elements are remarkably similar. The principal variation seems to be the degree of openness. In Muslim societies, recruiting can be very open. It may begin with young students in radical madrassas, where hatred of the infidels may be part of the curriculum. Before September 11, there were reports of teachers at religious schools in Pakistan marching with their students to Afghanistan. Or recruits may come from the most militant Islamic missionary organizations that are not themselves violent but that facilitate recruiting. In non-Muslim societies, recruiting has always been more circumspect, especially since 9/11.

Jihadist recruiting techniques are sophisticated, distilled from centuries of recruiting history. One can find parallels in the recruiting for the Christian military religious orders of the Middle Ages, the Ismaili assassins admired by today's jihadists, secret societies and religious cults through the centuries, even modern military elites.[48] The basic components of jihadist recruiting include indoctrination—the jihadist cause is God's will, the community must be defended against its enemies, bloodshed is justified, God will reward martyrs; the imposition of a strict code of behavior, which may include an ascetic lifestyle and sexual abstinence; voluntary isolation from the debilitating and corrupting influences of ordinary society; advancement by tests and proofs to identify the most committed; progressive revelation of secrets with advancement; training to harden spirits and sharpen skills; contracts and oaths to formalize commitment and prevent backsliding; and finally, assignment to a mission. Instilling a jihadist mindset—the introduction of a dogma based upon faith and ideology—is more important than merely signing up a soldier. The recruiting vocabulary focuses on humiliation, shame, and guilt, contrasted with dignity, duty, and honor.

A volunteer doesn't sign up for jihad and board a bus to basic training. Initiation into jihad is a multistep process that usually begins in a religious setting, at a mosque, religious school, or study group, but it can also start at a student meeting, bookstore, street corner, cybercafe, or cellblock—anywhere young men assemble.

The job of the recruiter is to incite men to carry out jihad. Radical imams may themselves be recruiters, but more often, it is their task to incite, while regular recruiters troll at the edges of the most radical mosques, spotting those who, by their enthusiastic responses to fiery sermons or by hanging around to ask questions, identify themselves as potential recruits. Recruiters may be men respected in the neighborhood where they engage with young idlers, deride their dissolute lifestyle, challenge them to reject the mediocrity and meaninglessness of their lives, and invite them to come and talk when they are interested in restoring their dignity as men. Recruiters visit hospitals. They offer small gifts, a cultural custom to encourage obligation. They may be prison chaplains or Muslim prisoners who have been elected to lead prayers, offering useful advice to new and frightened inmates, not initially exhortations to faith, but practical help on how to get by in prison.

Many of the early recruiters were veterans of the Afghan war against the Soviet Union or men who had fought in jihads in Kashmir, Bosnia, or other fronts. This experience, which at some point is revealed to potential converts, gives the recruiter status among younger men. "I saw their scars," recalls one acolyte, "and that made me want to dedicate myself even more." But the requirements of clandestinity demand discretion, while the belief that jihadist warriors are merely instruments of God imposes modesty. Some recruiters are ex-convicts who have served time in prison for petty crime or involvement in terrorist activities, also a source of prestige.

Recruiting begins with a quiet word, not a drum roll. A subtle seduction, it is hard to say who leads the first dance—the experienced recruiter spotting a prospect or the curious wannabe, feigning adolescent indifference or openly displaying interest. The recruiter invites the candidate to a meeting with some of the brothers away from the mosque or for a one-on-one conversation in which the discussion revolves around the unhappy personal circumstances or empty spiritual life of the candidate and the need to find the right path through God. Effective recruiters are, of course, shrewd observers of human behavior and skilled communicators. "Believe me, these guys knew how to wield words," observed one French convert to jihadism. "They knew all the nooks and crannies of my brain. They knew the course of my life very well, which allowed them to touch me easily. . . . They are good at detecting people who had a weakness. . . . Very cleverly, they gave courage to the most disadvantaged, who, in turn, let themselves be enrolled very easily."[49]

Conversations increasingly turn political, with discussions of current events, the aggression of the infidels, the suffering of the devout, the injustice of situations in Muslim communities, the humiliation inflicted upon the faithful. Recruiting stresses the necessity to take action against these wrongs, the opportunities for heroism, and the spiritual rewards that await. "I read a traditional Quran," recalled one recruit, "then the instructors gave me a Quran to which they had added pages."[50] He may have been referring to *Interpretation of the Meanings of the Noble Qur'an,* in which the authors add footnotes to the Quran, inciting hatred of the Jews, elevating jihad (which they describe exclusively in terms of armed struggle), and exalting martyrdom.[51]

Jihad videos containing gruesome displays of atrocities committed against Muslims in Bosnia, Chechnya, and other places, accompanied by rousing music and narrative, elicit both sympathy and anger. "Everyone who is not a Muslim is the enemy of Muslims. It is written in Quran: one must kill the infidels, the Jews first, then the Christians," the narrator says on one video. Other videos exalt the heroism of the jihadists or offer the last testaments of martyrs.

Early in the recruiting process, the candidate may be invited to participate in martial arts or some other type of physical training organized exclusively for the brothers. Jihadists don't expect to defend Islam with karate chops, but it is useful to see who shows up regularly. It is a test of individual commitment, one of a series of gateways to selection that instills combativeness, allows identification of individual skills, contributes to bonding, and provides opportunities for further indoctrination. An evening of martial arts may be followed by an invitation to weekend paintball battles, pistol practice, white-water rafting, or other physical adventures, which again test commitment, cement closer bonds, and allow spotters to identify potential tactical skills or natural leadership qualities. For the candidate, it offers a chance to join a brotherhood, develop pride, and demonstrate his own prowess as a pretend warrior.

At some point, the recruit may be called to go on a *jamaat*. The word literally means group or congregation, but it can also refer to a kind of pilgrimage—a jihadist jamboree. A *jamaat* may last from a few days to several months. It is a more serious test of commitment of both time and money. It may require the recruit to leave his family and job for a period, and often he is expected to pay his own way, even to a foreign country. The journey provides stronger bonding and a safer environment for further indoctrination.

The recruit is encouraged to isolate himself from all outside contact; he is expected to avoid infidels, less-committed Muslims (who are just as bad), family, old friends. Instructors control the flow of all information. Television and music are the "works of Satan," recruits are told. Journalists are "manipulators in the service of Jews." "There was no television, but many prayer books," recalled one recruit. Cut off from the outside world, the recruit is never left alone. He may be assigned to an older "brother" who will be his guide and mentor. He may move into an apartment to live communally with other brothers, where sermons and prayer are endless. Recruits immerse themselves "all day long in the same discussions," watch jihad videos, engage in endless talk of jihad. In these tiny universes, cut off from reality, it is easy to slide into feral fanaticism, to yearn for death and destruction. "The desire to go to battle on the side of my martyred brothers took hold of me more and more. I was obsessed by the idea," said one graduate.

The long process of indoctrination produces profound mental transformations, according to another former jihadist who later fought free of the mental grip of the movement. "We never spoke of death, but instead of paradise that awaited us," recalls another. Interviews with jihadists detained in Singapore indicate that guaranteed passage to paradise figured prominently as a motive. (Recruiters emphasize the rewards of paradise, but the avoidance of hell is also part of the pitch.)

Do jihadists believe that deliberately sacrificing their lives in the process of killing infidels will bring them the pleasures of a sensuous eternity surrounded by virgins? Suicide bombers who succeed cannot be interviewed, and we have no X-ray for a man's soul. We can only observe behavior and wonder. There are numerous reports, from the training camps in Afghanistan to the jihadists fighting in Iraq, of volunteers clamoring for suicide missions, impatient with headquarters for not offering enough opportunities for martyrdom. And even today, in Iraq, Afghanistan, Israel, and the Palestinian territories, martyrs' graves remain the destination of believers seeking favors on the other side. We have witnessed mass suicides in religious cults, of course; Islam has no monopoly on revered martyrs. Behavior suggests belief.

With each step, the recruit reaches a higher level, a smaller, more elite circle to which new secrets are revealed. Promotion brings status and satisfaction. "For the first time in my life, I had achieved a goal that I had set for myself," one jihadist said. "I was finally succeeding at something." The recruit may adopt a new name, not for security purposes, but to shed his past life, announce his new commitment.

Discussions of jihad eventually turn hard-core, from simply agreeing that something must be done to the question of what the candidate is personally willing to do. One jihadist leader in Singapore formalized the process with a written survey form from which recruits could select statements indicating how far they would go for the jihad.[52] The choices included offering supplications for the fighters, performing missionary work, contributing ideas, contributing funds, conducting sabotage outside of Singapore against U.S. interests, supporting any activity against U.S. interests, conducting sabotage inside Singapore against U.S. interests, and volunteering to be a suicide bomber against U.S. interests. Peer pressure tends to drive up commitment. It is hard to stay at the supplication level when those around you are volunteering for action. Three of the 36 people detained in Singapore had indicated on their forms that they were willing to die for the cause.[53] Whether formally or informally elicited, this commitment becomes a contract with dire penalties in the afterlife for reneging.

Recent terrorist attacks may be discussed with the candidates, hypothetical ones talked about. Weapons and tactics may also be discussed, but there may still be no formal terrorist training—how to conduct operations, how to build bombs. Some recruits will decide early that jihad is not for them, and others may drop out along the way or prove to be unreliable, but the most eager recruits will continue to push forward, to take the next step.

The next step may be a longer *jamaat*, perhaps a trip abroad where one receives further indoctrination and terrorist training. Before 9/11, the final leg of the journey meant traveling to a jihadist training camp in Afghanistan; after 9/11, al Qaeda instructed recruiters to stop sending recruits to Afghanistan, but to utilize other locations. This journey often requires deception, possibly traveling on a fake passport, and represents the first step into illegality.

In the absence of signed surveys and sworn oaths, it is difficult to say exactly when a recruit becomes a jihadist. Spiritually, it is a slide. Legally, we are obliged to look for a line. Hatred in one's heart is a blight on society but not a crime, nor is reading jihadist literature or watching jihadist videos. Martial arts training, pistol practice, and paintball battles are all legal and popular pastimes in America. Instruction in bomb-making can be found in local libraries, in bookstores, and on the Internet. Does doing all of these activities constitute a crime? A new law in the United States makes "providing material assistance to a terrorist group" a crime. Material assistance includes attending terrorist training, but can terrorist training consist merely of attending a radical madrassa or does it require some kind of paramilitary exercises?

Once one becomes a jihadist, getting out is hard. Being considered a traitor by former jihadist brothers while still a suspect in the eyes of the authorities is only the external problem. The real challenge is internal. Khaled al-Berry, an Egyptian who made the journey both ways and describes his recruitment, training, imprisonment, self-examination, and liberation in a book with the revealing title *Earth Is More Beautiful Than Paradise,* says that, freed from prison, he still had to liberate his mind. It took months after leaving the extremists for him to rediscover his ability to think independently, outside of the texts and slogans that had been engraved in his brain.[54]

Recruiting is a slow process; 18 months used to be the usual time frame, but the transformation from curious candidate to committed jihadist could take several years, allowing individuals to float along the spiritual current before diving into jihad's deep end. That changed with 9/11, after which no one could claim not to know what al Qaeda stood for. With authorities closely monitoring developments, recruiting became more dangerous for both recruiters and recruits.

Recruiters continue their efforts, but the presumption of more surveillance requires more caution. Greater clandestinity is required. Greater concerns about surveillance and infiltrators also mean tighter conspiracies that are harder to detect, shorter recruiting and planning horizons. And with the loss of the training camps, recruiters now have more influence over the destinations of recruits.

One can no longer leisurely slide into jihadism by degrees. Joining up means a faster leap into full clandestinity. Recruits may react either with greater caution, avoiding any overt commitment, or by more rapidly embracing greater risks because of superior commitment. The post-9/11 cohort of recruits is likely to be more fanatical, more violent, but possibly less reliable, since the indoctrination process may be accelerated. Post-9/11 recruits include fewer Mohamed Attas, more of the wild bunch, harder men with less to lose, possibly with more genuine psychological problems, ready for death.

Reconnaissance of targets and planning for attacks are also continuous activities. Planning itself is considered a way to participate in jihad. Target folders and embryonic plans are surrogate operations reflecting the planners' ambitions and fantasies. Planning is based on manuals, playbooks, and observed tactical lessons. Previous operations are examined in order to perfect techniques and to surpass predecessors. At the same time, planning is entrepreneurial, offering the opportunity for any jihadist to take the initiative.

Jihadist Profiles

Profiles of jihadist recruits vary greatly, which is not surprising in a global enterprise that draws followers from mosques, religious schools, universities, mountain tribes, desert villages, city slums, and prisons. The ranks of the jihadists include scions of wealth and petty thieves, university students and juvenile delinquents, physicians and mechanics, schoolteachers and taxi drivers, civil servants and prison inmates.

Some recruits appear to be carrying on long family or local traditions of Islamic extremism and political rebellion. Indonesia's contemporary jihadists, for example, include members who can trace family ties back to armed Islamist rebellions of the 1950s. The father of Ahmed Ressam, the would-be millennium bomber arrested on his way to Los Angeles with a trunk full of explosives, fought against the French in the Algerian War. Some recruits are second- or third-generation immigrants struggling with identity problems. Others have converted to Islam in life crises.

Most are young. As is done in all armies, jihadist recruiters target impressionable adolescents and men in their twenties. Few recruits are married or have children. More often they are lonely young men seeking to belong to something. Joining a secret elite gives them a special sense of power. Most appear to be of average or above-average intelligence. Educational levels range from less than high school to advanced university degrees.

Interviews show jihadists to be high on religion, seeking the right path to paradise, but tired of endless searching. They want a "no-fuss" belief system that takes them to paradise.[55] Khaled al-Berry has said that recruiters look for people who show a high degree of obedience, meaning obedience to God's word. An al Qaeda "employment contract" listed "abiding by al Qaeda rules" and "obedience to the leaders in charge" as the first and second requirements of a recruit.[56] Psychological testing reveals compliant, low-assertiveness personalities.[57]

After religion, the second most important values listed by captured Singaporean jihadists were comfort and wealth—hardly surprising in that industrious and prosperous nation. Social values—concern for the well-being of others, doing good, helping the Muslim community—were third. Guilt seems to be prevalent.

But if the group portrait of the jihadists depicts an army of obedient religious fanatics ready to die for the cause of Islam, individual portraits underscore human diversity.

Ahmed Ressam, who would have placed a large bomb in the Los Angeles Airport had he not been stopped at the Canadian border by a suspicious U.S. Customs agent, fits the pattern described above almost perfectly. An émigré from Algeria, he first moved to France, where he lived illegally for two years; he then went to Canada on a forged passport and promptly requested political asylum. Awaiting his hearing, he supported himself with welfare payments and by robbing tourists. After being arrested several times, convicted once, and fined, he moved on to trafficking in stolen drivers' licenses and other identification documents. When his request for asylum was turned down, he gave himself a new identity and continued living underground.[58]

Cut off from his roots, unemployed, with no girlfriend, living on petty crime, Ressam tumbled into the orbit of a radical mosque in Montreal, where a skillful recruiter with direct connections to al Qaeda gradually reeled him in. Ressam began hanging around with others on the fringes of the jihadist movement, smoking cigarettes, sharing rent and rants, plotting imagined terrorist operations.

Two years later, Ressam made the inevitable trip to Afghanistan, where he was approved for terrorist training. He returned to Canada the following year, a determined al Qaeda terrorist operative with a new name. Ressam's journey from Algerian refugee to petty criminal in Canada had taken four years. His transformation from thief to terrorist had taken another four.

Some recruits, like Raed Hijazi and Dhriren Barot, appear to be wandering warriors, pulled along by visions of fantastical destruction. Hijazi, born to comparatively well-off Palestinian parents in San Jose, California, followed a conventional path until he enrolled in university, where he planned to study business. Instead, he was swept up into jihad, making the pilgrimage to Afghanistan, where his aptitude for weaponry earned him the new name "Abu Ahmed the Mortarman." When the Soviet forces withdrew, Hijazi moved his jihad to Jordan, where he planned a spectacular bombing. It became his life's goal. The plan matured slowly, with Hijazi working as a taxi driver in Boston, engaging in robbery and forging documents on the side to help finance the operation in Jordan. In 1996, he asked al Qaeda for technical assistance, which led to his incorporation into the Jordanian end of the 1999 millennium plot, a foiled plot to detonate 16 tons of explosives in downtown Amman while Ahmed Ressam was to have detonated his bomb in Los Angeles.[59]

Dhriren Barot, British-born of Indian descent, converted to Islam at the age of 20, becoming Issa al-Hindi, "Issa the Hindu," or sometimes Issa al-Britani, "Issa the Brit." He went off to fight in Kashmir, writing a literate but romanticized field manual and memoir of his adventures. Barot then found al Qaeda's orbit. As Hijazi was finalizing his end-of-millennium spectacular, Barot was dispatched to scout targets, first in Kuala Lumpur, then, in 2000, in the United States, where he devoted months to reconnoitering symbols of America's "economic might" and "Jewish targets." To Barot, this meant big bank headquarters in New York, New Jersey, and Washington. His carefully researched target folders show his desire for dramatic visual destruction—glass-clad skyscrapers tumbling to the ground. Back in safer territory in England in 2001, he continued to refine the New York project while working on new terrorist schemes in London until his arrest in 2004.[60]

Both Hijazi and Barot were failures, arrested before achieving their violent goals. But both men demonstrated absolute devotion, single-mindedly pursuing their projects for years. No prayer-house hotheads, these were determined fanatics with high hopes. Had they been arrested earlier in their trajectories, the seriousness of their intent might easily have been dismissed—a cautionary note for how we assess terrorists who are apprehended early in their schemes.

The 9/11 hijackers were a different sort of recruit. Not lowlife thieves, they were bright students with the possibility of successful careers. Yet something in their temperament or circumstances propelled them toward the same destination.

The Egyptian leader of the 9/11 team, Mohamed Mohamed el-Amir Awad al-Sayed Atta, the man we call Mohamed Atta, but whose friends knew him simply as Amir, was variously described as very intelligent but not creative, mathematical rather than artistic, analytical but close-minded, respectful of authority but argumentative, polite but awkward, never warm, with little interest in personal conversation. Hardly the perfect date, his attitude toward women ranged from dismissive to hostile.[61]

A prig, Atta flaunted his disgust at any display he considered immodest. Self-contained, inwardly focused, he displayed an "aggressive insularity." The more fervently he committed himself to jihad, the more introverted he became. Any deviation from established routine made him visibly upset. He hated the lack of order in the West, which to him, was chaos. "Joy kills the heart," he said. Perhaps not clinically psychotic, Atta clearly was a candidate for counseling.

In a strange way, Atta reconciled his mission to demolish the World Trade Center, the icon of Western economic power, with his own profession of urban planning. Even as plans for 9/11 were being finalized—plans that would end in his death—Atta worked to complete his master's thesis. Dedicated to Allah, its subject was the protection of traditional neighborhoods in Aleppo, Syria, against the destructive forces of modernization. The 9/11 attacks became his testament against progress.

Another of the 9/11 plotters, Ramzi bin al-Shibh, adopted the name Omar, the successor to the Prophet Muhammed. Bin al-Shibh and Atta, who met in Germany, constituted the core of the Hamburg group. Bin al-Shibh was slated to be the fourth pilot on September 11, but when he could not obtain a visa to the United States, he instead became the key contact between team members in the field and the operation's planners. He was arrested in 2003.

Bin al-Shibh could not have been more different from the dour Atta. Acquaintances describe him as having an exceptionally sunny disposition, charming, open, rarely downcast, happy-go-lucky, always smiling. Bin al-Shibh's qualities gave him a good understanding of human nature and made him an effective proselytizer and recruiter.

While Atta imposed order, bin al-Shibh gave his comrades a sense of purpose. That purpose, in his view, was religion, specifically jihad. Coming from Yemen, he saw himself as a warrior who, like generations of holy warriors before him, would face a coming test of his faith and commitment. He happily embraced the idea, casually accepting death. "What is life good for?" he asked. "Paradise is better."[62]

Ziad Jarrah, the pilot of the second plane to hit the World Trade Center, came from Lebanon. A bright but inattentive student, more cosmopolitan than the others, he was also more easygoing in his religion; he drank alcohol and was somewhat of a playboy.[63] He alone among the principals had a wife, although he grew more distant from her as he plunged deeper into jihad. His domesticity did not relieve his sense of dissatisfaction with life. He wanted to do something meaningful—it was the lure of jihad that captured his soul and gave his life new purpose.

Marwan al-Shehhi, the pilot of the plane that crashed into the Pentagon, was a soldier in the armed forces of the United Arab Emirates who arrived in Germany on an army scholarship. Acquaintances describe him as laid back, dreamy, good-humored, docile, lumbering, even clumsy. He loved to eat and satisfied a constant sweet tooth with an ever-present bag of candy. He entertained friends with Arab fairy tales. The son of a muezzin (a man who calls Muslims to prayer), he took his religion seriously, strictly followed its dictates, avoided alcohol, and never spoke to women unless compelled to do so.[64]

Hani Hanjour, the fourth pilot on 9/11, whose plane crashed in a Pennsylvania field, was a last-minute replacement for bin al-Shibh and the erratic Zacarias Moussaoui, who proved too unreliable for the 9/11 mission. Hanjour was a Saudi who already had a commercial pilot's license but no job as a pilot. Devout but drifting, he took off to Afghanistan, where he was readily recruited for the operation.[65]

All of these men seemed to be tumbling through life. Broken off from their roots, they found one another and clung together. They shared a sense of destiny but had no sense of direction until they rediscovered religion and, within it, an angry ideology that commanded jihad. Much seems explained by mere chance. Believers would say it was written.

While to most Americans, Osama bin Laden is a distant figure, the al Qaeda terrorist that Americans got to look at up close was Zacarias Moussaoui, often incorrectly described as the 20th hijacker on 9/11. What they saw was a chaotic personality and erratic behavior. The only consistent features were Moussaoui's undisguised hatred of America, his undiminished commitment to violent jihad, and his unconcealed contempt for its victims. Clearly a complex man, Moussaoui was described by a psychologist at his trial as a paranoid schizophrenic, prompting Moussaoui himself to mockingly offer his own diagnosis—"a beautiful terrorist mind."

Moussaoui's journey to an American criminal court began with a turbulent childhood in France. His father was abusive; his mother fled, but, unable to support her family, she abandoned the boys in an orphanage. She later retrieved them, but Moussaoui never forgave her.

As a young student, Moussaoui had been the target of pervasive and sometimes violent racism. He seemed culturally adrift. According to his brother, he was "a Frenchman not at ease with being French . . . a Moroccan who can't speak Arabic." Moussaoui hated the French.

Determined to advance his career in London, Moussaoui lived for months a precarious solitary life in a charity-run shelter—a rough place. He took up bodybuilding to protect himself against assault. Faced with what he regarded as even greater racism, he came to hate the English too.

Moussaoui's original goal in life had been simply to get rich, and he successfully obtained a master's degree in business. But his education was also proceeding in another direction.

According to his brother, Moussaoui had no interest in and a total ignorance of religion, preferring to go to town instead of to the mosque. Alone in London, estranged from his family, disappointed in love, angry at the world, Moussaoui was the perfect candidate for jihadist recruiters. His conversion to extremism took years, but by the late 1990s, he was in an al Qaeda training camp.[66]

Even here, Moussaoui was marginalized. Although he boasted that he was a favorite of bin Laden's, volunteered for martyrdom, and, along with dozens of others, was sent to flight school, he was considered by Khalid Sheikh Mohammed, 9/11's central planner, to be unreliable. He talked too much, broke security rules, and was likely to get caught—and he was.

In custody, he at first denied any knowledge of the 9/11 plot but then later confessed to being part of a follow-on plot to crash a hijacked plane into the White House. On the witness stand, he changed course again and testified that he was to have piloted a fifth plane on 9/11 with Richard Reid, the "shoe-bomber." An improbable story, it appeared motivated by Moussaoui's desire to achieve glory as one of the 9/11 hijackers. Moussaoui later recanted, and even Osama bin Laden issued an unusual audiotape to confirm that "Brother Moussaoui" had not been a part of the 9/11 operation.

Jose Padilla is an argument against al Qaeda's global recruitment for jihad. A teenage gang member in Chicago, he was arrested several times for petty crime before the age of 14, when he moved up to robbery and assault, including a brutal stabbing. For that he spent time in a youth detention center, where he apparently learned little. Back on the street, he continued his existence as a lowlife predator. More arrests followed, and after a 1991 shooting in Florida, the outcome of a road-rage incident, he went back to prison for another ten months. It was around this time that he found religion, converted to Islam, and began to slide into the jihadist orbit, changing his name to Ibrahim. In 1998, he left his wife and headed for Afghanistan, changing his name again, this time to Abdullah al-Muhajir (Abdullah the Immigrant).[67]

One wonders whether the street tough from Chicago conned his jihadist commanders into thinking he had underworld connections. Or did al Qaeda's senior planner, Abu Zubaida, who was captured in 2002 and fingered Padilla, play a trick on his interrogators, giving up Padilla as the point man for al Qaeda's Manhattan Project? Or did Padilla's U.S. captors exaggerate his role? We don't know what Zubaida or Padilla said, only what authorities have reported, which is that Padilla had been sent to the United States to scout targets for a "dirty bomb" attack. This was later amended to the claim that he was planning to blow up apartment buildings. All of these claims were dropped in Padilla's final criminal indictment, and he currently faces the lesser charge of supporting al Qaeda.

Padilla's transformation from desperado to revolutionary field commander should not be dismissed. Pancho Villa's rise during the Mexican revolution is a good example of such a transformation. Abu Musab al-Zarqawi was al Qaeda's version. Zarqawi's early acquaintances recall him as an ill-tempered, violent teenager, inciting quarrels among others, quick to pick a fight himself, the "neighborhood lout," called the "green man" because he covered his body with tattoos (which Islam forbids). He was arrested for shoplifting and drug dealing, and he went to prison for knifing a man.[68]

A school dropout, unable to hold a job, leading a dissolute life, yet dreamy and idealistic, drifting through life, eager to give it some meaning, Zarqawi was the perfect recruit for radical religious politics and the call of jihad. He arrived in Afghanistan too late to fight Soviet soldiers, but he took part in the vicious internecine warfare that followed.

A new name marked his metamorphosis. He became Abu Musab, the "Father of Musab," one of the Prophet's warriors, who lost both hands in battle and is now the patron saint of suicide bombers. For his last name, he took the name of his home village, becoming al-Zarqawi. Increasingly steeped in religion, Zarqawi memorized the Quran. He spoke of a dream he had one night of a sword engraved with the word "jihad" splitting the sky. He forced the women of his family to adopt the strict dress of Afghan women under the Taliban, forbade his brothers to watch television, and plotted terrorist attacks.

Charismatic, a natural leader, a skillful recruiter, but a brutal tyrant who tolerated no criticism, Zarqawi was sworn to the destruction of all unbelievers, not just Christians and Jews, but also Shi'ites—indeed, all Muslims not sharing his own narrow interpretation of the faith. He became the "Sheikh of the Slaughterers" in recognition of his bloody-mindedness, which caused even jihadists to wince.

It is a trajectory we often see in terrorist organizations. Well-educated ideologues like Osama bin Laden and Ayman al-Zawahiri initiate the campaign. Violence is for them a means to an end, but as the organization grows, it recruits "soldiers" who share their beliefs but who also gain psychological fulfillment from participation in terrorist operations, ranging from the status offered by clandestinity to, in this case, martyrdom and the guarantee of paradise. The 9/11 attackers fit this category. As the violence continues and the earlier veterans are killed off or picked up, a third generation emerges. It usually lacks the intellect and ideological grounding of the first generation, which still dominates the leadership; it is more attracted by death and destruction. This is the generation in which we find the thugs, including, until his death, Zarqawi.

Invariably, tensions arise between the strategists of the first generation and the harder men of the third generation, who push for ever-escalating violence without concern for its longer-term political consequences. This is not to argue that bin Laden and Zawahiri are gentle souls. They are the leaders who hoped to kill tens of thousands on September 11, 2001, who seek weapons of mass destruction, and who would have no qualms about using them to kill millions of infidels. They do, however, have qualms about slaughtering fellow Muslims. The third-generation thugs accept no constraints at all. For them, escalation is always the answer.

Zawahiri once warned Zarqawi that his bloody attacks on Shi'ites to foment a civil war in Iraq could provoke a backlash that would undermine the long-term goals of al Qaeda. But the distant ideologues, on the run, sometimes in prison, are always at a disadvantage in dealing with their third-generation rivals who naturally come to dominate the front line. Any attempt to rein in the third generation may imperil the authority of the leadership or fragment the enterprise itself. In an organization made up of extremists, it is difficult to be less extreme than the most extreme and still maintain control. The first generation can admonish, but it must go along. Zarqawi, who delighted in reminding al Qaeda's leaders that he was on the front line and they were not, ignored Zawahiri's cautions.

A Briefing in Waziristan

How does the situation look to the jihadists nearly five years after 9/11? We know what Washington says, but what might a briefing to bin Laden look like?

The briefing would probably begin with a reminder of al Qaeda's objectives:

> To incite the largest number of the faithful to enter the battle, to maximize their opportunities for participation in the jihad, and to facilitate decentralized operations in order to exhaust the enemy with continuous attacks.

Any al Qaeda briefer would have to acknowledge that the past five years have been difficult:

> The Taliban were dispersed, and al Qaeda's training camps in Afghanistan were dismantled. Thousands of jihadists have been captured or killed worldwide. More important, some of al Qaeda's top planners—talent that is hard to replace—have also been killed or captured. In addition, the organization's cash flow has been restricted. Zawahiri himself has acknowledged financial problems.

> Infidel armies occupy Afghanistan and Iraq; they operate throughout the region, assisted by apostate regimes in Saudi Arabia, Kuwait, Iraq, Bahrain, the Emirates, Qatar, Oman, and Jordan. Americans threaten Syria and Iran, while American puppets in Kabul and Islamabad hunt jihadists with the assistance of mercenary tribesmen. Muslims are everywhere persecuted.

Our fictional briefer in Waziristan would also have to concede that the operational environment worldwide has become more difficult.

> Because of increased intelligence efforts by the United States and its allies, transactions of any type—communications, travel, money transfers—have become more dangerous for the jihadists. Training and operations have been decentralized, raising the risk of fragmentation and loss of unity. Jihadists everywhere face the threat of capture or martyrdom.

Yet despite all this, the al Qaeda briefer might conclude that the jihadists are succeeding.

> We have survived the infidels' mightiest blows with our top leadership intact, evidence of divine protection. America's arrogance and aggression have angered Muslims and alienated its own allies. The shadow of 9/11 still hangs over the American economy. Oil remains its great vulnerability.

Our briefer could also point out that proselytization for jihad continues.

> Communications from the top have not been shut down. Video and audiotapes continue to arrive at al Jazeera and other outlets, where they are broadcast to the world, although not always in their entirety. They are then replayed

in the Western media, authenticated by the intelligence services, and commented upon by government officials and the numerous experts who populate television, radio, newspapers, and the Internet. How many hear the original message or pay attention to it is harder to gauge, but distant terrorist attacks signal positive responses. Communication among jihadists also continues on a growing number of web sites, exhorting attacks, discussing strategy and tactics, and exchanging technical information.

A cadre of dispersed Afghan veterans provides continuing connections and a source of local leadership for future operations. The recruiting of new acolytes continues, albeit with greater caution. Training is dispersed. To a certain extent, instruction can be provided on the Internet, but this does not provide the deep bonding that derives from the shared hardships and dangers in the old training camps.

Our jihadist briefer could nonetheless boast that operations continue at a swift pace.

And armed resistance is again on the rise in Afghanistan.

The briefer might cleverly remind bin Laden that the leader himself had correctly anticipated the American invasion of Iraq, which surely is a gift from Allah.

America's quick "victory" over the army of Saddam Hussein put its soldiers in a situation where they are vulnerable to the kind of warfare the jihadists wage best: lying in wait to attack; carrying out assassinations, kidnappings, ambushes, and suicide attacks; destroying the economy; making the enemy's life untenable. Iraq will be to America what Afghanistan was to the Soviet Union. Few would have believed at the outset of that conflict that a band of determined jihadists could have defeated the Soviet armed

> forces, but after ten years of hard fighting, bloodied and unwilling to bear the terrible burden of continued war, the Soviets withdrew in exhaustion. Shortly afterward, the mighty Soviet empire collapsed.

In the eyes of the jihadists, the Americans are pampered weaklings who have even less spine and stomach for losses than did the Soviets.

> As long as the fight continues, American soldiers die, costs mount, the anti-war movement in the United States grows more powerful and popular, and the ranks of elected officials opposed to the war in Iraq grow.

The Americans will not last ten years, our briefer says.

> The Americans are already talking about withdrawing their forces. Since we know they came to stay as permanent occupiers, any withdrawal—partial or conditional—represents a reversal of the infidels' original intentions and a great victory for jihad, as Sheikh al-Zawahiri has pointed out.
>
> While the fighting continues, foreign jihadist volunteers are coming to Iraq, where they are mastering the techniques of urban guerrilla warfare and sabotage of economic infrastructure. This new cohort of veterans will eventually disperse, raising the operational skills of jihadists worldwide. Thanks to the blessed American invasion, Iraq has become a university of jihad.

The briefer would remind bin Laden that when the Americans depart, chaos will ensue in Iraq, giving jihad new space in which to operate.

> And with the collapse of the American effort, the apostate regimes in the region will tremble and fall, clearing the way

> for reestablishment of the caliphate and the eventual restoration of Islam's glorious past. The oil wealth of the region will be in jihadist hands. The West will be forced to abandon Israel, and the Holy Places again will belong to their rightful owners—believers in the one true faith. As you have pointed out, Osama, victory is inevitable.

Above all, the briefer might boast, the jihadists have demonstrated their conviction, their courage, and their prowess, which will inspire the Muslim world and demonstrate their worthiness before God.

> It is confirmed in the timeline laid down by the Prophet centuries ago, when he warned his followers that he would be followed by "rightly guided caliphs," but that these, in turn, would be followed by less-virtuous princes, who would be succeeded by kings. Then would come the tyrants, Muslims in name only, who would persecute the true believers to the ends of the earth. During the time of tyranny, only the most zealous will adhere to their beliefs, but in doing so, they will lead the revival and reestablish the unity that will bring about the return of the Mahdi, or Messiah.

The current travails, our jihadist briefer might conclude, only prove the correctness of the Prophet's words.

They are a test of faith, a prelude to future triumphs.

What Does bin Laden Really Fear?

We cannot gauge the depth of bin Laden's belief, whether there might be dark moments when disillusion and doubt cloud his determination, but recurring themes in his speeches suggest certain concerns. What worries bin Laden the most?

It is not death. Bin Laden exhorts others to martyrdom, and although he does not seek it himself, he has said several times that he will not be taken alive. Of course, one would hardly expect him to announce that, if cornered, he will meekly surrender. But for the past quarter-century, he has chosen a path of danger from which there is no return. We concede his willingness to face death.

If not death, then what does bin Laden fear? The almost continuous communications themselves, despite the obvious risks they pose to a man on the run, suggest that the uppermost fear on bin Laden's list is the loss of voice—the inability to communicate with his constituency. He has proclaimed his mission to incite believers to take up arms and join jihad. To be silenced by circumstances or increasingly ignored would destroy this mission. The objective of 9/11 was to amplify the voice of bin Laden. This is why, before 9/11, bin Laden could not resist dropping hints of something big about to happen, much to the dismay of the operation's lead planner, who worried that it would compromise the security of the operation.[69] It is why there has been a continuing flow of communications promising new attacks since 9/11. Bin Laden's voice is his authority.

Given bin Laden's loss of direct control, his appearing to be in charge requires skill and a willingness to inflate his own self-importance that would make even the most pompous politician blush. He may not be able to order new attacks, but he can appeal, he can point the direction. He also can anticipate where future clashes may occur and can position himself to take credit if an attack does occur. He correctly forecast the U.S.-led invasion of Iraq and positioned himself to exploit Muslim anger. His marching orders point to all directions. In a message broadcast in April 2006, bin Laden marched across the globe extolling the resistance in Iraq, denouncing the Saudi government, urging resistance to Western military intervention in Sudan. He summoned jihadists to help their brothers in the Horn of Africa, called for action against Pakistan, and supported the struggle in the Palestinian territories, Kashmir, and Chechnya. He lamented the plight of Muslims in Bosnia, sided with Indonesia on the issue of East Timor, denounced Western aggression in Afghanistan, and demanded the punishment of Danish cartoonists. Subsequent actions in any of these places will send analysts scurrying to find coded signals in his messages, but bin Laden is merely surfing, not making the waves.

Bin Laden is not the only voice of jihadism. Zawahiri has become a more frequent communicator, while bin Laden lately has communicated less frequently. While Zawahiri does not seem likely to openly challenge bin Laden's nominal leadership, he could gradually eclipse his authority. To avoid being overshadowed by his own lieutenants, bin Laden must continue to address his audience directly.

A serious threat to bin Laden's vision of a global jihad could arise from disunity. Unity is a frequent theme in his messages. In the jihadists' interpretation of history, it is the lack of unity that repeatedly has hampered Islam's response to Western aggression. With the loss of al Qaeda's own centralized training camps, its greater difficulty in disbursing funds, and its leaders on the run, bin Laden may worry that without a strong center, the al Qaeda–led jihad will fragment and disperse.

Loss of relevancy also would rank high on bin Laden's list of worries. This is the fate of most terrorist enterprises. Circumstances that inspired their creation and developments that galvanized their followers change with time. The world moves on, leaving behind aging underground warriors locked in past dialectics.

For bin Laden, rejection and ridicule would be worse than death. He berates those who do not heed God's call to jihad. Denunciations of jihadist attacks that kill Muslims—even from militant groups like the Muslim Brotherhood and Hamas—cause him concern. He must justify the violence.

We in the West sometimes seem to pay more attention to bin Laden's latest screeds than do those in the community he addresses. It is hugely entertaining for the Muslim world to watch the jihadist torment the tiger, but to many Muslims, even those angered by U.S. policies, bin Laden is a crackpot.

Some believe that bin Laden today is no more than a voice, limited to exhortation, a cheerleading chairman, emeritus but toothless. Indeed, much of his power is undeniably an illusion. Like the Wizard of Oz, bin Laden hides behind a facade of smoke, papier-mâché, noise, and bluster. Yet, as we have seen in many cults, even humbugs can attract fierce, to-the-death loyalty.

Many Visions of the Future

How do the jihadists think they will eventually win? There are many jihadist visions of the future. In all of them, Iraq has become the central battlefield. Many jihadists believe that the United States, bloodied and exhausted by the insurgency, stripped of its allies, will eventually withdraw. They believe this defeat alone could bring about the collapse of the United States, just as collapse followed the Soviet defeat in Afghanistan. At a minimum, the U.S. withdrawal will open the way for the post-withdrawal struggle, which will lead to jihadist control of at least a portion of Iraqi territory and a base for expansion.

As our jihadist briefer might point out:

> America's retreat from Iraq will also expose the neighboring states—Jordan, Kuwait, the Emirates, and above all, Saudi Arabia—to an expanding jihad fed by veterans of the Iraqi conflict. Without American protection, the Saudi ruling regime will crumble. The United States either will be forced to occupy the country to defend its supply of oil, thus provoking further resistance, or will withdraw, losing direct control of Saudi oil reserves.
>
> When jihadists are in control of the region's oil, they will be able to force the Europeans, and eventually the Americans as well, to choose between their continued support of Israel and their own economic survival. Without foreign support, Israel must eventually collapse.
>
> A wealthy caliphate will stretch from the Mediterranean to the Arabian Sea, marching west across the Maghreb and into Central Africa. It will spread east to Bangladesh, Malaysia, Indonesia, and the Philippines. It will recover Afghanistan and Pakistan and spread into

> Central Asia and Western China, although it is possible that the events may occur in a different order, with the fall of Pakistan's government or the eventual withdrawal of Western occupying forces from Afghanistan. Or events still unimagined could disrupt America's schemes.

How long will it take? A decade? A generation? As bin Laden says, until Judgment Day.

What is the point of analyzing Osama bin Laden's communications, distilling the jihadists' operational code, or speculating about how they might assess their situation? For one thing, the analysis provides a completely different perspective on the war, one that hardly intersects with the prevailing American perspective. This does not mean that we should fight the jihadists' war, but if we are going to do more than run them down one at a time, we must try to affect their perceptions.

In examining the words of their leaders, we see that their pronouncements are not mere lists of grievances or political demands—detail, or lack of detail, is not the issue. Their words are a narrative aimed at the home front, intended above all to incite action. They convey a message that has resonance and undeniable appeal.

The jihadists have developed a style of fighting that is drawn from their traditions, understood by all, and suitable to their circumstances. Again, it is completely different from the way Americans approach war.

For us, warfare is about defeating the enemy in battle. In contrast, the jihadists' actions are aimed at maintaining unity and attracting more recruits. We mobilize an army to fight. They fight to mobilize an army.

Whether we get the briefing exactly right is not as important as understanding that the jihadists measure progress differently. Their beliefs and fighting concepts make it difficult to dent their determination. This fight will go on for a long time, especially if we fail to see it through their eyes. But once we do, we can formulate a new set of strategic principles better suited to the conflict.

Historic American Engineering Record/Jet Lowe

Armed force alone cannot win this war.
The real battle is ideological.

CHAPTER FOUR

A Sharper Sword: Strategic Principles for Defeating Today's Enemy

American actions after September 11, 2001, were a response to a catastrophic attack without precedent in the annals of terrorism. Immediate action was required to prevent further attacks. There was no time for lengthy planning. Action and strategy evolved concurrently, which is not unusual in war. It was no different in World War II, when well into the fighting, the allies were still formulating their grand strategy.

America's strategy in response to 9/11 was initially sketched out in a series of speeches by President Bush and was later elaborated in a number of official documents. On September 20, 2001, the President first spoke of the "war on terror." Later expanded to the "global war on terror"—GWOT in government-speak—the concept has continued to frame American strategy, although perhaps in a somewhat less expansive form today. There was a conscious effort in 2005 by some national leaders to replace GWOT with GSAVE (for "global struggle against violent extremism"), but President Bush rightly brushed it off as a meaningless phrase.

Although "global war on terror" is direct, concise, and conveys action, the particular choice of words struck me at the time as ominous, but not because of the word "war." Military force had been a part of America's counterterrorist arsenal since the mid-1980s, when then–Secretary of State George Shultz fought hard against those in the Pentagon who had resisted the use of military force in any circumstances short of an all-out conventional war that we could win quickly. "We cannot allow ourselves to become the Hamlet of nations, worrying endlessly over whether and how to respond," he said in his famous 1984 speech at the Park Avenue Synagogue in New York City.[70] The speech marked a turning point in American policy, although the military establishment continued to resist.

In an essay written immediately after 9/11, I argued in favor of framing the U.S. response as war, for several reasons.[71] To begin with, it would distinguish America's response to this attack from previous patterns of response. Until 9/11, U.S. counterterrorist efforts were officially referred to as "combating terrorism," a term that correctly implies an enduring task. But the response to 9/11 had to be different. While the United States would continue its efforts to combat terrorism, after 9/11 it was necessary to utterly destroy the al Qaeda organization, the entire jihadist network, and the jihadist ideology. Doing so would entail a global effort against a global enterprise and certainly would include the sustained use of overwhelming military force, in contrast to the isolated incidents of targeted strikes applied against terrorism in the past. The use of the term "war" would make it easier to mobilize the necessary national resources. It would enable the United States to seize the initiative rather than wait for terrorist attacks. It would set aside strict requirements of timeliness and proportionality. It would enable us to attack when, where, and with weapons of our choosing. And it would not obviate concurrent law enforcement efforts. Crushing the jihadist enterprise, not payback, would be the objective.

Moreover, as a Vietnam veteran, I was skeptical of fickle public opinion and feckless politicians. Never again, in my view, should American soldiers be sent into combat without a clear mandate from Congress and the American people. A declaration of war, or its close equivalent, was a way to ensure this mandate. "Global war" did not strike me as an overstatement. It was the choice of the word "terror" that gave me pause.

The Terminology: "Terrorism" or "Terror"

The terms "terrorism" and "terror" both have well-established lineages, but they mean different things. "Terror" entered the political lexicon during the French Revolution's Reign of Terror, when extremists in control of the government sent cartloads of condemned counterrevolutionaries to the guillotine in order to strike terror in the hearts of any who dared oppose the new regime. Since that time, the term has been generally applied to actions used *by governments or their secret agents*, including assassinations, arbitrary arrests, disappearances, concentration camps, the torture of prisoners, summary executions, forcible relocations of entire populations—all calculated to discourage dissent. Historically, terror was a government tool.

During the Cold War, however, the concept of "terror" took on an additional meaning as it was extended to the strategic discourse: A "balance of terror" between the superpowers, both of whom had sufficient nuclear weapons to destroy the planet, would deter the use of those weapons. Terror thus came to imply weapons of mass destruction.

"Terrorism" also entered the political lexicon in France, when Napoleon's chief of police ordered the roundup of terrorists responsible for an attempt on the emperor's life. The word gained currency during the 19th century, when bomb-throwing revolutionaries, who wanted to obliterate property and terrorize the ruling classes, readily called themselves terrorists. Since then, "terrorism" generally has applied to certain tactics used *by those seeking to bring down governments*, tactics such as assassinations, bombings, kidnappings, and hijackings.

The use of the two terms implies no moral comparison. Terrorism from below is no worse than terror from above, although government terror has claimed far more victims than revolutionary terrorism has. The tactical repertoires of those engaged in terrorism and of those engaged in terror overlap considerably. The contemporary definition of terrorism makes no distinction with regard to actors.

The distinctions between terrorism and terror began to blur in the 1990s as terrorists became increasingly determined to engage in large-scale, indiscriminate violence. This was the "new terrorism."

The collapse of the Soviet Union and fears about the security of its vast nuclear arsenal, followed by the 1995 terrorist attack on Tokyo's subways by cult members using a nerve agent, generated growing concerns that terrorists would acquire and use weapons of mass destruction. At the same time, several countries that had sponsored terrorist attacks against their adversaries abroad were known or suspected to be developing nuclear weapons. The nightmare scenarios of terrorists being armed with nuclear weapons by renegade states or by rogue elements in these countries became a presumption. Iraq was a particular suspect. It had developed and used chemical weapons against its own population and against Iran during the 1991 Gulf War. After that war, arms inspectors discovered that Iraq had a nuclear weapons program that was more advanced than Western intelligence services had known.

The 9/11 attacks clearly fell in the domain of terrorism rather than terror. Why, then, did the President on September 20 use the term "terror"? Was it merely imprecise language, the product of a speechwriter who did not understand the arcane distinctions analysts made between terrorism and terror? Did the sheer scale of the attack push the vocabulary out of the realm of seemingly ordinary terrorism and into the strategic domain where the word "terror" seemed more appropriate? Did the President suspect the involvement of a foreign government? It crossed my mind at the time that we probably were going to war with Iraq.

In the autumn of 2001, I envisioned a narrow campaign to destroy al Qaeda and its jihadist affiliates. This was the enterprise that had declared war on the United States, carrying out attacks on U.S. installations in Saudi Arabia in 1995 and 1996, the American embassies in Kenya and Tanzania in 1998, and an American warship in Yemen in 2000; it had attacked the United States on September 11, 2001. The destruction of al Qaeda was justified and necessary, and it had to be the priority.

But Washington, where Mars ruled, had a much broader view of its mission. Propelled by equal parts of fear and hubris, the global war on terror grew in scope. From the start, there was a lot of chest-thumping. The United States would not only destroy al Qaeda, officials said, it would settle scores with all the groups that had American blood on their hands. Asked if the United States was going to expand its campaign against al Qaeda to include Hezbollah, a high-ranking State Department official responded, "Just like a wrestling meet. We are going to take them one after another." In return for the support of other nations, the United States stood ready to assist their local counterterrorist campaigns, which meant adding their foes to the list of our foes. The United States would lead an international effort to raise counterterrorist capabilities worldwide. The United States itself would focus on terrorists with "global reach." The United States would see to it that terrorists did not acquire weapons of mass destruction. Determined to rid the world of terror, the United States would deal with Iraq, Iran, and North Korea. In this global war on terror, President Bush gave nations around the world the choice: You are either with us or against us.

Too Much Under One Tent

Clear strategy requires clear thinking, based on objective analysis rather than anger or emotion. First, we must be clear about what we are fighting against. The global war on terror covers too much under one tent. It is an overly ambitious attempt to combine the campaign against the al Qaeda–inspired jihadist terrorist enterprise, future campaigns against other terrorist organizations, and efforts to attack the phenomenon of terrorism itself, while also dealing with ongoing insurgencies in Afghanistan and Iraq. It includes efforts to prevent nuclear proliferation on the grounds that the development of nuclear weapons by states such as Iraq, Iran, and North Korea will facilitate the future acquisition of these weapons by terrorists. And it encompasses efforts to deal with failed states to prevent them from becoming breeding grounds or sanctuaries for terrorists.

These are all serious national security concerns, and they are related to one another, but connecting them to a single framework ignores the diversity of the challenges. It impedes understanding of different foes by lumping them together. It creates pressure to find links between things that may have little or no connection. It discourages specific responses to specific threats. It distorts the allocation of resources by encouraging government institutions, which are always competing for resources, to invent counterterrorist missions, to affix counterterrorist labels to other missions that should be pursued anyway, or, worse, to bend the missions themselves. For example, piracy in the Malacca Strait and off the coast of Somalia is a serious problem that should be addressed, but not because there is any evidence connecting pirates with terrorists.

Putting all the counterterrorism efforts into a single framework leads to the unsupportable assertion that fighting terrorists in one place eliminates the need to fight terrorists in another place. It narrows space for maneuver by imposing policies from one dimension onto another. The United States does not negotiate with terrorists, and there is nothing to negotiate with al Qaeda's leaders. But this should not prohibit U.S. assistance in negotiations to resolve other conflicts whose participants may include terrorists, or to negotiate with insurgents in Iraq to bring them into the political dialogue.

Nuclear proliferation poses a major challenge, but for more reasons than the presumption that new nuclear-armed states will make their arsenal accessible to terrorists. The conflation of foes and phenomenon leads to vague, unachievable objectives that provoke cynical speculation about real agendas. It condemns the United States to a perpetual state of war, with profound consequences for governance and society.

Our cause would be better served by treating the various components of the global war on terror as related but separate, recognizing that the United States is engaged not in one war, but in many overlapping campaigns. The goals of destroying al Qaeda, eliminating the jihadist threat, combating terrorism, reducing the violence in Iraq, and limiting the spread of nuclear weapons remain the same. Coordination will continue. Implementation will depend on the situation and the terrain.

Strategic Principles

In a long conflict, a strategy can be only theoretical. Application must be specific to the circumstances of each situation. This is especially true in a multidimensional, multifront global campaign against an evolving adversary. New situations require changes in strategy. Events initiated by the enemy or of one's own making will alter the situation and require new calculations—not mere midcourse adjustments, but significant changes.

The chronology of events since September 11, 2001, illustrates this perfectly. The Taliban were quickly removed, but there is now an escalating insurgency in Afghanistan. The United States then chose to invade Iraq. The invasion succeeded, but armed resistance escalated, demanding the continued commitment of large numbers of troops, causing American and allied casualties and requiring huge investments of money, which dismayed even the war's initial supporters and which could force the United States to withdraw. How such a withdrawal would take place and what would happen next would, in turn, create a completely new set of conditions. The strategic calculations of 2006 differ significantly from those of 2001. Our actions should be governed not by a strategy leading to a distant, undefined victory, but by a set of enduring strategic principles.

Destroy the Jihadist Enterprise

The United States should focus its continuing counterterrorism campaign on the destruction of the global jihadist enterprise. This enterprise remains the principal immediate threat to U.S. national security. The pursuit of the jihadists must be implacable, unrelenting. The terrorist enterprise—its historic center and its affiliates in their current and future forms—must be defeated and destroyed. Its adherents must be dispersed, scattered, divided, deprived of glory, disillusioned, demoralized, and kept on the run, no matter how long it takes. Terrorist operational capabilities have been reduced considerably since 2001, but the jihadists have proven to be adaptable, resilient, and capable of continued action. And as the analysis in Chapter Three sug-

Immediately after September 11, 2001, I wrote an essay that began to lay out a strategy for countering al Qaeda. The essay grew into a series of briefings, which were delivered to various government agencies in Washington. The briefings were expanded and updated to reflect later developments and in 2002 were published in a RAND monograph. The proposed strategy comprised the following key elements:

- The destruction of al Qaeda must remain the primary aim of the American campaign.
- The pursuit of al Qaeda must be single-minded and unrelenting.
- The campaign against terrorism will take time—decades.
- The fight in Afghanistan must be continued as long as al Qaeda operatives remain in the country.
- Pakistan must be kept on the side of the allies in efforts to destroy the remnants of al Qaeda and the Taliban and to dilute Islamic extremism.
- New networks must be created to exploit intelligence across frontiers.
- The war on terrorism cannot be accomplished unilaterally—international cooperation is a prerequisite for success.
- This is a war against specific terrorists—the goal is to combat terrorism.
- The current U.S. strategy should be amended to include political warfare.
- Deterrent strategies may be appropriate for dealing with the terrorists' support structures.
- It must be made clear that terrorist use of weapons of mass destruction will bring extraordinary responses.
- Homeland security strategies must be developed that are both effective and efficient.
- The war against the terrorists at home and abroad must be conducted in a way that is consistent with American values.

SOURCE: Brian Michael Jenkins, *Countering al Qaeda: An Appreciation of the Situation and Suggestions for Strategy*, Santa Monica, CA: RAND Corporation, 2002.

gests, their determination is not easily dented. We should not let the initial U.S. successes translate into dangerous complacency. Ideologically, the jihadists are still on the march. Unpursued, they will be able to quickly repair the damage done to their organization and escalate the violence.

At the same time, the United States must continue to encourage and assist efforts to combat terrorism worldwide, making the operating environment more hostile for all groups using terrorist tactics. However, we are not going to take them all down one after another.

Circumstances may arise where the United States may even find tactical advantage in dialogue and cooperation. Whether we treat other groups like al Qaeda will depend on their behavior. This puts a deterrent component into the U.S. strategy. It does not make terrorism tolerable. It provides an incentive for groups, including those actively engaged in armed conflict, not to resort to terrorist tactics and not to attack the United States. At the same time, it allows the United States to focus its counterterrorist efforts on the most urgent threat.

And although the emergence of al Qaeda and its jihadist ideology reflects a unique confluence of events, the jihadist enterprise is the prototype for the amorphous and criminal networks that will figure prominently in the 21st century. Therefore, we must seek not only to destroy the jihadist enterprise, but to develop the skills, institutions, and relationships that will be necessary to conduct a global war against non-state actors.

Conserve Resources for a Long War

America's efforts to combat terrorism may be divided into several distinct phases. The first phase began with the recognition of the threat in the early 1970s and was characterized by efforts to build both international consensus on outlawing terrorist tactics and institutional capabilities to respond more effectively. When the United States increasingly became the target of sustained terrorist campaigns in the early 1980s, a thorough policy review led to significant increases in security and a tougher response, including the use of military force—but we were still reactive. With 9/11, we seized the initiative, carrying the battle to the terrorists wherever possible and redefining homeland security, accomplishing a lot but sometimes going too far, riding roughshod over domestic rules, squandering international support. Now we have to arrange our policies and carry out actions in ways that can be sustained and will be supported over the long run.

Historical experience suggests that the jihadist conflict will go on for a long time. It took Germany and Italy more than a decade to effectively suppress the tiny terrorist formations operating on their territory. It took the British a quarter of a century to persuade the IRA to give up its armed struggle, and the IRA was a much smaller organization than the global jihadist enterprise—its operations were confined, for the most part, to British territory. A small number of Basque separatists were able to continue their campaign of terrorism in Spain for nearly 40 years. Insurgencies last even longer. Guerrillas in Guatemala fought for nearly half a century. The insurgency in Colombia is now in its fifth decade, with no signs of ending soon.

Even capturing al Qaeda's leaders could require a lengthy pursuit. They could be killed or captured tomorrow or ten years from now. It took nearly two decades to apprehend Carlos, the overrated terrorist celebrity of the 1970s. Abu Nidal, who personified international terrorism to many in the 1980s, was never apprehended and died of natural causes 20 years later. In 1916, General John Pershing led the U.S. Army into Mexico in pursuit of Pancho Villa, who had waged his own war against Americans. Villa escaped Pershing and was not caught until Mexican gunmen assassinated him 12 years later.

The United States must conserve its resources for the long haul. These include blood, treasure, the will of the American people, and the support of needed allies. This means picking future fights carefully, making security measures both effective *and* efficient, maintaining domestic support, avoiding extreme measures that alienate the people, and cultivating rather than bullying other countries.

Wage More-Effective Political Warfare

Armed force alone cannot win this war. The real battle is ideological. In the continuing campaign against al Qaeda and the insurgencies raging in Afghanistan and Iraq, political warfare must be an essential part of America's arsenal. It is not enough to outgun the jihadists. We must destroy their appeal, halt their recruiting. It is not enough to kill or apprehend individual members. Al Qaeda's jihadist ideology must be delegitimized and discredited.

Few Americans understand political warfare, which, in its broadest sense, can encompass every aspect of conflict other than military operations, from assassination to political accommodation. Reversing Clausewitz's famous dictum that war is the extension of politics by other means, political warfare is the extension of armed conflict by other means.

Political warfare is not concerned with advertising American values or winning hearts and minds, an effort that addresses the attitudes of the broader population—the sea in which the jihadist fish swim. We must, of course, attempt to understand the sentiments of the Islamic world, their antipathies toward us and toward the terrorist fanatics who threaten them as well. Where possible, we should try to address these within the limits of our own national interests. But we also must be realistic about our limitations.

There is, today, great ferment among devout Muslims in the broader community about how they should relate to political authority, the application of law, the basis of economic development, the challenge of globalization, the onslaught of Western culture, the problems of integration in non-Muslim societies. Notions of dividing this vast Islamic community into progressive or fundamentalist belief systems or energizing the "moderates" to take on the jihadists fail to acknowledge the complexity and fluidity of the current debates. The United States is seen neither as a qualified commentator nor as a respected source of opinion on these topics.

Political warfare, rather, comprises aggressive tactics aimed at the fringes of the population, where personal discontent and spiritual devotion turn to violent expression. But political warfare does not focus exclusively on enemies who are at large, nor does it end with their capture. It targets those on their way into the enemy ranks, those who might be persuaded to quit, and those in custody. Political warfare sees the enemy not as a monolithic force, but as a dynamic population of individuals whose grievances, sense of humiliation, and desire for revenge, honor, status, meaning, or mere adventure propel them into terrorism. Certainty of death may not dissuade the most committed zealots, but there are many others in both the process of commitment and supporting roles who can be reached. Political warfare accepts no foe as having irrevocably crossed a line; it sees enemy combatants as constantly calibrating and recalibrating their commitment. It sees every prisoner not merely as a source of operational intelligence, but as a potential convert. Political warfare is infinitely flexible and ferociously pragmatic. It accepts local accommodations to reduce violence, offers amnesties to induce divisions and defections, and cuts deals to co-opt enemies. And while it may be silly to talk about the mindset of the "Arab street," political warfare could also target the sea of passive supporters who permit the extremists to operate.[72]

The United States, of course, engages in some political warfare now, but its efforts are the uncoordinated by-products of diplomacy, intelligence, law enforcement, or military operations, and they lack coherence. Moreover, attitudes get in the way. Americans are suspicious of psychological operations beyond the distribution of battlefield leaflets, fearing that propaganda will contaminate the U.S. media or be used to generate domestic support for administration policies. America is a nation of laws, and Americans believe in punishment. We bridle at deals with those who have been our enemies, we object to amnesties, we miss opportunities. Before carefully considering how the United States might exploit a propaganda opportunity, government officials are pressured to make ill-considered remarks in public to make news for short-term advantage.

The U.S. government has many information offices whose staffs are tasked with advertising American values, public diplomacy, placing favorable articles in hostile press environments, and conducting tactical psychological operations, but it has no organization and no strategy for political warfare. We are behind the enemy in this area.

As long as we see political warfare as merely advertising American values, as a dangerous deception unbefitting democracy, or as dancing with the devil, we are condemning ourselves to taking down our opponents one at a time in endless combat—a strategy that amounts to stepping on cockroaches. Even as we kill some, the others will multiply.

"Improving our efforts will likely mean embracing new institutions to engage people around the world," wrote Secretary of Defense Rumsfeld in the essay quoted in Chapter Two. "During the Cold War, institutions such as the U.S. Information Agency and Radio Free Europe proved to be valuable instruments for the United States. We need to consider the possibility of new organizations and programs that can serve a similarly valuable role in the war on terror."[73] This is true, but the United States will need more than new organizations and more-effective delivery of messages. It will need a political warfare strategy based on a thorough knowledge of our terrorist foes.

Break the Cycle of Jihadism

The U.S. strategy against the jihadist enterprise must be broadened to address the entire jihadist cycle, from entry to exit. The cycle begins with radicalization of eager acolytes and ends with their rehabilitation, lengthy imprisonment, or death. The diagram below illustrates the cycle from the outsider's perspective. First, self-selected volunteers willingly accept indoctrination and recruitment. Recruitment, as we

American Counterterrorist Efforts Focus on Jihadist Operations but Ignore Phases in the Jihadist Cycle That Fall Below the Surface

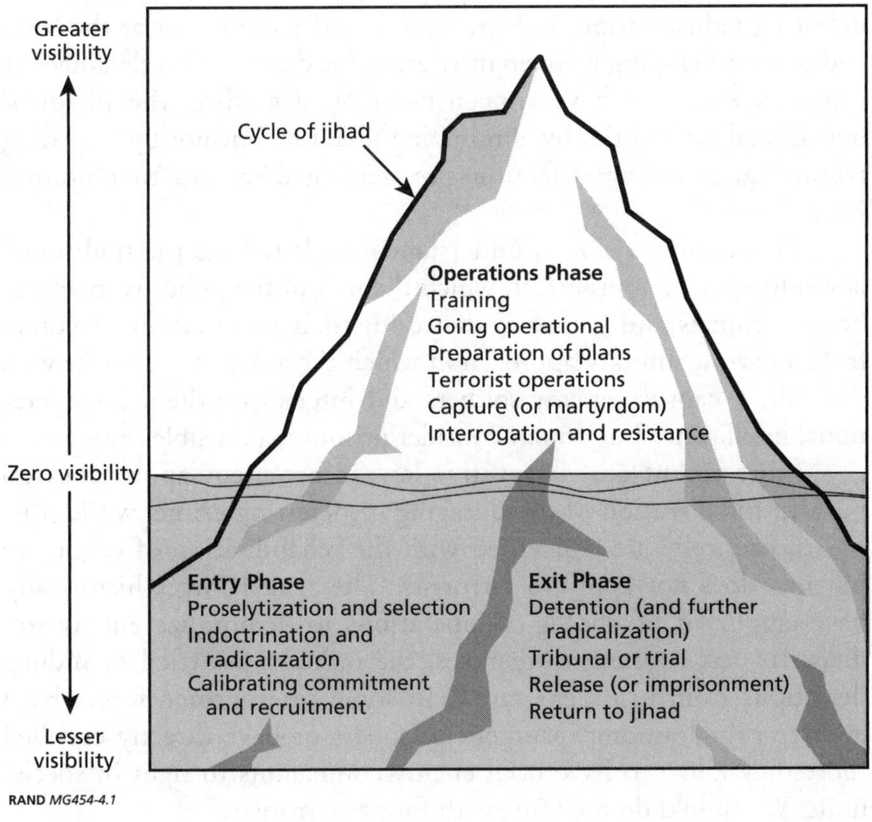

RAND *MG454-4.1*

saw in Chapter Three, is itself a multistep process in which recruits must provide proofs of commitment to advance. Going operational—recruiting others, preparing and participating in terrorist operations—is the step that may result in death or capture. But capture does not end the jihad. Interrogation, trial, and captivity, however long, do not quash the jihadist's commitment—only death can do that. We expect the same of American soldiers who, even as prisoners of war, follow a code of honor that requires them to continue to behave as soldiers at war, to resist their captors, to escape if possible, to continue the struggle. Only death, demobilization, or the end of hostilities ends their efforts.

U.S. counterterrorist efforts focus on only the operational portion of this cycle, the visible tip of the iceberg: from late in the recruitment process to death or capture. Insufficient attention is paid to defeating radicalization, indoctrination, and recruitment at the front end or to developing a coherent strategy for dealing with detainees at the back end. We have concentrated on degrading the jihadists' operational capabilities by eliminating jihadists, but not by impeding recruiting, inducing defections, or getting detainees to renounce jihad.

This narrow vision is understandable. It reflects the traditional law enforcement approach in which the task of the police is to apprehend criminals and gather evidence for their prosecution. It comes from a narrow military approach in which the armed forces close with and kill or capture enemy soldiers and interrogate them for operational intelligence but do not consider prisoners a possible resource.

More recent and innovative law enforcement approaches do push in the direction of discouraging or deterring crime, while prisons theoretically are concerned with the rehabilitation of criminals; but this does not apply to terrorists. The armed forces historically have employed psychological operations to demoralize enemy soldiers. In past counterinsurgencies, the military has tried to induce defections from insurgent ranks. In some cases, armed forces have even recruited among insurgent prisoners or have directly enrolled those they know to have been enemy combatants to fight in special units. We should do the same with former terrorists.

Impede Recruitment

Reducing jihadist recruiting is essential to reducing the terrorist threat. There are several possible approaches. One would be to remove the sources of discontent by addressing the root causes. Resolving the Palestinian problem; ending conflicts in Chechnya, Kashmir, and the Philippines; reducing poverty while expanding economic opportunities; encouraging democracy; and better integrating Muslim immigrant populations—these are noble causes on their own merit and should be pursued. But although jihadist recruiting exploits these issues, it also specifically includes bringing down the governments of Saudi Arabia, Afghanistan, Iraq, and Jordan; destroying the state of Israel; driving the United States and non-Muslims out of Muslim lands; reestablishing caliphates in the Middle East and among the Muslim populations of Malaysia, Indonesia, and the Philippines. These are obviously demands we can never agree to. As a result, jihadists are prepared for perpetual war against the infidels.

Moreover, there is little evidence linking poverty or political oppression with terrorism. The history of modern terrorism, in fact, suggests otherwise. Liberal democracies—including Uruguay, Italy, Germany, France, the United Kingdom, and the United States—have spawned terrorist movements, with many members coming from middle- and upper-class families and having college degrees. Neither al Qaeda's leaders and key operational planners, the 9/11 hijackers, nor many other jihadist operatives are products of poverty or oppression. Individual discontents, not the ills of society, determine who joins.[74]

This is not to say that policies don't count. The United States pays a price for its support of Israel and the House of Saud. The invasion of Iraq upset much of the Muslim community. The photographs of the abuses at Abu Ghraib prison provoked deep anger. And if an entire community moves several percentage points in a negative direction, it considerably increases the population of extremists on the tail of the curve where jihadist recruiters operate. They don't need a million volunteers, only a few alienated souls.

The expansion of jihadist recruiting may reflect not only accumulating social and political grievances or fundamental spiritual revival, but also the proliferation of "sales points": the physical and virtual places where individuals are exposed to the jihadist message. Marketing, not message, often explains growing congregations. If so, then merely reducing the number of jihadist sales points would reduce jihadist recruiting.

Until the world can be made a better place, it is the actual practice of indoctrination and recruiting that must be cracked. Governments have tried to reduce recruiting by attacking incitement and outlawing oral or written speech that encourages hatred and violence. This provokes hostile reactions in societies that protect free speech, but such restrictions are increasingly being expanded. Governments in these societies can also go after the inciters, expelling foreigners—but not native citizens—who preach violence.

Experience from previous wars and counterterrorism campaigns gives us numerous examples of efforts to impede recruiting, encourage defections, and turn prisoners around. Known recruiting sites can be shut down or so obviously kept under surveillance that they are seen by potential recruits as unsafe. Respected communicators can be deployed to warn of jihadist recruiters and counter their messages. Informants can be recruited to provide information; even their suspected presence obliges recruiters to move with greater care. Recantations and denunciations can be elicited and broadcast. False recruiting sites can make volunteers nervous or be used to circulate repellent material.

Measures that have little impact on civil liberties are preferable. Even if known recruiters cannot be arrested or expelled, authorities can identify and frequently interview them. Making surveillance obvious removes the cloak of clandestinity and can create uncertainties and suspicions. As part of the campaign to reduce Ku Klux Klan violence in America, FBI agents conducted aggressive interviews that informed Klan members that their identities were known, that there were informants in their ranks, and that if trouble occurred, they would be under suspicion.[75]

Preemptive recruiting is another approach. During the Vietnam War, U.S. Special Forces soldiers recruited highland tribesmen and rural villagers to the South Vietnamese side, knowing that if the

United States didn't give them rifles, the Viet Cong would. In the same way today, recruiting large numbers of Iraqis into government security forces at least keeps them employed and, it is to be hoped, out of the clutches of the resistance. Recruitment into government service works best in an insurgency, but there may be other ways to draw off the energies of angry young men, including aggressively recruiting them into special units of the armed forces. A few of those who join might start out intending to infiltrate the "enemy's camp," but intense military training and the bonding that comes with it has a way of changing attitudes. It can be no riskier than the past practice of taking into the army young delinquents who were offered the alternatives of jail or joining up.

Educational efforts can also be launched to explain how the jihadists have twisted the religion of Islam. Singapore has enlisted unpaid religious teachers to study the jihadist ideology, identify its distortions, and give lectures at mosques. (This program is described further below, in the discussion of getting detainees to renounce terrorism.)

Yet another approach involves interfering with recruiting. As part of their campaign against terrorists in the 1970s, German authorities deployed hundreds of young undercover agents to likely terrorist recruiting spots. Their mere presence caused the already paranoid terrorists to suspect every new volunteer. Surveillance—real and imagined—at every likely jihadist center since 9/11 has forced jihadist recruiters to be more circumspect.

Encourage Defections, Facilitate Exits

Luring those in the terrorist fold back to society is another strategic approach. Terrorists say they are all determined to fight to the death, an assertion they underline by pointing to suicide attacks. But the ranks of even the most fervent fanatics include less-committed individuals, even latent defectors who might quit if offered a safe way out. They may come to fear the mad leaders who would happily have them die, yet they also fear what might happen to them in American hands. Dropping out and defection may be more frequent occurrences than we suspect. The images of Abu Ghraib should not be seen as the only alternative to martyrdom.

The Chieu Hoi (Open Arms) program during the Vietnam War persuaded more than 100,000 enemy soldiers to defect to the South Vietnamese side by offering them amnesty, cash, job training assistance, and homes.[76] Some of the "ralliers," as they were called, eventually drifted back to the communist side, but overall the program was an economical and certainly less-dangerous way of removing a sizable number of enemy combatants.

When I was a member of the U.S. Army Special Forces in Vietnam, we created yet another program, called the Civilian Irregular Defense Group (CIDG), in the remote areas of Vietnam where ethnic minorities often predominated. We devised the CIDG initially to enhance local self-defense capabilities but also to compete with Viet Cong recruiting. The CIDG grew to a force of over 50,000 fighters, more than a few of whom had once been in the Viet Cong.

These were individuals who did not want to leave their tribal areas and who, as ethnic tribesmen, would not have been treated well in the camps for the ralliers—even less well in the prisoner-of-war camps. But hungry, tired, the tribesmen showed up to join the CIDG, never admitting their prior Viet Cong service but having obvious military skills that marked them as ex-guerrillas. Rather than turning these "irregulars" over to South Vietnamese authorities, the Special Forces camps often took the risk of enlisting them directly into the CIDG and, when possible, bringing their families into the camps as well, hostages to their good behavior. It did not always work, and there were some deliberate infiltrations with terrible results, but many of the enlistees proved to be effective fighters on our behalf.

Although it may be difficult to convert committed jihadists, it is not impossible. Khaled al-Berry did it on his own, as discussed in Chapter Three.[77] Faced with a direct terrorist challenge from al Qaeda, the government of Saudi Arabia has cracked down hard, but it also has offered the terrorists amnesty and financial assistance for their families. Only a few have openly accepted, but the program has established that there is another road, and it has given greater legitimacy to the government's continuing campaign against those who have rejected the offer.

In 2004, Iraq's interim president first floated the idea of a broad amnesty for the insurgents in that country. The objective, he said, was to split the insurgency between nationalists fighting to evict foreign troops and foreign fighters engaged in jihad. Iraq's new president revived the idea in 2005, restricting the offer to Iraqi insurgents who turned away from the resistance.

American officials reacted negatively. "We don't think it's appropriate to give amnesty to people who have killed American or Coalition forces," observed a State Department spokesman. It is an understandable sentiment, but one that narrows exit scenarios. Can the fighting end only when the last American soldier in Iraq kills the last Iraqi insurgent?

Get Detainees to Renounce Terrorism

Political warfare does not end with terrorist captivity. Lacking a strategy, we have competing views of what should be done with suspected terrorist detainees: interrogate them for operational intelligence, detain them for the duration of the war, bring them to trial before military tribunals or civilian courts, hand them over for imprisonment in their countries of origin. But turning detainees against violence should be considered as important as interrogation. Rehabilitation is more important than prosecution, especially if it can be used to discourage jihadist recruiting. Those in custody should be offered the opportunity to quit the jihad, to repent, to publicly recant. We should not let our own desires for revenge or our determination to see justice done get in the way. We must be pragmatic. We are not settling blood debts, we are waging a political war.

The objective cannot be to accumulate ever-growing numbers of detainees, nor should it be merely to reduce the number held. The United States has requested that some countries take back their own nationals among the detainees, but the recipient country must sign an agreement that it will not abuse the prisoners in its custody and that it will permit inspections by a third party. This concern for the detainees' welfare is legitimate; however, given the U.S. record, it is viewed in other nations as extraordinary hypocrisy. Not surprisingly, thus far there are few takers.

One of our top objectives should be to identify those who never were enemy combatants but were picked up in error and held for long periods. The authorities should avoid any temptation to cover initial errors by obtaining false confessions as a condition for prompt release. We have no right to hold these people, but we should also facilitate their reentry into society, assist them if we can, enlist their assistance if they are willing, and ensure as much as possible that their understandable anger does not lead them directly into the jihadist camp.

Those who truly are jihadists will, of course, require a different approach. The experience of other countries offers a number of examples. Determined to reduce the number of IRA detainees, British authorities compiled evidence to justify the release of those individuals whose family or community backgrounds suggested that they could be moved away from violence. This reduced both the population of detainees and the alienation in the communities from which they came. The British also encouraged (and covertly assisted) paramilitary leaders in exploring their political options.

Italy, a Catholic country, used an appropriate religious term to encourage Red Brigades prisoners to renounce terrorism and cooperate with authorities. Those who did so were called "repentants," and their sentences were reduced accordingly. The mere fact that some repented dismayed those still at large, and the information the repentants provided was crucial in cracking the terrorists' campaign.

Other innovative approaches are being pursued today by other countries. In Yemen, Islamic scholars challenged a group of defiant al Qaeda prisoners to a theological debate. "If you convince us that your ideas are justified by the Quran, then we will join you in the struggle," the scholars told the terrorists. "But if we succeed in convincing you of our ideas, then you must agree to renounce violence." The scholars won the debate, and a number of the prisoners renounced violence, were released, and were given help in finding jobs. Some have since offered advice to Yemeni security services—indeed, a tip from one led to the death of al Qaeda's top leader in the country.[78]

Turning terrorists around is not easy, and it doesn't always work. Reportedly, some of those released in Yemen have slipped back into jihadist circles, but we should not expect, nor do we need, 100 percent success.

Saudi Arabia has launched its own campaign by mobilizing some of its most militant clerics, including one whom Osama bin Laden tried to recruit as a spiritual guide of the jihad, to discourage recruitment and reeducate imprisoned jihadists. The program involves teams of clerics and psychiatrists who daily engage individual prisoners in intense religious discussions that can go on for hours at a time. It is almost a mirror of the intense indoctrination that jihadist recruits receive on their way in. If the conversion is considered successful, the individual is released and helped to find a job, or even a wife, but is also kept under close surveillance. At the same time, counselors employed by the government infiltrate jihadist web sites and chat rooms to argue with al Qaeda sympathizers.

It is difficult to assess results. Saudi authorities claim that they have succeeded in changing the thinking of 250 online sympathizers, but how do we know whether they truly think differently now? About 500 jihadists have completed the prison course and been released, but critics charge that 85 to 90 percent might be faking.[79]

With only 36 detainees, Singapore has developed a comprehensive strategy that could provide a model for the United States. In 2003, it approached Islamic religious teachers, asking them to assist in counseling the detainees. The effort grew into the Religious Rehabilitation Group. Unpaid volunteer religious teachers studied the jihadists' literature, identified specific areas where it contradicted or misinterpreted the Quran, prepared a training manual, and recruited other Islamic teachers to participate in the effort.[80]

The group has provided hundreds of counseling sessions to reeducate and rehabilitate the detainees. The teachers admit it is slow work. Some of the detainees remain obstinate; only a few have been released, and they are required to continue attending classes at the mosque. The program has been expanded into lectures at mosques aimed at insulating the community against the jihadists' extremist interpretations.

A separate community program in Singapore, set up with government encouragement in 2002, provides support to the detainees' families. The program will facilitate the reintegration of those detainees who are released. Being aware that their families are being helped is a source of comfort to them, and it creates a better environment for the counseling.[81]

Success in any of these programs may not be validly measured by the percentage of individuals who claim to have abandoned jihadism or the sincerity of that claim, which lies beyond our ability to assess. The same was true of Vietnam's ralliers and Italy's repentants. But public recantations, explanations of how people succumbed to jihadist recruiting, descriptions of recruiting techniques, invitations to come in with one's honor intact—even a few of these can be used to undermine recruiting and create uncertainty in jihadist ranks.

Americans have not done well here. Despite holding hundreds of detainees, some for four years now—including many whose participation in jihad was minor—not one detainee has been publicly turned. One doubts that they are all so dedicated. Is it instead because the interaction is limited to confinement and interrogation, which produces only resistance and radicalization? Would it not be better to try to enlist at least some of them as spokesmen against al Qaeda's brand of jihad, having them tell their stories to would-be jihadists—explaining their initial illusions, their decision to cooperate with those who see jihad exclusively as war, and their eventual disillusion?

Undoubtedly such personal accounts would be dismissed by many as propaganda, and their authors would be described as turncoats saving their own skins, especially if they were obliged to read prepared testimonials. But if they were allowed to express their own internal conflicts, their words could ring true to those on the same path. And the public debate would be shifted from terrorists versus government spokesmen to terrorists versus former terrorists.

The United States could use foreign assistance in this endeavor. It might require setting up a venue other than Guantanamo and Kandahar, perhaps under multilateral supervision, dedicated to rehabilitation.

Maintain International Cooperation

One of the major reasons for the successes that have been achieved in the struggle against the jihadist network is unprecedented international cooperation among intelligence services, law enforcement agencies, and the military. Some of this may be credited to muscular American diplomacy, but most of it is due to a shared sense of threat, especially as the jihadists have expanded their terrorist operations.

The United States cannot afford to waste allies. It simply cannot defeat its terrorist adversaries by itself. International cooperation is a prerequisite to success in the long run, a precious commodity not to be squandered by bullying, unreciprocated demands, indifference to local realities, or actions that repel even America's closest friends. Maintaining the world's support also requires continued demonstration of resolve even when things go badly.

The United States cannot mandate international support. It must build and strive to keep it. Without lessening the determination behind the American effort to contain, reduce, and ultimately destroy the global jihadist enterprise, the United States would be wise in some cases to speak softly, hold back, and let others take the lead. The war against terrorism should not be America's war. Having captured the world's sympathy and support immediately after 9/11, the administration in Washington fumbled by claiming the war as its own. The message "You're either with us or against us" may have been initially useful to get the attention of some uncommitted states, but as a constantly repeated refrain, it was insulting and it complicated cooperation, which could then be perceived only as yielding to American ultimatums.

International support in defeating the jihadists is a dynamic alliance. The United States must accept different degrees of support on different fronts at different times. There is not one coalition, but several overlapping coalitions. One is engaged in hunting down al Qaeda operatives, another is engaged in pacifying Afghanistan, another is engaged in Iraq, and still others will assemble to meet new challenges.

The United States will have to accept imperfect allies. Pakistan is one such ally. One of the few nations to back the Taliban, it dramatically reversed its policy after 9/11. But the Pakistani government still confronts pockets of strong antipathy toward Americans on the part of its own officials and population, and especially among the quarrelsome tribes on its own frontiers that have never been entirely pacified and that remain close to al Qaeda and the Taliban. Pakistan faces a growing insurgency in Baluchistan. It remains sympathetic toward Muslim guerrillas in Kashmir despite their increasingly jihadist complexion. It is a society deeply divided along sectarian lines, with widespread hostility toward the United States among its citizens. Despite these internal difficulties, Pakistan has been helpful in tracking down al Qaeda operatives on its territory and in trying to keep the pressure on al Qaeda and Taliban guerrillas operating on its border with Afghanistan. The relationship between the United States and Pakistan will remain a difficult work in progress.

Saudi Arabia also poses difficulties for the United States. The historically close relationship between the two nations is strained by Saudi Arabia's continuing state-supported expansion of an intolerant and aggressive form of Islam known as Wahabism, which many see as the ideological gateway to jihadism. Textbooks used in Saudi schools perpetuate hostility toward Christians and Jews. The so-called "Noble Quran," used by jihadist recruiters to justify hatred of infidels and exhort violent jihad, is a Saudi production. It was endorsed until just after 9/11 by the country's religious leadership, which itself is historically close to the ruling family.

The campaign against jihadist terrorism is not a religious war, but until the Saudis seriously address officially sponsored Wahabi extremism, jihadists worldwide will be able to claim religious legitimacy. Changes will come slowly. Religious devotion runs deep in this conservative kingdom, and the ruling family, its legitimacy already challenged by al Qaeda, does not want to fuel further opposition. If we have difficulty grasping the Saudi reality, we should keep in mind that the United States itself is not free of influential but troublesome religious leaders who espouse intolerance and violence. While these individuals have no official standing, unlike the Wahabi clerics in Saudi Arabia, they do wield considerable political clout.

At the same time, Saudi Arabia has been vigorous in its pursuit of al Qaeda operatives on its soil, publicly vowing to wipe out the

Saudi branch of the jihadist enterprise. And at the international level, Saudi Arabia has taken a lead in drawing attention to the problem of jihadist terrorism in the world and facilitating cooperation. It would certainly not be in the interest of the United States to destabilize the country.

Russia is a third nation with which the United States confronts difficulties but which could play a greater role in combating the threats that both countries face. The terrible situation in the Caucasus poses major problems for Russia. In addition to the jihadist challenge, the human and physical destruction that has accompanied the wars in Chechnya continues, the Caucasus offers a base for transnational organized crime, and Russian forces themselves are exposed to corruption. The United States is not obliged to endorse Russia's methods for dealing with these problems, which it regards as brutal and counterproductive, but neither is it in a position to offer lectures on human rights.

In the late 1980s, at the height of the Cold War—indeed, at the very moment the United States was arming the mujahedin against Soviet forces in Afghanistan—a little-known initiative began to explore the possibilities of Soviet-American cooperation against terrorism.[82] The terrorism Soviet officials worried most about was the spread of Islamic extremism from Central Asia into the Soviet Union itself. The discussions, which began informally, were later taken up in a series of bilateral meetings at the official level, but the dialogue was interrupted by the momentous events taking place in the Soviet Union itself.

The Soviet collapse raised new issues for the bilateral discussion, with much of the focus on the security of the country's nuclear arsenal and the disposition of the scientists working in sensitive areas of weapons research. More general exchanges of intelligence pertaining to terrorism also have taken place, but the resurgence of old antagonisms and new suspicions about U.S. intentions now impede the closer cooperation that should be pursued in the mutual interest of both countries.

The challenge for both nations will be to get past real policy differences and old confrontational habits to build a compartment of cooperation in the area of terrorism. Defeating the jihadists is in the interest of both countries. Both would also benefit from a resolution of the conflicts in the Caucasus. Neither country's interest is served by nuclear proliferation or by weapons of mass destruction ending up in the hands of terrorists. The sharp political and economic differences that exist even among traditional allies have thus far not impeded close cooperation in the area of terrorism. The same can work for the United States and Russia.

The United States can also learn from its international partners. Reality has by now undermined the arrogant presumption that Americans know best how to defeat terrorists. The United States has vast resources and high technology, but this is a human contest where the knowledge and experience of others can be valuable.

The idea of not just getting intelligence but actually learning from Saudis, Singaporeans, Yemenis, Egyptians, or Malaysians—or from the relevant historical experiences of the French, the British, the Italians, the Germans, and the Spanish in their long struggles against terrorists—may still strike many in Washington as exotic. Some efforts to learn from other countries are circulating in the research community, but this work has a hard time getting translated into U.S. government programs. And in some cases, the United States may simply be the wrong venue for implementation.

Rebuild Afghanistan

Afghanistan is an initial success that could easily slip away. A representative government rules in Kabul, though not far beyond the city. In contrast to the situation in Iraq, NATO forces are present and expanding in Afghanistan. The insurgency in the country has been growing, but the level of violence there is nowhere near that in Iraq. Ethnic and tribal antagonisms remain an obstacle to national unity, but the vicious sectarian violence seen in Iraq is not taking place in Afghanistan. Afghanistan's population is so poor and its infrastructure is so undeveloped that the investment of even modest resources could have a significant effect.

We have learned the lesson of neglecting Afghanistan once. We cannot walk away again. With continued serious engagement and ample international assistance, Afghanistan could eventually become a progressive bastion in a key part of the world.

Preserve but Narrow the Principle of Preemption

The determination of today's terrorists to carry out large-scale attacks, together with their growing destructive power, requires that preemption be preserved as an option, but it is important to distinguish between preemptive action and preemptive war. In the late 1970s, I argued that the United States should take and publicize the position that in order to prevent terrorists from acquiring or using weapons of mass destruction, America would take whatever measures it deems necessary, including unilateral preemptive military action. What I had in mind, however, was something far narrower than preemptive war.

Circumstances could arise in which terrorists would be known by us to be fabricating, accepting delivery of, or already possessing weapons of mass destruction. The preferred option would be to notify local authorities, but there could be situations in which the local government was unable or unwilling to take action, or possibly even where the government was an accomplice of the terrorists. If the threat were imminent and the terrorists were poised to act or to go underground where we might lose track of them, delay could be dangerous.

Such circumstances are extremely unlikely to occur. Rarely would we have that kind of precise intelligence, but if we did, we would be obliged to act and to make a strong case afterward that the action was entirely justified. When I first floated the idea of preemptive military action, there was no notion in my mind that the United States would launch a preemptive war—a gradually prepared, publicly advertised, full-scale invasion, ultimately wrong in many of its presumptions.

The invasion of Iraq, following on the 1998 launch of cruise missiles against a pharmaceutical plant in Khartoum suspected of producing biological weapons, has called into question U.S. intelligence capabilities and has raised the issue of possible government misuse of information as a pretext for bringing down a foreign government. The invasion also has allowed foes of the United States to portray preemption as disguised aggression. The subsequent problems in Iraq have further discredited the principle of preemption. Nonetheless, this option should be preserved; however, it should be limited to precise actions, not regime changes, and it should be taken as a measure of last resort when no other options are available.

Reserve the Right to Retaliate—A Muscular Deterrent

The world has had limited success in preventing states determined to acquire nuclear weapons from doing so. In order to build a second line of defense between nuclear proliferation and nuclear terrorism, we need to review and revise our thinking about deterrence.

Claims by some that bin Laden has acquired tactical nuclear weapons, which he has already smuggled into the United States to ignite an Armageddon scenario of death and destruction, merit skepticism.[83] If they were true, what is he waiting for?

Although a nuclear attack appears to be beyond the capacity of today's terrorist groups, there is concern that renegade states with nuclear capabilities, or rogue elements within states, will transfer know-how, material, or actual weapons to terrorist groups for pure profit or for the purpose of surrogate warfare. The concern is appropriate, but the empirical evidence suggests that we may have exaggerated the willingness of national governments to risk equipping uncontrollable terrorists with weapons of mass destruction. Apart from commissioning the murder of troublesome exiles, when it comes to high-stakes terrorist operations, even those governments identified as state sponsors of terrorism have tended to employ their own agents rather than trust terrorist groups. This was the case in North Korea's assassination of South Korean officials in Rangoon in 1983 and the sabotage of a Korean airliner in the Middle East in 1987. A Syrian agent was found to be behind the attempted sabotage of an Israeli airliner in 1986. Libyan agents were behind the sabotage of Pan Am 103 in 1988 and a UTA airliner in 1989. It is a matter of governments wanting to maintain control. But in every case, sooner or later, the state sponsors have been exposed.

Terrorists themselves must be prevented from acquiring weapons of mass destruction, especially nuclear weapons or contagious pathogens that could spawn dangerous epidemics if disseminated. Derivative substances such as botulinum toxin, ricin, or anthrax, along with chemical substances such as nerve gas and radioactive material for use in a so-called "dirty bomb," are dangerous as well. But unless terrorists were able to acquire large amounts of these agents and disperse them effectively, they would not produce casualties equivalent to those that would result from an epidemic or a nuclear explosion. Panic, dislocation, social disruption, and long-term economic effects (in the case of radioactive contamination) could result, but the direct threat to human life would be likely to equal that of a large-scale conventional explosion. This is not to diminish the indirect effects of such weapons, which could ascend to the catastrophic. An attack with these weapons also could provoke severe curtailments of civil liberties, but this would depend on our reactions, not the direct effects of the weapons themselves.

In contrast, contagious diseases or a nuclear explosion, depending on the details of the scenario, could vault direct casualties into a realm two or three orders of magnitude greater than that of the 9/11 attacks—to the tens of thousands, hundreds of thousands, possibly even millions of fatalities. The important difference between bioterrorism and nuclear terrorism is that while casualties in the case of nuclear terrorism would be confined to the target, a local outbreak of highly contagious disease could quickly become a global pandemic. This fact itself offers a deterrent strategy.

Either a bioterrorist attack or a nuclear attack would produce unpredictable societal, economic, and political effects. All calculations would change. Either type of attack would unleash unprecedented fury and would fuel a demand for all-out warfare, with relatively few constraints against any group or government known or perhaps even suspected of being responsible. Everyone, including our adversaries, should understand that.

The difference between a deadly epidemic and a nuclear bomb suggests different approaches to dealing with each. Our public discussion of the consequences of a biological terrorist attack in the United

States should emphasize not how many *Americans* might die. The crowded cities of Asia, the Middle East, and Africa, with their much weaker public health systems, are far more vulnerable to a pandemic than are American towns and cities. The crowded cities of the developing world could potentially suffer deaths on the scale of the Black Plague of the Middle Ages. Contagious diseases, we should remind our foes along with their constituents and sympathizers, can be only initiated, not confined. And there would be pressure to respond in kind. Bioterrorism is a threat to the world, not to any single country, and could actually wind up causing more deaths in the home country of an attacker than in the target of the attack.

All governments should understand that any attack involving a nuclear weapon will demand responses governed by completely new rules and against which considerations of sovereignty will provide little protection. A terrorist cutout will offer no cover. Any government found to have provided the material, aided in the attack, or provided asylum to the terrorist attackers will bear the same consequences as the attackers themselves. Because governments have national territory, infrastructures, and populations to protect, they are much more vulnerable to retaliation.

The threat of assured destruction might even be broadened to encompass deterrence not only against a single state but against any suspicious nuclear programs. Potential foes, bent upon the development of nuclear weapons, might be informed that in the unimaginable aftermath of a terrorist nuclear attack, the United States may not feel obliged to wait for proof of a particular country's involvement, but may instead choose to strike on suspicion alone or simply on the grounds that the world can no longer afford the risk of nuclear programs that are not under strict international controls. Any clandestine or suspected nuclear weapons development that is outside of the Nuclear Non-Proliferation Treaty and international controls could be considered a legitimate target.

The objective of such a policy would be to expand uncertainty. The threat would not be specific, and methods would not need to be specified, but it would make the point that in the wake of a devastating terrorist-initiated pandemic or terrorist nuclear attack, a post-apocalypse world would be unpredictable. Massive retaliation, preemptive attacks, actions by other states that feel threatened, even actions by independent groups bent upon revenge are all possible, perhaps inevitable.

Iraq: The Search for a Strategic Principle

The decision to invade Iraq was a huge strategic gamble. Like many gambles, it seemed a sure thing at the start. Failure seemed inconceivable. Military victory came swiftly. Then things began to go awry.

More than three years later, the stakes are increasingly higher. Armed resistance has become a bloody insurgency. Foreign and local jihadists have exploited the situation and will benefit if the United States fails. Americans are deeply divided, with a majority now opposed to the government's handling of the war. Failure will further deepen the political divide.

With so much now riding on the outcome, it is still not possible to be certain how things will turn out. There is no easy way forward, but there is also no easy exit. Military experts have outlined counterinsurgency strategies based on proven methods as sensible alternatives to what the United States is doing now, and in the very long run—a presumption in all of the suggested strategies—some might work.

After a difficult beginning, lacking sufficient forces—hampered by official refusal to admit that there was a growing insurgency, ordered to deliver knockout blows, but without an operational doctrine—American soldiers and Marines on the ground in Iraq are starting to figure it out. They are training Iraqi soldiers and detaching Americans to serve in their units. They are dispersing their forces to live with Iraqi units and provide better security for the Iraqi people. They are getting out of armored vehicles to patrol on foot. They are devoting more attention to understanding the local culture and interacting more successfully with the local population—their past failure to do so has been a source of major criticism. They are spending more time with local officials and tribal sheikhs, learning the local power structure.

Again, in the long run, such measures could bring success, but in the short run, they expose Americans to continuing casualties at a time when there is an effort to keep casualties down and thereby reduce growing political pressure to get out. Accordingly, U.S. Army units are being redeployed into garrisons and reducing their combat operations except for providing necessary support to the Iraqi forces. This redeployment, however, puts a heavier burden on the still insufficient and poorly equipped Iraqi forces and risks ceding portions of the country to the insurgents.

Conflicting issues of unorthodox soldiering and institutional rigidity are not new, nor are political pressures to limit casualties, turn things over quickly to inadequately prepared local forces, and get out. We have been there before—in Vietnam, for example. What is being accomplished in the field now may be too little, too late, the dreams of military mavericks who write brilliant memoirs but rarely make it to positions of high command.

For many Americans, withdrawal has become an independent objective to spare further cost, protect political power, save the Army. But like staying in, withdrawal is a gamble. Token reductions in forces, coupled with dubious claims of progress merely to serve domestic political agendas, are likely to provoke cynicism and increase opposition. However, a rapid withdrawal would almost certainly guarantee failure (proponents would counter that withdrawal would merely recognize it). Withdrawal would diminish American influence—our ability to coax the Iraqis toward political solutions or constrain their worst instincts. Americans would quickly become mere bystanders. Too rapid a withdrawal could precipitate a civil war and a humanitarian disaster that would cry for intervention. How ironic would it be if a U.S. departure led to conditions that demanded our return? Withdrawal could leave behind a failed state of 27 million people, a huge chaotic mess in the heart of the Middle East, and a power vacuum that Iran might try to fill.

It is true that the continuing presence of American forces may not prevent these things from occurring anyway. It is also true that some aspects of the continuing U.S. presence may be helping to perpetuate the violence. However long the United States remains in Iraq, its behavior must change. American forces must be guarantors of, not a threat to, the security of ordinary Iraqis.

There is no obvious solution. It is a matter of judgment that will depend on the course of events. My own view is that while the outcome is not yet known in Iraq, the cause is not yet lost. Much can still be done: Keeping American forces at their strength of 130,000–140,000 troops in the spring of 2006, adopting smarter tactics, and changing rotation policies while building up Iraqi forces would give the Iraqi government, with continuing Coalition military participation, a growing capability to deal with both the insurgent and independent militia challenges while preserving hard-earned local experience.

We must be realistic about what we can achieve in Iraq. It is clear that the dream of quickly turning the country into a prosperous, Western-style secular democracy where Americans are considered beloved liberators and all factions live in peace and harmony is just that—a dream. But just because we can't achieve everything we dream of in Iraq doesn't mean we can't achieve anything.

Reducing insurgent, sectarian, and predatory criminal violence to a level that permits social and economic progress is a more realistic and possibly still achievable goal. To do so will require a continued and significant military presence and substantial economic investment. Can we offer the Iraqis both freedom from a brutal tyrant and a better life? We have not done so yet.

It is admittedly a hard sell in America. The costs are obvious. Gains will be subtle and slow. The consequences of failure remain abstract and arguable. And we must remain prepared to accept, although perhaps not just yet, that we cannot do it. Whatever we do next must be carefully calibrated so as not to make the situation worse. With respect to Iraq, that has become the overarching—and perhaps the sole surviving—strategic principle.

Historic American Engineering Record/Jet Lowe

The defense of democracy
demands the defense of democracy's ideals.

CHAPTER FIVE

A Durable Shield: Strategies for Strengthening Ourselves

Are we safer now? Since 9/11, it has, not surprisingly, become Americans' most frequently asked question. On that date, the United States suffered its most violent day since the major battles of the Civil War, worse than Pearl Harbor, worse than D-Day, 18 times worse than the terrorist bombing in Oklahoma City. Americans had little experience with violence on this scale. Security became our paramount concern.

But securing the homeland requires more than proliferating bollards and barriers. It requires strengthening ourselves, and that requires acceptance that the world has changed. Wide oceans no longer provide protection. Distance means little today. Borders have blurred. Walled frontiers will not keep out the world or its conflicts. We must continue our relentless campaign against terrorists abroad while improving intelligence and increasing vigilance at home.

But strengthening ourselves also requires that we know ourselves, understand how we think about threats and how this affects our calculations of risk. The terrorist threat is real, of course, but the way it is portrayed and perceived in the United States adds layers of fear to the point that we sometimes seem determined to terrorize ourselves. How did America come to be so afraid?

An Age of Alarms

Millennial anxieties began to build well before the turn of the century. Instead of foreseeing a post–Cold War era of peace, political observers warned of a new world disorder, of ethnic and religious conflict and transnational organized crime accelerated by the sudden collapse of the Soviet Union and the rapid globalization of the economy.[84]

Rapidly advancing technology provided no comfort, only new dangers. To many people, it seemed that scientific advances merely opened up more opportunities for misadventure and malevolence. Some worried about the possible effects of genetic modification of foodstuffs, others worried about mutant or deliberately designed super germs, the reemergence of old plagues and the appearance of new viruses, the collapse of our computer-dependent society triggered by the end of the century itself, the consequences of good chemistry gone bad, the survival of the planet in the face of man's unrelenting assaults on the environment.

A lot of this was the same sort of *fin de siècle* apprehension that had haunted the closing years of the 19th century, now supplemented by New Age anti-science, the obsession with "endism" that is a peculiar feature of American spiritual thinking, the eternal search for the signs of the Apocalypse, the ever-ready American market for doomsaying. But the fear was real. As one psychiatrist observed, "Our historical moment is fraught with a new kind of dread, for we live with the real, scientific possibility that either through nuclear warfare or choking pollution, or vastly increased rates of disease . . . we could actually end human existence . . . indeed, to completely ignore the forms of our potential destruction itself requires an act of imagination."[85] In 1999, I scribbled in my notebook that we were entering the "age of alarms." Imagining doom was easier than imagining its avoidance.

Bracing for the Apocalypse

Defense analysts worried about the security of the Soviet Union's nuclear arsenal and the rapid spread of scientific knowledge throughout the world that would accelerate the proliferation of weapons of mass destruction. Meanwhile, terrorism experts wrote about the "new terrorism," violence without constraint aimed at causing mass casualties by bringing down airliners, detonating huge truck bombs in city centers, or releasing nerve gas on subways. The terms "bioterrorism" and "cyberterrorism" entered the vocabulary and the national psyche. These new threats, difficult to assess, harder to prepare for, ascended to the level of national security concerns.

Several national commissions were convened in the 1990s to examine the new dangers. One after another, they issued sober findings. In 1999, the Deutch Commission warned of the diversion of weapons of mass destruction from Russia, possession of weapons of mass destruction by unfriendly states, clandestine delivery of a nuclear weapon, and terrorist use of weapons of mass destruction in the United States.[86] The following year, the Bremer Commission warned of large-scale terrorism in the United States, including chemical, biological, and radiological attacks.[87] The Gilmore Panel warned of attacks in the United States with weapons of mass destruction, terrorist attacks on U.S. agriculture, and cyberterrorism.[88] All three commissions agreed that the United States had to prepare for catastrophe. They also warned that national panic in the face of such threats could imperil civil liberties.

As imperatives to action, the threat assessments conveyed in the commission reports had to arouse what their authors saw as a sclerotic government and a complacent population—they had to frighten. To convey a sense of immediacy in its warnings, the Deutch Commission presented several scenarios. One involved the dispersal of anthrax in Boston's subway; another assumed that North Korea had ten nuclear bombs; another described a disgruntled Russian scientist selling plutonium; a fourth postulated an Iraqi launch of sarin-tipped missiles.

An anthrax attack at a sports arena, a cyber attack on the nation's financial system, and the sinking of a cruise ship in the Panama Canal were among the scenarios that former National Security Advisor Anthony Lake used to underscore the new security challenges faced by the nation in his 2000 book, *6 Nightmares.* Well-crafted, displaying the credibility of a former White House official, the scenarios provided riveting drama and effectively intensified the threats.

We were crossing a divide, from events that had occurred to those that might, from history to imagination, from intelligence to literary narrative. Novelists had played with nuclear Armageddon, usually averting it at the last minute through the dogged heroism of a fictional protagonist. Scary war games including scenarios involving super-terrorism were played out at think tanks and in the bowels of the Pentagon, but these were seldom published.

The line began to blur between government portrayals of hypothetical events and pure fiction. If analysis becomes more speculative, then well-informed fiction is not so different. Either one could influence policy. A well-crafted novel about biological terrorism reportedly helped persuade President Bill Clinton that the country needed to devote more attention to the threat. Publicized government concerns sparked new headlines that further inspired novelists and screenwriters. Everything lurched toward the lurid, especially as television news broadcasts increasingly adopted the attributes of popular entertainment. As fact and fiction blended, public perceptions of the threat were limited only by Americans' imagination.

Analysts and policymakers had debated these issues among themselves for decades. Looking at past trends, at the capacity of terrorist groups, at evidence of manifest intent, some experts remained skeptical of the more-elaborate scenarios being offered. They saw tomorrow's terrorist simply as a more ambitious, more brutal version of the terrorists then in circulation. Others, even before 9/11, saw historical patterns as unreliable indicators; believed in sudden, unpredicted events; didn't trust intelligence to provide warning. Possibility, not probability, sufficed to take action. Yet in retrospect, the alarm did not lead to the threat being taken seriously enough before 9/11.

The 9/11 attacks were diabolically low-tech, possessing none of the devices favored by the armchair alarmists or their scenarios—no sarin, no anthrax, no disgruntled Russian nuclear scientist—but they were still devastating. The attacks redefined plausibility, demonstrating that catastrophic terrorist attacks on U.S. soil, as many had anticipated, had become reality.

And within days, the country confronted the mysterious and deadly anthrax letters, while an especially vicious computer virus concurrently raced through the Internet. Although unrelated, these events seemed to confirm the dire predictions of the most fervent Cassandras. All agreed that this was not simply a one-time anomaly, but the violent birth of a dangerous new world. There was an immediate expectation of further catastrophic terrorist attacks. If these terrible things could happen and could happen here, were there any limits?

Terrorism on 9/11 escalated by an order of magnitude. The 9/11 Commission subsequently blamed intelligence for a "failure of imagination." Imagination could not fail again. Our thinking about terrorism vaulted to the edge of imagination. In an attempt to anticipate and prepare for what terrorists might do next, virtually no scenario could be dismissed. Sending waves of suicide bombers to America's shopping malls, demolishing Boston's waterfront with a sabotaged liquefied-natural-gas (LNG) carrier, bringing down the George Washington Bridge in New York City, crashing a plane into the White House or a nuclear reactor, spraying a major urban center with anthrax, sinking tankers to block narrow straits, unleashing hoof-and-mouth disease, bringing down the banking system, spreading smallpox, vaporizing Manhattan with a nuclear bomb, all once considered far-fetched, became presumptions.

The Country on Edge

Public warnings of new terrorist threats helped to keep the country on edge. Six months after 9/11, the government unveiled a new color-coded public warning system. The system was a shorthand way to communicate a judgment—"judgment" being the operative word—based upon available intelligence, to federal agencies, states, local authorities, and those with security responsibilities in the private sector. A sensible step, the government needed a single system to replace the multiple warning systems already in effect. If intelligence reports indicated taking security up a notch, it was important that everyone with security responsibilities have the same understanding of what that meant.

Critics said the alerts were too frequent. But in the shadow of 9/11, as intelligence efforts intensified, information began to pour in from new sources and recently captured terrorist operatives. New terrorist attacks were occurring at the same time authorities were uncovering new terrorist plots. Understandable apprehension and pressure to share information resulted in five nationwide alerts raising the threat one level, from yellow (significant risk) to orange (high risk), between September 2002 and December 2003. One of these alerts coincided with the invasion of Iraq. Although no terrorist incidents occurred, it still seems a sensible precaution. Two more partial alerts were issued between January 2004 and July 2005, the latter just after the London subway bombings—again, a reasonable step. Undoubtedly, there were false alarms, but seven alerts over a 45-month period does not seem extraordinary when jihadists were carrying out attacks worldwide on an average of one every ten weeks.

It can be argued that the threats were too vague, but when authorities have precise information, direct action is possible—they can arrest someone—and public warnings are not necessary. Threats communicated to the public, therefore, will almost always be credible enough to be worrisome but too vague to allow direct intervention.

On the other hand, the government might be criticized for needlessly publicizing the threats, and it does seem that some should have been quietly communicated only to local authorities. Going public looks like bureaucratic tail-covering. But America's pervasive and aggressive news media also make it almost impossible to communicate threat information exclusively to thousands of recipients in government and law enforcement, who will then visibly increase security measures, without attracting some attention. Absent a public statement, reporters will seek their own sources of information, and many different versions will emerge, along with the inevitable rumors, causing uncertainty and possibly even greater alarm. On balance, it is better sharing with the public what the authorities know—and don't know—and relying on everybody's common sense.

What does merit unqualified criticism is the often breathless, needlessly melodramatic language in which the threats, especially the earlier ones, were communicated. Press conferences called to broadcast terrorist threats became political theater and, not surprisingly, led to allegations that they were motivated by political agendas.

The announcements also had a schizophrenic quality. Dire warnings of imminent danger were accompanied by admonitions for Americans to go on about their business as usual. At best, this made citizens cynical about the threats. At worst, it heightened anxiety. Public warning has utility only when the recipients of the message can or should take some action—and when they know what that action is. Lack of public education and public engagement remains a conspicuously neglected component of homeland security.

Although the color-coded alert system still exists, it has not been used on a national level since December 2003. This may reflect a change in policy as much as it reflects a diminishing threat. Nonetheless, circumstances could arise in which a national or local alert would be appropriate. How that alert is communicated will reflect whether any lessons have been learned.

From Terrorist Capabilities to Our Vulnerabilities

Part of our continuing national anxiety also derives from a subtle but significant change in the way we now assess threats. Traditional threat assessments are based on an analysis of the enemy's intentions and capabilities. That was easy during the Cold War. Soviet intentions were manifest. Threat assessment focused on capabilities.

Terrorists are more difficult foes to fathom. Intelligence is harder to get. Their actions are harder to predict. Their targets are virtually unlimited. This uncertainty caused analysts to shift from threat-based assessments to vulnerability-based assessments.

Vulnerability-based assessment starts by identifying a vulnerability; it then postulates a hypothetical terrorist foe and constructs an invariably worst-case scenario, which usually begins something like, "Suppose that terrorists were to attack a nuclear reactor. . . ." Although this approach can be useful for assessing the potential consequences of certain terrorist attacks and evaluating response preparedness, it is not a substitute for threat assessment. Nevertheless, these scenarios are often transformed into real threats. What begins as hypothetically possible evolves into a scenario that is probable, which then somehow becomes inevitable, and, by the bottom of the page, is imminent.

In a large industrial country, vulnerabilities are virtually unlimited. A complete catalog would include commercial aircraft and airports, subways and trains, cruise ships and ferries, cargo vessels and port facilities, bridges and tunnels, refineries and pipelines, power lines and transformers, nuclear power plants, reservoirs and waterworks, food-processing facilities, financial institutions, government buildings, foreign embassies, landmark properties, tourist sites, churches, synagogues, temples and mosques, hospitals, sports arenas, shopping malls, any place people gather. All of these meet the al Qaeda training manual's criteria for target selection: "sentimental value" or "high human" intensity. All have been targets of terrorists in the past. All vie for attention and resources today.

Threat Advocacy

This competition encourages threat advocacy in which individuals, propelled by professional knowledge or constituents' concerns, champion specific threat scenarios. Threat advocacy is not threat-mongering, but the need to be heard and often to overcome the political clout of industries that are anxious to avoid additional expenditures for security requires that public and government concern be aroused. Advocates lead with the worst-case scenarios.

In an open democracy, all of this takes place in public. We advertise America's vulnerabilities in congressional testimony, government reports, the news media, and a steady stream of books, as well as on the Internet. Every imaginable scenario enters the popular culture, then circles back into government, where it inspires new concerns that prompt yet further intelligence inquiries. The inquiries themselves create an eager market for information about new threats—where there are buyers, there will be sellers—and some of the information will inevitably fan the initial fears that had prompted the inquiry.

Our terrorist foes do not live on another planet, however. Even in their isolated universes, they watch what we watch, read what we read. A highly publicized vulnerability inspires them to contemplate whether they actually might be able to exploit it. When our intelligence in turn learns what terrorists are talking about, the feedback loop is completed, seeming to confirm our own worst fears.

Our obsession with new terrorist threats affects us. The inevitable by-product is public dread. Free-floating anxiety in an individual can lead to depression, irrational fears, edginess, the inability to think clearly, hypochondria, and hysteria. On a national scale, it can turn us into a herd cowering before imagined horrors, vulnerable to doomsayers and demagogues, ready to pawn liberty for security.

Facing the Foe Within

Fear is the biggest danger we face. Fear can erode confidence in our institutions, provoke us to overreact, tempt us to abandon our values. There is nothing wrong with being afraid, but we have spent the past five years scaring the hell out of ourselves.

We need to spend the next several years doing things very differently. We need to get more realistic about risk. We need to increase preparedness by educating and mobilizing all Americans to participate in homeland security. Amid the proliferating bollards and barriers and gates and guards, we need to understand security better and to accept its limitations—yet we must also take the opportunity to rebuild America's decaying infrastructure. We need to improve local intelligence without succumbing to national paranoia about "sleeper cells" and fifth columns. We need to build a better legal framework for preventive interventions against terrorists, but we also need to ensure proper oversight to prevent the abuse of those preventive interventions. In all these areas of conduct, we need to remember our core national values and to uphold them as we move forward. Otherwise, the terrorists will truly have won, even without following through on any of their plans of attack. Their terror alone will have sufficed. We will have unilaterally surrendered.

Get Realistic About Risk

Authorities will never be able to uncover and thwart every terrorist plot. It is not a prediction, but it should be our operative presumption that further terrorist attacks will occur on U.S. soil. Nonetheless, we can reduce the terror they are intended to create through a more realistic assessment of personal risk.

Terrorism is actual or threatened violence calculated to create an atmosphere of fear and alarm, which will in turn cause people to exaggerate the strength of the terrorists and the threat they pose. It often works. Since 9/11, most Americans have exaggerated the danger posed by terrorist attacks. This is because spectacular events, not statistics, drive our perceptions.

We see events involving multiple fatalities differently from the way we see multiple events involving one fatality each. Not surprisingly, events with multiple fatalities have much greater impact. Psychologists have learned that we rank such events by almost squaring the death toll per event. An automobile accident with one fatality is seen as one fatality. One hundred accidents with one fatality each are still seen as 100 deaths. But a single event with ten fatalities has almost the same psychological impact as 100 individual fatalities, and an event with 100 deaths has the psychological impact of almost 10,000 deaths. This is why we pay more attention to increasingly rare airline crashes, which usually involve many fatalities, than we do to the much larger national death toll from automobile accidents. The terrorist attack on 9/11, with nearly 3,000 dead, had the psychological impact of millions dying.[89]

Vivid visuals have greater effect than statistics—remember the gory pictures from high school driver's education courses. Deaths that are random have greater impact on us than those that have "rational" explanations. Murder resulting from domestic quarrels is comprehensible. We see it every day on television. But terrorist attacks are random, inexplicable tragedies, and therefore they are more frightening. One can avoid rough neighborhoods. But how do we avoid all the places terrorists might strike?

Now look at the numbers. The average American has about a 1 in 9,000 chance of dying in an automobile accident in a given year and about a 1 in 18,000 chance of being murdered. During the past five years, including the death toll from 9/11, an average American had a 1 in 500,000 chance of being killed in a terrorist attack. And if we extend the actuarial chart to the ten-year period from 1997 to

2006, the probability of dying at the hands of terrorists drops to 1 in a million. The heightened probability of a terrorist attack does not significantly increase the danger to the individual citizen unless we move up into the territory of truly catastrophic scenarios with tens of thousands or hundreds of thousands of deaths.

True, the long-term trend is worrisome. The bloodiest terrorist incidents in the 1970s caused tens of fatalities. The bloodiest attacks in the 1980s caused hundreds of fatalities. This remained the case in the 1990s, although large-scale attacks occurred somewhat less frequently. In 2001, terrorists crossed into the thousands—an order-of-magnitude increase every 15 years. Had the World Trade Center towers collapsed before the evacuation, tens of thousands conceivably might have died.

But there are very few scenarios where fatalities on this large a scale are likely. If we look at the worst explosions, fires, floods, and hurricanes in the history of the United States, the total numbers of fatalities are in the hundreds or thousands. Only huge natural disasters such as the earthquakes and tsunamis that have occurred abroad reach higher death tolls, as do major wars. Conventional explosives and even most realistic chemical attacks simply do not produce this scale of death. The only plausible terrorist scenarios that would achieve this larger scale of destruction would involve the deliberate spread of a contagious disease or the detonation of a nuclear bomb in a crowded city.

These possibilities are frightening, but we have faced such dangers before. For four decades, we lived under the shadow of potential nuclear war. Further back in our history, Americans confronted outbreaks of contagious diseases. The most devastating epidemic in our history, the Spanish flu in 1918 and 1919, killed 1 in 200 Americans. Today, the lifetime odds of an average American being killed in a traffic accident are 1 in 77.

Of legitimately great concern, however, is the fact that lesser terrorist attacks involving lethal chemicals or radioactive material might still produce mass psychological effects, causing panic and social disorder, which could cause more casualties than the attacks themselves. This is where public preparedness comes in.

Enlist the Public

The best way to increase our ability as a nation to respond to disasters, natural or man-made, is to enlist all citizens through education and engagement, which also happens to be a very good way to reduce the persistent anxieties that afflict us. We have not done this.

Girding for all-out war after 9/11, U.S. officials and al Qaeda's leaders took divergent approaches to rallying their supporters. Osama bin Laden sought to arouse his followers to take action. Jihadist ideology demands that every individual participate in jihad as a warrior or an active supporter of war. Al Qaeda's call was a summons to arms.

In contrast, the United States government sought the political support of its citizens but not their active participation. From a strictly operational perspective, this made sense. The United States had sufficient military power to defeat any foe, and once government agencies were properly focused on the terrorist threat, given adequate resources, and equipped with sufficient authority, the federal government could fulfill its traditional task of ensuring national security.

Post-9/11 psychological and political dynamics were closely linked. There was little debate about the need to respond forcefully to the terrorist attack—we were going to war! The real policy choice was how best to wage the war on the home front. The nation was already frightened, which, given the events and continued uncertainty, was inevitable. As shaken as everyone else—and perhaps more so—officials in Washington seized on every vulnerability, issued alarming alerts, holed up at secret sites, offering a performance that further fueled national fears. Citizens were consigned to the role of frightened passengers.

What useful action could citizens perform anyway? Calls to individual action might provoke vigilante behavior, which no one wanted. Apart from exhortations to "be vigilant," Americans were advised to go on with their lives. The global war on terror was not to interfere with the good life. Except for military families, no sacrifices were necessary.

Security visibly increased, which did little to allay anxieties. The hastily drafted Patriot Act increased government powers. The Executive Branch claimed even more authority while covertly undertaking additional measures without discussion or debate: secret detentions, ignoring existing oversight procedures, authorizing the secret collection of data on citizens. If members of Congress were told about these, the legislative body asked no questions and raised no challenges. The public was left to cheer fictional heroes in fictional wars against terrorism on television.

Although it is unclear how much of this "stand-aside-we'll-do-it" approach was by design, it suited the attitude of an administration that was convinced of the necessity to take extreme measures, determined to restore executive authority, and naturally secretive.

As the shock of 9/11 eventually wore off and fears gradually subsided, there was little permanent gain. National threat alerts had become the subject of jokes, precious homeland security resources had been squandered with only modest improvement in local preparedness, and the public was just as vulnerable to alarm as it had been on the morning of September 11. Inevitably, some of the covert programs were discovered, prompting a previously supine Congress and a disturbed public to belatedly address what clearly were critical issues for the country, but this led to an unenlightening debate between those who unquestioningly endorse anything in the name of national security and those who reflexively resist any alteration. A half decade later, it is difficult to argue that as a nation we are now stronger.

An alternative strategy, more consistent with American tradition, would have been to reduce public fear through a different style of communication and governance and by more actively engaging citizens in their own preparedness and response. Such a strategy would attack the terror, not just the terrorists. This approach would have seen the administration working closely with the legislative and judicial branches to increase security without trespassing on liberty. It would aim at preserving national unity. In sum, it would be a strategy that seeks lasting strength. Then, we would be less inclined to reactively repeal needed measures and programs as fear declined in the absence of attack. And if further attacks did occur, we would be more able—mentally and physically—to respond.

It is amazing how many people want to actively assist in homeland security—not to just "be vigilant" without further instruction or keep shopping when alert levels are raised. The federal government does not provide homeland security. Citizens do. This nation has powerful traditions of self-reliance and resiliency, as it proved on 9/11. We must build on them.

Self-reliance, reinforced by mutual assistance, is a fundamental American virtue. Writing his observations on *Democracy in America* in 1835, the French author Alexis de Tocqueville remarked upon the readiness of Americans to sacrifice their own time and resources to ensure the welfare of the group. This was not because the government required it, but because Americans perceived this virtue as "enlightened self-interest."[90] So it should be today.

Al Qaeda's call to arms was also a summons to faith. Washington's pronouncements emphasized fear. Different politics. Unfortunately, to be continually reminded of imminent threats while at the same time being told to go on about our business as usual was advice that only increased anxiety. Worse yet, it encouraged Americans to think of themselves as victims instead of protagonists in a long struggle, thereby reinforcing a long-term trend in law and litigation of displacing individual responsibility and treating all risk as someone else's legal obligation.

By making homeland security a purely Washington affair, the government was signaling that it would take responsibility for both security and response. Instead of promoting self-reliance, the government encouraged dependency. (And if expectations were not fulfilled, Washington had set itself up to be blamed.)

Security is a fundamental human right, but it should not become an individual entitlement. Americans are going to have to accept a measure of risk, even if the risk is minuscule, as we have seen. Yet the acceptance of risk should never become an excuse for negligence.

Public education is the first step toward strengthening ourselves. We need more than Homeland Security web sites and Government Printing Office pamphlets; we need to aggressively educate the public through all media, in the classrooms, at town halls, in civic meetings, through professional organizations, and in volunteer groups. This means more than speeches in front of the American flag. The basic course should include how to deal with the spectrum of threats we face, from "dirty bombs" to natural epidemics, with the emphasis on sound, easy-to-understand science aimed at dispelling mythology and inoculating the community against alarming rumors and panic.[91]

More-advanced training, including specialized first aid and family protection measures, can be offered through youth organizations and other groups. Our goal should be that all American teenagers, adults, and able-bodied senior citizens are capable of taking care of themselves first, then taking care of their families, then taking care of their neighbors who need assistance.

The second step in strengthening ourselves is to ensure individual and family preparedness against an array of natural disasters and terrorist events. Information and home protection kits are available now, but their dissemination is haphazard. Federal funding should be aimed at improving local capacity. The U.S. Department of Homeland Security should make its mission "to ensure the preparedness of every home."

With a population of 300 million people, the United States has enormous untapped capability that can be organized in advance and quickly mobilized when a crisis strikes a community. In addition to public employees, the National Guard, the Red Cross, and other official and volunteer groups, we have a "standing army" of 2 million men and women in the private security industry whose capabilities can easily be increased through mandated improvements in training.

Beyond the doctors and nurses already working in hospitals, volunteer medical professionals can be mobilized to staff predesignated neighborhood MASH units. They could provide emergency care, administering vaccines and offering concerned citizens sound advice that will have far more credibility than the advice given by talking heads on television.

Citizen volunteers, from schoolteachers to CEOs, could be assigned emergency roles, which could then be practiced in drills. We can learn from others here. London engages business executives in exercises and real-life episodes to rapidly assess the impact of terrorist attacks and other disasters on the financial system and to ensure business continuity. The Nordic countries practice a concept of total defense in which virtually every citizen has a preassigned role in a national emergency. Israel actively engages its citizens in homeland defense. Psychologists have learned that knowing what to do and having an assigned task in preparation, planning, and response not only increases preparedness but also reduces stress.[92]

Become More Sophisticated About Security

Not every terrorist plot can be thwarted, no matter how much is spent on security. We have to be savvy about security, accept its limitations, and ensure that measures taken in the name of security do not destroy our open society or disrupt our economy. We cannot banish danger.

Security against terrorism differs from both security against ordinary crime and defense in conventional war. A lot of difficulty has arisen because the public and many of our public officials do not understand the nature of security itself in this unique circumstance. Security against terrorism at home is governed by some basic principles.

For starters, terrorists will always have the advantage. They can attack anything, anywhere, anytime. We cannot protect everything, everywhere, all the time. This makes it difficult to allocate security resources with any precision. There is no such thing as 100 percent security. Despite the best efforts of intelligence and increased physical security, terrorists will sometimes succeed.

Security against terrorism will almost always be reactive. The problem is that terrorists and terrorism analysts can conjure up more attack scenarios than security can possibly cover. Defenders must always decide how much they can devote to protect against events that are plausible but that have not happened anywhere, have not happened domestically, or have not happened in a long time.

Aviation security provides a splendid example. The White House Commission on Aviation Safety and Security, convened in 1996, was well aware of the shortcomings in the security screening at U.S. airports. Contracts to private companies hired to perform this difficult task had gone to the lowest bidders. The turnover rate for the low-wage screeners was extremely high, which complicated training and hampered learning on the job. There were egregious lapses. At best, performance across the country was patchy, good in some places, poor in others. Commission members, including myself, discussed how the situation might be improved. But we considered any recommendation to create a federal security agency to be a nonstarter. As it was, even some of the more modest security recommendations ran into stiff resistance from Congress and the airline industry. Proponents of the measures were repeatedly asked, "When was the last hijacking in the United States?"

Within months of 9/11, the federal government took on the task of airport screening, creating the Transportation Security Agency (TSA), a step that had been unimaginable before the attacks. Even after 9/11, Congress—on ideological grounds—built in exceptions and inserted the possibility of airports opting out of TSA and returning to private screening. The opt-out option was then accelerated in subsequent legislation.

Protecting commercial airliners against man-portable surface-to-air missiles is an excellent example of how security against terrorism will almost always be reactive. We know that these missiles are probably in the hands of terrorists and that terrorists have used them against civilian aircraft, although almost always in conflict zones. Outfitting the entire U.S. commercial fleet of nearly 7,000 aircraft initially would cost at least $10 billion. According to a RAND study, the total cost of acquisition, deployment, maintenance, and operation over a ten-year period would cost $40 billion—a massive government expenditure.[93] Political leaders debate whether we should start now.

But if a missile attack on a commercial airliner were to occur in this country, there would be angry criticism, and pressure to deploy antimissile technology would be irresistible, illustrating another fundamental dilemma. Extraordinary security precautions, which are hard to justify in advance, become grounds for allegations of negligence after an attack, along with criticisms that we are locking the barn door after the horses have escaped.

Yet it still makes sense to increase security around certain targets after one has been attacked. Terrorists tend to be imitative. One attack, when seen by terrorists as successful, inspires similar attacks. We need only to look at airline hijackings and subway bombings.

We must avoid lurching from one nightmare scenario to another and instead formulate broad security strategies that estimate comparative risks and set priorities. After its initial and necessary effort to rapidly raise security across the board nationwide, the Department of Homeland Security has recently embarked upon a more sophisticated risk-based approach, which means allocating more resources in some areas while accepting greater risk in others. It will take time to develop and implement these new analytical approaches, will require public education, sometimes will provoke intense debate and criticism. But ultimately, the effort should reflect how the country wishes to deal with risk.

The concept of security itself must be broadened from deterrence and prevention, which in public places is nearly impossible to ensure, to include effective response procedures to mitigate casualties and ensure rapid recovery. In some cases, the emphasis will be on the front end—deterrence and prevention, as is the case with commercial aviation. In other cases, where prevention is not feasible, the emphasis will necessarily be on response and recovery. In government and in the corporate world, we need a broader understanding of the full spectrum of security and its traditionally separate functions of risk management, physical security, crisis management, emergency response, disaster recovery, and business continuity.

We must recognize that the extraordinary security measures imposed now will become a permanent feature of the landscape. They must be acceptable and sustainable. And if we are to avoid gradually choking our own economy, the security measures must be not only effective, but efficient and practical. We need to more effectively exploit America's enormous capacity for invention and innovation. In addition to its direct costs, security can have insidious adverse consequences, from productivity loss to depriving the United States of foreign talent. There is no easy way to measure these indirect costs, and currently there is no systematic effort to do so.

Finally, the American people themselves need to become more sophisticated about security. Americans abhor security that is intrusive and selective. We insist that our security be passive and egalitarian. We resist the use of personal data to better focus screening. We reject the idea that some people may be inspected more thoroughly, while others are permitted to pass through rapidly. We fear that selective searches will inevitably lead to profiling based upon race or ethnicity. To prevent this, we demand strict mathematical randomness, but we then criticize the system when, for example, little old ladies are subjected to secondary inspections at airports. These cultural biases condemn us to the repetition of mindless, ineffective, and inefficient rule-based, production-line security procedures. Changing this will require a fundamental change in mindset.

Favor Security Investments That Help Rebuild America's Infrastructure

Given the uncertainty of terrorist attacks, compounded by the uncertainty of indirect security costs, funding should favor investments that have benefit even if no attack occurs. Improving the nation's public health and emergency care systems is one obvious example. We also need to calculate and compare the continuing costs of security against the costs of replacing vulnerable infrastructure with more robust, redundant, or resilient structures and systems. Homeland security should provide a basis for renewing America's crumbling infrastructure.

We should not isolate the security function from other national strategies. The consolidation of agencies with security responsibilities into a single Cabinet department had positive results. But in some cases, as in the area of transportation, the consolidation separated those professionals concerned exclusively with security from those concerned with safety and efficiency. In some cases, the solution to a security problem may lie outside the realm of security. How much do we spend on aviation security versus how much should we invest in high-speed intercity rail, which has significant security advantages?

Much of America's vital infrastructure is privately owned, and security mandates in the realm of infrastructure will affect major business sectors. The private sector must be enlisted as a partner with government, but there will be friction. Corporations are reluctant to spend money on security that reduces their bottom lines. Industries contribute directly to the political campaigns of the same elected officials from whom government agencies must seek money. The fact is, the airline industry for decades successfully opposed measures to improve aviation security. Currently, America's biggest retailers are opposing certain measures to increase the security of shipping containers, which some terrorism analysts fear may be used to smuggle weapons of mass destruction into the country. In some cases, vital infrastructure, even though privately owned, may have to be treated as a vital public resource and required to meet higher security standards.

Security measures should seek a net security benefit, not merely the displacement of risk. This is especially true in the case of security for public places, from airport lobbies to subway stations, which are the most difficult to protect because they are public places. There may be occasions when it is necessary to protect some public place for a period of time—a football stadium during a Super Bowl, a convention center during a political convention. We do so knowing that we cannot prevent determined terrorists from attacking under all circumstances, but by making an attack more difficult, we may persuade them to attack at another place or time. For permanent security measures, we have to achieve a net security benefit. For example, if costly and disruptive security measures at airport ticket counters or subway stations serve only to push determined terrorists toward shopping malls or crowded city streets where they can attain the same results, there is no net security benefit to society, and the resources are wasted.

Improve Local Intelligence

Most of the jihadist terrorist attacks since 9/11 have been at local initiative, carried out by local cells inspired by al Qaeda's ideology—the 2005 bombings in London fall in this category. Some of the local cells are connected, others are entirely autonomous. As a consequence, there are fewer communications that can be intercepted, fewer border crossings that can be monitored, fewer transfers of money that can be traced. An entire terrorist plot may proceed under the radar of national intelligence services. Therefore, it is necessary to enhance domestic intelligence collection and analysis capabilities.

Disappointment with the failures of intelligence prior to 9/11 has led some in Washington to speak about creating a separate domestic intelligence agency, like Britain's MI-5, but there is understandable public resistance to a federal agency devoted exclusively to spying on Americans. Instead, the FBI has expanded its domestic intelligence operations and substantially increased the number of Joint Terrorism Task Forces (JTTFs) to improve intelligence-sharing with local law enforcement agencies. The JTTFs bring together intelligence, homeland security, and law enforcement authorities of the federal, state, and local levels under FBI supervision to collaborate on intelligence and terrorism prevention. JTTFs exist in all of the major metropolitan areas of the United States. At the same time, state law enforcement agencies and some local police departments have increased their own intelligence operations. According to a 2004 RAND report, 75 percent of states and 16 percent of local police departments, mainly in the larger cities, have specialized counterterrorism units.[94]

A more recent RAND study identifies some of the continuing problems.[95] Most local police departments have little capacity for intelligence collection and analysis. Local police departments have no funds to support intelligence activities; what they spend comes out of existing budgets, and financially strapped local governments have been unable or unwilling to increase police budgets for this specific purpose. Those police departments that now have intelligence operations focused on terrorists may not be able to count on continued resources. This also reflects variations in the perception of the terrorist threat across the United States.

Local police also lack doctrine and guidance for intelligence operations and are insufficiently trained. This is particularly dangerous, because it increases the probability of unintentional abuse in a very sensitive area.

Information-sharing has improved since 9/11, but problems remain. The JTTFs control the information flow, which tends to make it one-way toward Washington. There are also some complaints that the JTTFs still tend to be case-driven, always looking for opportunities to arrest suspects, rather than developing long-term sources.

Outmoded security classifications still impede sharing information with local police officials who do not have security clearances. Nor is there adequate sharing of information among local police.

Clearly, we need to enhance the intelligence capabilities of local police, not just those of the FBI. The more than 600,000 sworn police officers in the United States are in the best position to monitor potential homegrown terrorists.

They know their territory. Recruited locally, they are likely to be ethnically closer to the communities they serve, they are more aware of local changes, and they are more acceptable to local community leaders. Unlike federal agents, local police do not rotate to another city every few years. They are in the best position to identify "hot spots" for terrorist recruiting, talk to local merchants and community leaders, and develop local sources of intelligence. As we have seen in many cases, local police, through routine criminal investigations, community policing, or dedicated intelligence efforts, may be the first to pick up leads to terrorist plots.

Local police report to local political authorities, which allays some of the concerns about civil liberties. Undeniably, however, many police intelligence units have abused their authority in past decades. Some of these incidents were the consequence of misguided policies. Many resulted from inadequate supervision. Certainly, safeguards will be needed to protect civil liberties.

At the same time, local police need to be given adequate resources, to be properly trained, and to be introduced to the culture of intelligence, which differs from making cases for prosecution. They also need to be connected with other police departments, at home and abroad, and with the national intelligence apparatus. This requires the creation of networks of horizontal and vertical collaborative relationships between intelligence and law enforcement agencies, not hub-and-spokes structures or the imposition of cumbersome new hierarchies or procedural requirements that impede the flow of information.

RAND's research suggests a division of labor in which the FBI continues its targeted intelligence inquiries on the basis of information that local authorities do not have, while local law enforcement agencies, through their routine law enforcement and criminal investigations, provide the eyes and ears on the street. Analysis would be done at the federal level, since local police departments lack this capability. Others might argue that such an arrangement perpetuates the current hierarchy, puts too much distance between intelligence collectors and the analysts, and leaves local agencies dependent on what federal officials choose to tell them.

The New York Police Department (NYPD), the nation's largest police force in the city where most terrorist attacks in the United States have occurred, has taken the lead in creating its own ambitious counterterrorist intelligence capability. By combining skilled former CIA operators with experienced city detectives and recruiting talented civilian analysts, the department has revolutionized police intelligence. All of this has been accomplished within legal guidelines.

Mindful that the 2005 bombings in London were planned and prepared in Leeds, more than a hundred miles away, the NYPD has established close working relationships with surrounding police jurisdictions to extend its early warning capabilities. At the same time, it has deployed liaison officers to selected police departments abroad. The mission of these officers is not to interfere with local investigations or to compete with existing intelligence-sharing arrangements, but to ensure the rapid transfer of information about the latest terrorist attacks, tactics, and technology so that security measures can be immediately modified to meet new terrorist threats.

The New York program reflects the city's sense that it cannot count entirely on the federal government. That alone creates some tension between the NYPD and the FBI, although the two entities have learned to work together.

At the other end of the United States, where perceptions of the threat of terrorism are not as strong as they are in New York, the Los Angeles County Sheriff's Department has taken the lead in creating the Terrorism Early Warning Group. This group brings together officers from the county's multiple police jurisdictions and other agencies with responsibilities for security or response, including private agencies. Members of the group develop and exchange information, review terrorist threats, and ensure preparedness.

Neither of these local initiatives is intended to supplant the existing structure of JTTFs that combine local police and the FBI. In fact, intelligence collection from the ground up differs from and complements the more traditional case-driven investigative approach of the JTTFs, although some in law enforcement will insist on seeing this as competition.

The NYPD's counterterrorist intelligence program is not likely to be replicated across the country. There are more than 18,000 police jurisdictions in the United States, but only about a thousand have 100 or more sworn officers. But combining the best practices developed in New York with the multijurisdictional Terrorism Early Warning approach in Los Angeles could enhance police intelligence in several major metropolitan centers.

Inevitably, such efforts provoke institutional resistance. Direct police-to-police national and international networks are not readily accepted by federal investigative or national intelligence agencies. Although one might think that 9/11 ended all bureaucratic wars in the intelligence domain, old habits resurface. Those accustomed to compartmentalized worlds or to total control of the information flow see these flat networks as chaotic, even dangerous.

But enhancing local police intelligence is preferable to creating a Washington-run domestic intelligence agency, and the former may fit well with the Department of Homeland Security's own increasingly sophisticated intelligence analysis role. One can envision an arrangement in which the Department of Homeland Security sponsors the building of a nationwide network connecting local police department intelligence operations and participates in analysis. That would keep collection under local control while ensuring nationwide connectivity. Such an approach would be more compatible with U.S. traditions of strong local authority, especially in this very sensitive area.[96]

Build a Better Legal Framework for Preventive Intervention

The determination of today's terrorists to carry out large-scale violence and their fascination with unconventional weapons make a traditional, reactive law enforcement approach risky. We cannot possibly protect all possible targets; and prosecution of a handful of perpetrators, if any are still alive after they have inflicted massive carnage, would be an unsatisfactory solution. The nature of the growing terrorist threat pushes society toward prevention and preemption, not just apprehension and prosecution.

As in most democracies, the legal framework for preventive intervention in the United States is poorly developed. Moving against potential terrorists sooner means either preventive detention under presidential authority during wartime or, where possible, arrests on lesser charges such as immigration violations, fraud, and petty crime. It also means acting upon imperfect information, often from confidential informants, before terrorist plans are fully matured. This complicates prosecution. Sometimes authorities will be unable to prosecute on any charges but may feel compelled to move in anyway to break up terrorist plots and impede further terrorist planning. This allows critics, who look at the small percentage of convictions compared with the number of arrests, to conclude erroneously that the authorities are overreacting or harassing certain populations. Because there is always a possibility of error and abuse, judicial review is essential.

The U.S.A. Patriot Act allows arrests on the charge of providing "material assistance" to a terrorist group, an offense that courts appear to be interpreting broadly. Meanwhile, the President has asserted wartime authority to detain whomever he wants as an enemy combatant and hold them indefinitely, without judicial review. Even if it were arguably necessary in extreme circumstances, this type of extrajudicial action should not be allowed to become routine. It opens the way for abuse that could—in the worst case—allow innocent people to be held for years or even for their entire lives without any kind of trial. It would mean accepting the idea of permanent warfare, which would profoundly change our political system. Carefully crafted legislation is needed to provide a better legal alternative. Meanwhile, the nation's courts cannot abdicate their responsibilities to protect the innocent.

Guarantee Oversight

Adopting a more aggressive posture means that mistakes will inevitably be made in gathering intelligence and in making arrests.

Oversight through internal mechanisms, by judicial reviews (especially by federal courts), and at the national level of congressional committees is critical. The purpose of oversight is not to establish volumes of confusing rules or to encourage excess caution, which were problems before 9/11. Rather, oversight could provide appropriate guidance in an area where doctrine and approaches are still being developed and could protect intelligence operations against unwarranted and ideologically driven attacks when honest mistakes occur.

Domestic intelligence-collection activities—some treading close to constitutionally guaranteed rights—are governed by legislation plus federal and state guidelines. Traditionally, intelligence activities have come close to violating constitutionally guaranteed rights in two sensitive areas: electronic surveillance and physical searches. These sensitive areas were placed under the jurisdiction of a special court established by the Foreign Intelligence and Surveillance Act (FISA) of 1978. Until recently, to conduct secret searches or monitor telephone lines, investigators had to apply to a FISA court, where judges with appropriate security clearances reviewed the applications to proceed.

Although the FISA courts almost always approved the applications, the National Commission on Terrorism in 2000, well before 9/11, heard testimony that the FISA process could be slow and burdensome. However, the commission also noted that the process had been streamlined in the period leading up to the millennium. If anything, critics charged, the high approval rate of the FISA applications reflected excess caution on the part of the Department of Justice. In the atmosphere that prevailed after 9/11, it seemed unlikely that the FISA courts would pose any obstacle to prompt investigations.

Nonetheless, following 9/11, the administration chose to bypass the FISA courts altogether, claiming war powers of the President to do so. The later revelation that telephone conversations were being monitored without judicial oversight provoked a storm of criticism. In the subsequent debate, need became confused with method. Few argued that authorities should be forbidden to listen to telephone calls from suspected terrorists abroad or even related telephone conversations in the United States. But the real, neglected issue has been that we have systematically ignored the established oversight procedures. If these are, in fact, cumbersome, then Congress should change them. And if the FISA process cannot be adapted, then it should be replaced by some other oversight mechanism.

If existing oversight requirements or procedures are obstacles to keeping up with extraordinary circumstances or rapidly changing technology, they should be changed, not ignored. The current administration has claimed that all of its activities are lawful, but are they right? To eliminate all external review by courts or legislative bodies on the grounds of executive authority in wartime is to assert unlimited presidential power, which is incompatible with the practice of democracy.

Preserve American Values

The suggestion slithered out on the mahogany table like a poisonous snake: "*Assassination!*" A word hissed rather than spoken. I was irritated at the person who had brought it up, fortunately not one of the high-ranking government officials in the room, but one of several consultants brought in by the State Department to assist in the formulation of U.S. counterterrorist policies. True, we were meeting in the wake of a series of terrorist outrages in which Americans had been killed during the 1980s. True, also, we were frustrated at the paucity of options to combat them.

But assassination, in my view, was a dumb idea. And it was dumber still to bring it up in that particular meeting among that particular assemblage of public officials. We were meeting in 1986, when an Executive Order still outlawed assassination. Even if one of those present favored the idea, he would not dare say so in front of so many others. And it was rude to embarrass government officials for whom even discussing assassination risked impropriety. Several of the people in the room looked positively in pain. Throats cleared. Chairs scraped the floor. As we deliberated in the top floor of the State Department building in Washington, DC, 200 years of American history stared down at us from portraits on the walls. After a moment of uncomfortable silence, one of the officials spoke. "Assassination is wrong!" he asserted. "Whatever we do to combat terrorism, American values must be preserved."

Perhaps not his exact words, but I recall them as simple, straightforward, eloquent only because they were spoken with conviction. It was a tiny moment of history. Thomas Jefferson would have been proud. I was proud.

There is right and wrong, and there is good and evil. This man reminded us in that meeting in 1986 that we were supposed to be the good guys. In the darkest moment of despair, I never feared that terrorists would triumph. In the long run, they would fail. We would survive. But would we always manage to remain the good guys? Should we?

In the years that have passed since that meeting, terrorists have committed more outrages. Indiscriminate attacks have grown more common. As terrorism has become bloodier, the "gun 'em down, string 'em up" school of counterterrorism has understandably gained strength. The United States now engages in "targeted killings" of terrorist leaders rather than "assassinations."[97]

My own view is that in the current context of war, even though it is a war against an amorphous group of terrorists rather than a state, killing terrorist leaders—especially where circumstances prevent their capture—must be an option. Not routine practice, but an *option*, as it was in World War II when American fighters, authorized by President Roosevelt, were sent to shoot down the plane known to be carrying Admiral Isoroku Yamamoto, the commander of the Japanese fleet. This was war.

But the fact that even in the midst of a war for survival, Americans had qualms about killing the admiral of the enemy fleet reflects deeply felt national values that must also be safeguarded. The same applies to the treatment of those in our custody. In order to save the lives of future potential victims, should we not condone torture?

Assassination and torture have a certain atavistic appeal, especially for people who are frightened, frustrated, and angry. The 9/11 attacks and the steady stream of images of bloodied bodies and torn limbs since then have reduced our patience with those who remind us that combating terrorism will be a difficult and enduring task. How much more satisfying it is to hear that to end terrorism we need only to take off the gloves and put on the brass knuckles.

It is now established U.S. policy that military force may be used to rescue hostages held by terrorists, to prevent or respond to terrorist attacks, or to remove terrorism-sponsoring regimes or governments suspected of developing weapons of mass destruction. Recently, it has been asserted that the United States could even use nuclear weapons to destroy deeply buried terrorist bunkers.

The United States has demonstrated that it will secretly apprehend suspected terrorists anywhere in the world, turn them over to other governments for interrogation, or hold them indefinitely at known or secret bases. The United States has engaged in targeted killings of terrorist leaders. The President has authorized the apprehension and detention of U.S. citizens indefinitely without allowing them access to legal counsel or courts. The administration defended its "right" to use harsh interrogation techniques on suspected terrorists, without defined limits, until the U.S. Senate enacted legislation prohibiting abuse or torture of prisoners. In sum, the U.S. government recognizes very few constraints in its counterterrorist campaign.

Operational latitude requires moral certitude, to say nothing of superb intelligence and extraordinary competence. It also requires self-restraint. Today's terrorists believe they can defeat America's superior military technology with their superior convictions, and we have sometimes handed them ammunition to reinforce their beliefs. But we, too, have convictions. We must not be provoked or frightened into abandoning our values. They are part of our arsenal. The preservation of these values is no mere matter of morality; it is a strategic imperative, particularly in a battle rooted in ideology.

As a former soldier, I am cautious but not squeamish about the use of force when it is necessary. Historically, military force has been used to destroy destructive ideologies, turn back aggression, liberate societies from brutal tyrants—all for the good. And countries facing serious terrorist threats have been obliged to change the rules to facilitate the collection of intelligence, broaden police powers, create new laws, and change trial procedures. It is possible for democracies to change the rules and remain democracies. But I fervently believe that whatever we do at home and abroad must be consistent with our values, and here I think we in America are in some danger.

We have ignored our own strengths. We have too readily accepted assertions of executive authority as necessary for our security. We have confused the appropriate need to gather intelligence with the rejection of all rules to do it.

We have yielded too much to fear, and it is fear that could destroy us. No stranger to adversity and war, Abraham Lincoln said in one of his most memorable speeches, "If destruction be our lot, we must ourselves be its author and finisher. As a nation of freemen, we must live through all time, or die by suicide."[98]

Virginia Governor James Gilmore, the plain-speaking man who led the national commission that warned the country of massive terrorist attacks on U.S. soil, at the same time has warned us against transforming society in the name of security. "My principal concern is the impact that all this is having on American society," he said in 2005. "Right now, . . . the message is, 'we're all gonna die.' I think the American people will survive this. We have survived worse things than this."[99]

Existential fear is the only reasonable explanation for America's toleration of torture after 9/11. One of the unreasonable explanations is that many Americans were simply reacting out of anger. For them, it made little difference whether or not torture was an effective way to extract information; it was treatment the terrorists deserved.

But it was unimaginable to me that I would ever witness the highest officials of the United States of America arguing publicly against any restrictions on how we treat those in our custody. I found it even more amazing that the statements did not provoke widespread outrage. As a nation, we treated the issue with remarkable insouciance. Here was a direct violation of the most fundamental value of Americans at war—we don't torture—and we wobbled. "It has always been done," many said, "we just didn't know about it before." As if ignorance made it right. Or we dabbled in sophistry about the precise definition of torture, how much pain could be inflicted, under what circumstances it might be permitted, whether we should consider the obscene idea of a judicial warrant permitting torture.

The legal argument that terrorists do not meet the criteria of "privileged combatants" and therefore do not qualify for protection as prisoners of war under the Geneva Conventions is narrowly correct, but that still does not justify abuse. Interrogations might not be exercises in gentle persuasion, but neither are they excuses for physical beatings, suffocations, sexual humiliation, or any of the other abuses that some U.S. guards and interrogators have inflicted upon detainees in American custody.

Pain will make people talk, although we may question the quality of the information thus obtained. And the exquisitely crafted scenarios in which a prisoner knows the location of a nuclear bomb set to explode in an hour but refuses to talk are more the stuff of television drama than of reality. Moreover, there is a heavy cost to be paid when abuses are revealed, as inevitably they will be. Dubious returns must be measured against strategic risks.

The photographs from Abu Ghraib shocked the country. The staged tableaux of the prisoners were almost as disgusting as the smirking guards deriving amusement from the spectacle. Still, abuse had its defenders, and prosecutions were mostly confined to the lower ranks. It took distinguished and determined Americans, legal scholars, and real warriors to teach the Department of Justice a lesson in the law and in American concepts of morality. Johns Hopkins law professor Ruth Wedgwood and former CIA Director James Woolsey effectively demolished the Department of Justice's unfortunate position on torture with both legal and moral arguments. Writing in 2004, they pointed out that "interrogation methods for combatants and detainees must be framed in the light of the applicable law, even in the war against al Qaeda. . . . In a democratic country bounded by religious faith, there is no room for unbounded power over any human being."[100] It took a courageous senator, informed more than most about the topic because of his own experience as a prisoner in Vietnam and as a victim of torture, to remind the government and the country about American values when he sponsored legislation outlawing torture.

Torture is wrong. Outlawing torture would not prevent every abuse, but we must keep the threshold high. Torture must remain a crime. Violations must remain individual choices, with the consequences well understood. Abuse cannot be national policy. Officials who reject that position might be reminded that with authorization comes inescapable accountability.

The terrorist threats we confront today will continue for many years. We are still closer to the beginning than the end of what is likely to be a very long campaign. The United States must maintain the support of its own citizens and a measure of international support if it is to succeed in the long run. America will be judged not just by what we say but by what we do. We cannot claim to be a nation of laws, a champion of democracy, when we too easily accept a disturbing pattern of ignoring inconvenient rules, justifying our actions by extraordinary circumstances, readily resorting to extrajudicial actions based upon broad assertions of unlimited executive authority, and espousing public arguments against any constraints on how we treat those in our custody. The defense of democracy demands the defense of democracy's ideals. To ignore this is to risk alienation and isolation. And defeat.

Counterterrorism is not simply a matter of technique. Like any form of mortal combat, it confronts the warrior with decisions and dilemmas that may have unavoidable moral dimensions. Being objective, being nonpartisan, being rigorously analytical does not mean being indifferent to right and wrong or being blind to the profound consequences of what we do and how we do it.

Maintaining our values may at times be inconvenient. It may mean, in some circumstances, accepting additional risks, but America has fought wars to defend what its citizens regard as inalienable rights. The country has faced dangers greater than all of the terrorists in the world put together. Neither the terrorists nor those who would promise us protection against terror should cause us to compromise our commitments. The current campaign against terrorism is a contest not only of strength and will, but also of conviction, commitment, and courage. It will ultimately determine who will live in fear. The choice, ultimately, is our own. I believe that we can win, and we can win right.

An Unconquerable Nation

Let us keep the threat in perspective. We have in our history faced far worse threats. Our lives are not in grave danger. The republic is not in peril.

We must not overreact. We may suffer casualties, but we must not yield to terrorist violence or to the terror it creates. The less fear, the less public clamor there will be for responses that could threaten our liberties and destroy our hard-won reputation as a beacon of justice and freedom.

We should not be swept up by the sound and fury of misleading rhetoric. Flag-waving and podium-pounding will not defeat terrorism. Combating terrorism will be a long, enduring, and costly task.

We cannot expect a risk-free society. We cannot be protected against every misfortune.

In the final analysis, our most effective defense against terrorism will come not from surveillance, concrete barriers, metal detectors, or new laws. It will come from our own virtue, our courage, our continued dedication to the ideals of a free society. It will come from our realism in the acceptance of risk, our stoicism in the face of threats, our self-reliance, our humanity, our sense of community, too fleetingly expressed in times of disaster. It will come from our fierce determination, despite the risks, to defend our liberties and protect our values, for which we have fought many wars. These are the kinds of defenses—the ones that come from deep within—that will make our nation unconquerable.

APPENDIX A

Chronology of Selected Jihadist Attacks Since September 11, 2001

Between September 11, 2001, and April 30, 2006, jihadist extremists carried out 33 major terrorist attacks worldwide. This total does not include attacks that are part of ongoing insurgencies and political violence in Afghanistan, Iraq, Israel and the Palestinian Territories, Algeria, and Russia. And it excludes the violence inside Kashmir (but includes the major terrorist attacks in Delhi). It focuses on attacks that were aimed at the West, although in some cases, more locals than Westerners were killed.

The connections between these attacks and the historic al Qaeda leadership remain murky. Al Qaeda was under heavy pressure throughout this period, and its role as jihad's central command was certainly reduced. Most of the terrorist operations described seem to have been planned locally, inspired but not materially facilitated by al Qaeda, but suspicions of al Qaeda approval, training, or financing remain. Other operations, including the attack carried out in Saudi Arabia and those in Jordan, were the responsibility of al Qaeda in the Arabian Peninsula (Saudi Arabia) and al Qaeda in the Land of the Two Rivers (Iraq), both autonomous al Qaeda branches.

October 28, 2001, Pakistan. Six masked gunmen opened fire on the congregation of a church in Bahawalpur, killing 15 persons. Various Islamist extremists were suspected.

December 13, 2001, India. Five gunmen attacked the Parliament House in New Delhi. Six security personnel and a gardener were killed, along with the six attackers. The Lashkar-e-Tayyiba group was blamed for the attack.

March 17, 2002, Pakistan. Extremists threw grenades into a church in Islamabad, killing five persons, including two U.S. citizens, and wounding 46. The Lashkar-e-Tayyiba group was suspected.

April 11, 2002, Tunisia. A suicide bomber detonated a truck loaded with explosives outside a historic synagogue in Djerba, Tunisia, killing 19 persons and injuring 26. The Islamic Army for the Liberation of the Holy Sites claimed responsibility.

May 8, 2002, Pakistan. A car bomb exploded outside the Sheraton Hotel in Karachi, killing 13 persons and wounding 25. No group claimed responsibility.

June 14, 2002, Pakistan. A car bomb exploded near the U.S. consulate in Karachi, killing 11 persons and wounding 51. Al Qaeda and al Qanin were suspected.

August 5, 2002, Pakistan. Gunmen attacked a Christian school, killing six persons. The al-Intigami al-Pakistani claimed responsibility.

October 6, 2002, Yemen. The French oil tanker *Limburg,* anchored about five miles off the coast of Yemen, was rammed by a boat filled with explosives. One person was killed and four were wounded. Al Qaeda was suspected.

October 12, 2002, Bali. A car bomb exploded outside a discotheque in Denpasar, Bali, Indonesia, killing 202 persons and wounding 300. Seven U.S. citizens were among the dead. Jemaah Islamiya, an al Qaeda ally, was responsible for the attack.

November 28, 2002, Kenya. An attack on the Paradise Hotel in Mombasa, Kenya, by a three-person suicide car bomb killed 15 persons and wounded 40. Three of the dead and 18 of the wounded were Israeli tourists. Near Mombasa's airport, two SA-7 shoulder-fired missiles were fired at an Arkia Airlines Boeing 757 carrying 261 passengers back to Israel. Both missiles missed. Three groups claimed responsibility for both attacks: Al Qaeda, the Government of Universal Palestine in Exile, and the Army of Palestine. Al-Ittihad al-Islami was also suspected.

May 12, 2003, Saudi Arabia. Suicide bombers attacked three residential compounds for foreign workers in Riyadh. Thirty-four people were killed, including the nine attackers, nine U.S. citizens, seven Saudis, and one citizen each from the United Kingdom, Ireland, and the Philippines.

May 16, 2003, Morocco. Five targets in Casablanca were simultaneously attacked by a team of suicide bombers. The targets included a Spanish restaurant, a Jewish community center, a Jewish cemetery, a five-star hotel, and the Belgian consulate. Forty-three persons were killed and 100 were wounded. The North African terrorist group Salafia Jihadia claimed responsibility for the attacks.

August 5, 2003, Indonesia. A car bomb exploded outside the Marriott Hotel in Jakarta. Ten persons were killed and 150 were wounded. Authorities suspected Jemaah Islamiyah, which carried out the October 12, 2002, bombing in Bali.

November 8, 2003, Saudi Arabia. A suicide car bombing occurred at the Muhaya residential compound in Riyadh. Eighteen persons were killed and 122 were wounded. Al Qaeda in the Arabian Peninsula was suspected of responsibility.

November 15, 2003, Turkey. Two suicide truck bombs exploded outside two synagogues in Istanbul, killing 25 persons and wounding at least 300. The Great Eastern Islamic Raiders' Front, a Turkish militant group, initially claimed responsibility, but the next day, the London-based newspaper *al-Quds al-Arabi* received an e-mail from an al Qaeda affiliate called the Brigades of the Martyr Abu Hafz al-Masri, claiming responsibility.

November 20, 2003, Turkey. Two suicide truck bombs exploded at the British HSBC bank and the British consulate general in Istanbul, killing 27 persons and wounding at least 450.

February 26, 2004, Philippines. A bomb exploded on a ferry boat in Manila Bay, killing at least 118 persons. The bomb was planted inside a television set aboard the Superferry 14. Six suspects having ties with the Abu Sayyaf Group (ASG) were arrested and charged with the attack.

March 11, 2004, Spain. Ten bombs exploded on the Madrid commuter transit system, killing 191 persons and wounding approximately 1,900. The bombs were hidden in backpacks and left in various stations and trains along a single rail line. The Brigades of the Martyr Abu Hafz al-Masri on behalf of al Qaeda, along with several other groups, claimed responsibility.

April 21, 2004, Saudi Arabia. A car bomb exploded at the Public Security Department in Riyadh, killing five persons and wounding 148. Al Qaeda in the Arabian Peninsula was suspected, although no group claimed responsibility.

May 1, 2004, Saudi Arabia. Four gunmen attacked the offices of ABB Lummus in Yanbu, killing six persons and wounding 19 Saudi policemen. The gunmen then attacked a Holiday Inn, a McDonald's restaurant, and various shops before throwing a pipe bomb at the International School in Yanbu. Al Qaeda in the Arabian Peninsula claimed responsibility.

May 30, 2004, Saudi Arabia. Jihadists attacked two oil-industry compounds, housing offices, and employee apartments in Al-Khobar, killing 22 persons and wounding 25. Al Qaeda in the Arabian Peninsula claimed responsibility.

September 9, 2004, Indonesia. A car bomb was detonated by armed militants outside the Australian embassy in Jakarta, killing 10 persons and wounding 182. The car was packed with nearly 200 kilograms of explosives. Jemaah Islamiya claimed responsibility.

October 7, 2004, Egypt. Jihadist assailants drove a car bomb into the Hilton Hotel lobby in Taba, detonating the explosives. Thirty-four persons were killed and 159 were wounded. Tawhid Islamic Brigades, Jemaah Islamiya, and the Battalions of the Martyr Abdullah Azzam, al Qaeda in the Levant and Egypt, all claimed responsibility.

December 6, 2004, Saudi Arabia. Five attackers broke through the gate of the U.S. consulate in Jeddah, fired automatic weapons, and set off three explosives, killing five persons and wounding nine. Al Qaeda in the Arabian Peninsula claimed responsibility.

April 7, 2005, Egypt. A suicide bomber attacked a bazaar in Cairo, killing four persons, including himself, and wounding 18. The Islamic Glory Brigades in the Land of the Nile claimed responsibility.

July 7, 2005, United Kingdom. Four suicide bombers exploded their devices on public transportation in London. Three almost simultaneous attacks occurred on the London underground train system, and the fourth attack occurred about an hour later on a double-decker bus. Fifty-two persons were killed and approximately 700 were wounded. The bombers were apparently not connected to any formal group but acted on their own in support of the jihadist cause.

July 23, 2005, Egypt. Three simultaneous bombs exploded at tourist sites in Sharm al Sheikh. Two car bombs, one in the lobby of the Ghazala Gardens Hotel and one in the Old Market, and a suitcase bomb which exploded near a Moevenpick Hotel killed a total of 88 persons; about 200 were wounded.

August 19, 2005, Jordan. Four men fired three rockets from a warehouse, targeting two U.S. Navy Ships, the USS *Ashland* and the USS *Kearsarge*, which were docked in the port of Aqaba; an airport at a nearby Israeli port; and a Jordanian hospital. The first rocket flew over the bow of the USS *Ashland* and landed on the pier in Aqaba, killing one Jordanian soldier. The Martyr Abdullah Azzam Brigades claimed responsibility for the attacks. Subsequent reports indicate that the American vessels were not the initially intended targets of the attack. The rockets were supposed to be part of a more ambitious plan in Jordan, but tight Jordanian security obliged the terrorists to fire their rockets and flee.

October 29, 2005, India. Three bombs exploded within minutes of each other in Delhi, killing at least 61 persons and wounding about 210. The attack occurred on the eve of the Hindu festival of

Diwali and the Muslim Eid al Fitr. Police arrested a Kashmiri militant leader who had planned and funded the attack.

November 9, 2005, Jordan. Three nearly simultaneous suicide bombs exploded at three luxury hotels in Amman, killing 63 persons and wounding more then 100. A fourth device carried by a female suicide bomber failed to go off. She left the scene and was later arrested. Abu Musab al-Zarqawi (the leader of al Qaeda in the Land of the Two Rivers) and seven other persons were indicted for the attack.

February 24, 2006, Saudi Arabia. Suicide bombers attempted to drive through the gates of the world's largest oil facility in Abqaiq. Guards opened fire on the vehicles, causing them to explode, killing two of the militants and two of the security guards. Four others were wounded. Al Qaeda in the Arabian Peninsula claimed responsibility for the attack.

March 2, 2006, Pakistan. A suicide bomber detonated a car bomb outside the U.S. consulate in Karachi, killing a U.S. diplomat and three other persons. Fifty-two others were wounded in a hotel parking lot next to the consulate. The attack occurred one day before President Bush was to visit Pakistan. No group has claimed responsibility.

April 24, 2006, Egypt. Three time bombs exploded, rocking the resort city of Dahab at the height of the tourist season, killing at least 21 persons and wounding at least 80. The Egyptian government said the attackers were local Bedouin extremists linked to previous attacks in the area and without international connections. Others suspected al Qaeda involvement.

APPENDIX B

Failed Terrorist Plots: What Were They Thinking About Doing?

Although it is impossible to count things that don't occur, some analysts claim that more than 100 plots by jihadist terrorists have been thwarted and foiled in recent years. The following, all of which were reported in the news media, were at various stages of maturity when discovered by the authorities, from an idea in a notebook to a foiled or failed attempt. Although many of the schemes appear to be drawn from the same playbooks as the terrorist attacks that did occur, they indicate a broader range of terrorist thinking.

The list reveals intense activity, especially when combined with the list of successful attacks. Reviewing the two lists, a terrorist planner might conclude that it is best to attack soft targets and keep it simple. Attacks on unprotected public places were the most successful, while attacks on hard targets have the highest risk of failure. The lists also suggest a lot of luck on both sides.

Had the terrorists carried out every plot, 12 to 14 more commercial airliners would have been hijacked and crashed into various targets; another 15 would have been sabotaged or shot down with missiles. Several more ships would have been attacked. Many additional bombings would have occurred. Attacks involving lethal chemicals, botulinum toxin, and ricin would have occurred in Europe and Jordan. Killing as many as possible seems to have been the paramount criterion in most of the plans. Had all of these plans succeeded, thousands would have died.

Very few of the attacks involving chemical or biological substances such as ricin would have caused mass casualties. All were discovered by authorities, which suggests that there were plans still on the shelf when the plotters were apprehended. That, in turn, suggests that the terrorists themselves may have had difficulties figuring out exactly how to employ these substances.

February 1993. According to a statement presented in court, the World Trade Center bombers planned for their bomb to release cyanide in the explosion.

June 1993. In a planned sequel to the World Trade Center bombing, terrorists were going to blow up various landmarks in New York, including the Holland and Lincoln tunnels, the George Washington Bridge, the United Nations Building, and the FBI offices. They also discussed assassinating the president of Egypt and a U.S. senator.

December 1994. Islamic extremists who hijacked a commercial jet reportedly contemplated crashing it into the Eiffel Tower in Paris.

January 1995. Philippine authorities uncovered a plot by Islamic extremists to smuggle bombs on board and blow up 12 U.S. airliners over the Pacific Ocean. Terrorist plans also included the assassination of the pope during his visit to Manila and the crashing of a small plane into the headquarters of the CIA.

July 1997. Police thwarted a plot by Islamic extremists to carry out suicide bombings in New York's subways.

December 1999. The arrest of an Algerian terrorist on the U.S.-Canadian border foiled a plan to detonate a large bomb at Los Angeles International Airport. The same terrorist had studied how to place lethal chemicals in air-conditioning intakes.

December 1999. Jordanian authorities interrupted a plot by al Qaeda extremists to blow up biblical sites in the Middle East and a major hotel in Amman.

2000. According to published reports, the planners of the October 2000 attack on the USS *Cole* were sent to Kuala Lumpur to plan a similar attack on a U.S. ship visiting a Malaysian port.

January 2000. Al Qaeda terrorists in Yemen failed in their attempt to crash an explosives-laden boat into the U.S. destroyer *The Sullivans*.

December 2000. Authorities thwarted a plot to bomb the Christmas Market in Strasbourg, France. The plot also mentioned the terrorists' intention to blow up a synagogue. (In a related or possibly separate plot, Italian authorities said that terrorists had planned to blow up the cathedral in Strasbourg.)

2001. Malaysian authorities discovered and thwarted a plot by operatives belonging to Kumpulan Mujahedin Malaysia, a local jihadist group, to attack a U.S. ship visiting a Malaysian port.

September 2001. According to trial testimony of captured terrorist Zacarias Moussaoui, a fifth plane was supposed to have been hijacked on September 11 and flown into the White House. (Interrogation reports from Khalid Sheikh Mohammed, the captured planner of the operation, dispute this.) The fourth plane, which crashed in Pennsylvania, was supposed to hit the Capitol building. At one point in the planning process, al Qaeda planners considered hijacking and crashing ten planes, five on each coast. And according to an Arab reporter who interviewed the 9/11 planners after September 11 but before their capture, the initial plan called for crashing the hijacked airliners into nuclear power plants, but al Qaeda decided against it for fear "it would go out of control."

September 2001. Dutch authorities arrested three suspects and accused them of planning to bomb the U.S. embassy in Paris. (The defendants were later acquitted.)

December 2001. Richard Reid, an al Qaeda operative, failed to detonate a powerful bomb concealed in his shoe while aboard a trans-Atlantic flight and was overpowered by passengers. According to subsequent reports, there was to have been a second "shoe bomber."

December 2001. Singapore authorities arrested 21 members of Jemaah Islamiya involved in planning terrorist attacks on various targets in Singapore. The earliest plans dated back to the mid-

1990s. Three plans were relatively well-developed: In 1997, the terrorists put together a plan to attack a shuttle bus that carried U.S. military personnel from a metro station but later shelved it. The second plan, developed after September 11, 2001, envisioned the use of truck bombs against the U.S. and Israeli embassies, the Australian and British High Commissions, and commercial buildings housing U.S. and Israeli firms. The third plan involved attacks on U.S. naval vessels in Singapore. Other targets contemplated by the terrorists included water pipelines, Changi Airport, a radar station, the Ministries of Defense and Education, the American school, and the city's metro system.

December 2001. A terrorist suspect arrested in Bombay reported that hijacked planes were to be flown into Big Ben and the London Tower Bridge.

February 2002. An al Qaeda training manual found in Afghanistan suggested attacks on targets of "sentimental value" such as Big Ben, the Statue of Liberty, the Eiffel Tower, museums, and monuments. It also called for attacks on sites of "high human intensity," including skyscrapers, ports, airports, nuclear power plants, and places where large numbers of persons gather, such as football stadiums.

March 2002. Authorities uncovered a plot to blow up the U.S. embassy in Sarajevo, Bosnia.

March 2002. Italian police believe they uncovered a plot to disperse cyanide from tunnels beneath the U.S. embassy in Rome. In wiretapped conversations, one terrorist operative also talked about putting poison in cans of tomatoes.

June 2002. Authorities in Morocco thwarted plans by al Qaeda terrorists to crash boats loaded with explosives into American and British vessels in the Strait of Gibraltar. The plans were uncovered during the interrogation of captured terrorists.

Summer 2002. Saudi authorities uncovered a terrorist plot to sabotage the Ras Tanura pipeline and other pipelines.

November 2002. As part of a coordinated attack, al Qaeda terrorists with two surface-to-air missiles attempted to shoot down an Israeli airliner. Both missiles missed their target.

December 2002. French authorities uncovered a plot to attack the Russian embassy in Paris with chemical or biological weapons. It was later revealed that the plotters had also discussed attacking a crowded clothing store in Paris and the Eiffel Tower.

January 2003. Al Qaeda planned to release hydrogen cyanide on New York's subways.

January 2003. British police discovered a terrorist plot in London involving ricin. In March, traces of ricin were found in a locker at a train station in Paris.

February 2003. Plans by al Qaeda to bomb the American Fifth Fleet headquarters in Bahrain were uncovered during the interrogation of captured terrorists.

February 2003. British authorities discovered terrorist plans to fly a hijacked airliner into a crowded passenger terminal at London's Heathrow Airport.

June 2003. An individual was ordered by al Qaeda to reconnoiter how the Brooklyn Bridge might be brought down.

August 2003. The arrest of a key al Qaeda leader in Thailand led to the discovery of a plan to hijack an airliner and crash it into Singapore's Changi Airport.

December 2003. As a result of an arrest in Pakistan in early 2004, target folders were discovered indicating earlier terrorist reconnaissance of financial institutions in the United States, including the World Bank in Washington, the New York Stock Exchange, Citibank headquarters in midtown Manhattan, and the Prudential Bank in Newark, New Jersey. The reconnaissance was done before September 11, 2001, but the idea was proposed in late 2003 or early 2004. According to the folders, the favored target was the Citibank building, a glass-clad skyscraper.

January 2004. French authorities say they thwarted a planned terrorist attack involving botulinum toxin and ricin.

March 2004. British authorities seized a large quantity of ammonium nitrate, which was to be used by al Qaeda–inspired terrorists to carry out large-scale bombings in London.

April 2004. Jordanian authorities broke up an alleged plot by al Qaeda terrorists to carry out bombings in order to disperse a "deadly cloud of chemicals" (including blistering agents) in the heart of Amman. Among the targets were the office of the Jordanian prime minister, the headquarters of Jordanian intelligence, and the U.S. embassy.

August 2004. Police thwarted a plot by Islamic extremists to bomb a subway station in midtown Manhattan.

November 2004. British and European officials were reported to have thwarted a plan by al Qaeda terrorists to fly hijacked airliners into Canary Wharf (a London skyscraper).

February 2005. An American inspired by al Qaeda's ideology was accused of plotting to kill President Bush by shooting him or by using a car bomb.

April 2005. Al Qaeda–trained terrorists in London planned to place ricin on the handrails and in the lavatories of the Heathrow Express.

July 2005. A team of four bombers detonated defective devices at three locations in the London Underground and on one bus, duplicating the attack that occurred two weeks before, on July 7.

August 2005. Turkish authorities uncovered a plot to ram a speedboat filled with explosives into an Israeli cruise ship in Antalya.

August 2005. British authorities say that they thwarted a plot begun in 2004 to release deadly gas or chemicals at the Houses of Parliament in London; plotters reportedly were also considering the London subway system as a target.

October 2005. According to a White House statement, ten terrorist plots had been foiled since 9/11, including a plot in 2002 to use shoe bombs to access the cockpit, hijack a plane, and crash it into the U.S. Bank Tower, the tallest building in Los Angeles. The other plots listed included a plot to hijack airliners and attack targets on the East Coast; a May 2002 plot to bomb apartment buildings in the United States; a plot in mid-2004 to bomb targets in Britain; a plot in 2003 to attack Westerners in Karachi, Pakistan; a 2003 plot to crash a hijacked airliner into Heathrow Airport; a 2004 plot to conduct large-scale bombings in Britain; a late 2002 plot to attack ships in the Persian Gulf; a 2002 plot to attack ships in the Strait of Hormuz; and a 2003 plot to "attack an unnamed tourist site outside the United States."

November 2005. Australian authorities arrested terrorists planning to carry out bombings at train stations in Melbourne or Sydney.

February 2006. British Chancellor of the Exchequer Gordon Brown claimed that three terrorist attacks against Britain had been thwarted since July 21, 2005, but gave no details.

April 2006. Moroccan authorities arrested nine al Qaeda suspects allegedly planning to blow up a church in Bologna, a commuter train in Milan, the headquarters of French intelligence services in Paris, three other unspecified targets in France, and the U.S. consulate in Rabat.

April 2006. Abu Sayyaf guerrillas in the Philippines reportedly plotted the seizure of a passenger ship or ferry and the holding of its passengers as hostages. (The report in the press may actually refer to a 2005 plot.)

April 2006. Two days after terrorist attacks on hotels in Egypt, two suicide bombers attempted to attack personnel of the multinational peacekeeping force near the Gaza border in Sinai, Egypt. Both attacks failed; the suicide bombers killed themselves but caused no other casualties.

Combating Terrorism: A Reading List

The terrorist attacks on September 11, 2001, produced an avalanche of books and reports on the topics of terrorism, al Qaeda, and, later, the war in Iraq. This bibliography is not intended to include all of them, although it probably does contain a majority of the published works. It represents my personal collection and a recommended reading list. I have grouped the titles in broad categories for convenience. Some works have been deliberately omitted—the most polemic and most superficial did not make the cut. Inevitably, there also are some accidental omissions; I will include these publications in future versions as I become aware of them. I invite readers to recommend additional titles or make specific comments on the works included here.

Theoretical Works on Jihad

Bostom, Andrew G. (ed.), *The Legacy of Jihad: Islamic Holy War and the Fate of Non-Muslims*, Amherst, NY: Prometheus Books, 2005.

Cook, David, *Understanding Jihad*, Berkeley and Los Angeles, CA: University of California Press, 2005.

El Fadl, Khaled Abou, *Rebellion and Violence in Islamic Law*, New York: Cambridge University Press, 2001.

Firestone, Reuven, *Jihad: The Origin of Holy War in Islam*, New York: Oxford University Press, 1999.

Haleem, Harfiyah Abdel, Oliver Ramsbotham, Saba Risaluddin, and Brian Wicker (eds.), *The Crescent and the Cross: Muslim and Christian Approaches to War and Peace,* New York: Palgrave Macmillan, 1998.

Hashmi, Sohail H. (ed.), *Islamic Political Ethics: Civil Society, Pluralism, and Conflict,* Princeton, NJ: Princeton University Press, 2002.

Johnson, James Turner, and John Kelsay (eds.), *Cross, Crescent, and Sword: The Justification and Limitation of War in Western and Islamic Tradition,* New York: Greenwood Press, 1990.

Peters, Rudolph, *Jihad in Classical and Modern Islam: A Reader,* Princeton, NJ: Markus Wiener Publishers, 1996.

The Rise of Islamic Fundamentalism and Contemporary Jihad

Abu-Rabi, Ibrahim M., *Intellectual Origins of Islamic Resurgence in the Modern Arab World,* Albany, NY: State University of New York Press, 1996.

Ahmed, Akbar S., *Islam Under Siege: Living Dangerously in a Post-Honor World,* New Delhi: Vistaar Publications, 2003.

Akbar, M. J., *The Shade of Swords: Jihad and the Conflict Between Islam and Christianity,* London and New York: Routledge, 2002.

Ali, Tariq, *The Clash of Fundamentalisms: Crusades, Jihads and Modernity,* London: Verso, 2002.

Baker, Raymond William, *Islam Without Fear: Egypt and the New Islamists,* Cambridge, MA, and London: Harvard University Press, 2003.

Benard, Cheryl, *Civil Democratic Islam: Partners, Resources, and Strategies,* Santa Monica, CA: RAND Corporation, MR-1716-CMEPP, 2004 (http://www.rand.org/publications/MR/MR1716/).

Bonney, Richard, *Jihad: From Qur'an to bin Laden,* New York: Palgrave Macmillan, 2004.

Chasdi, Richard J., *Tapestry of Terror: A Portrait of Middle East Terrorism, 1994–1999,* New York: Lexington Books, 2002.

Deloire, Christophe, and Christophe Dubois, *Les Islamistes Sont Déjà La,* Paris: Albin Michel, 2004.

El Fadl, Khaled Abou, *The Great Theft: Wrestling Islam from the Extremists,* New York: HarperCollins Publishers, 2005.

Esposito, John L., *Unholy War: Terror in the Name of Islam,* New York: Oxford University Press, 2002.

Gerges, Fawaz A., *Journey of the Jihadist: Inside Muslim Militancy,* Orlando, FL: Harcourt Inc., 2006.

_____, *The Far Enemy: Why Jihad Went Global,* New York: Cambridge University Press, 2005.

Habeck, Mary R., *Knowing the Enemy: Jihadist Ideology and the War on Terror,* New Haven, CT, and London: Yale University Press, 2006.

Hiro, Dilip, *Holy Wars: The Rise of Islamic Fundamentalism,* New York: Routledge, 1989.

Huband, Mark, *Warriors of the Prophet: The Struggle for Islam,* Boulder, CO: Westview Press, 1999.

Jacquard, Roland, with Dominique Nasplezes, *Fatwa Contre l'Occident,* Paris, France: Albin Michel, S.A., 1998.

Juergensmeyer, Mark, *Terror in the Mind of God: The Global Rise of Religious Violence,* Berkeley, CA: University of California Press, 2003.

Kepel, Gilles, *The War for Muslim Minds: Islam and the West,* Cambridge, MA, and London: The Belknap Press of Harvard University Press, 2004.

_____, *Jihad: The Trail of Political Islam,* Cambridge, MA, The Belknap Press of Harvard University Press, 2002.

Lewis, Bernard, *The Crisis of Islam: Holy War and Unholy Terror,* New York: The Modern Library, 2003.

_____, *A Middle East Mosaic: Fragments of Life, Letters and History,* New York: Random House, 2000.

_____, *Islam and the West,* New York: Oxford University Press, 1993.

_____, *The Political Language of Islam,* Chicago: The University of Chicago Press, 1988.

Mamdani, Mahmood, *Good Muslim, Bad Muslim: America, the Cold War, and the Roots of Terror,* New York: Pantheon Books, 2004.

Mansour, Latifa Ben, *Frères Musulmmans, Frères Feroces: Voyage dans l'Enfer du Discours Islamiste,* Paris: Editions Ramsay, 2002.

Milton-Edwards, Beverley, *Islamic Fundamentalism Since 1945,* New York: Routledge, 2005.

Nafziger, George F., and Mark W. Walton, *Islam at War: A History,* Westport, CT: Praeger, 2003.

Noorani, A. G., *Islam & Jihad: Prejudice Versus Reality,* New York: Zed Books, 2003.

Palmer, Monte, and Princess Palmer, *At the Heart of Terror: Islam, Jihadists, and America's War on Terrorism,* Lanham, MD: Rowman & Littlefield Publishers, Inc., 2004.

Phares, Walid, *Future Jihad: Terrorist Strategies Against America,* New York: Palgrave Macmillan, 2005.

Pipes, Daniel, *Militant Islam Reaches America,* New York: W.W. Norton & Company, 2003.

______, *In the Path of God: Islam and Political Power,* New York: Basic Books, 1983.

Rabasa, Angel M., Cheryl Benard, Peter Chalk, C. Christine Fair, Theodore W. Karasik, Rollie Lal, Ian O. Lesser, and David E. Thaler, *The Muslim World After 9/11*, Santa Monica, CA: RAND Corporation, MG-246-AF, 2004 (http://www.rand.org/publications/MG/MG246/).

Rubin, Barry, and Judith Colp Rubin (eds.), *Anti-American Terrorism and the Middle East,* New York: Oxford University Press, Inc., 2002.

Ruthven, Malise, *A Fury for God: The Islamist Attack on America,* London: Granta Books, 2002.

Schwartz, Stephen, *The Two Faces of Islam: The House of Sa'ud from Tradition to Terror,* New York: Doubleday, 2002.

Spencer, Robert, *Onward Muslim Soldiers: How Jihad Still Threatens America and the West,* Washington, DC: Regnery Publishing, Inc., 2003.

Spitaels, Guy, *La Triple Insurrection Islamiste,* Paris: Librairie Arthème Fayard et Editions Luc Pire, 2005.

Stern, Jessica, *Terror in the Name of God: Why Religious Militants Kill,* New York: Harper Perennial, 2004.

Treverton, Gregory F., Heather S. Gregg, Daniel Gibran, and Charles W. Yost, *Exploring Religious Conflict*, Santa Monica, CA: RAND Corporation, CF-211, 2005 (http://www.rand.org/publications/CF/CF211/).

Wheatcroft, Andrew, *Infidels: The Conflict Between Christendom and Islam 638–2002,* London: Penguin Group, 2003.

Wiktorowicz, Quintan, *Radical Islam Rising: Muslim Extremism in the West,* Lanham, MD: Rowman & Littlefield Publishers, Inc., 2005.

Wright, Robin, *Sacred Rage: The Wrath of Militant Islam,* New York: Simon & Schuster, 1985.

Historical Precedents

Daftary, Farhad, *The Assassin Legends: Myths of the Isma'ilis,* London: I. B. Tauris & Co Ltd, 1994.

Dunn, Ross E., *Resistance in the Desert: Moroccan Responses to French Imperialism 1881–1912,* Madison, WI: The University of Wisconsin Press, 1977.

Galula, David, *Pacification in Algeria, 1956–1958*, Santa Monica, CA: RAND Corporation, MG-478-RC, 2006 (http://www.rand.org/pubs/monographs/MG478/).

Gommans, Jos, *Mughal Warfare: Indian Frontiers and High Roads to Empire, 1500–1700,* New York: Routledge, 2002.

Hart, David M., *Banditry in Islam: Case Studies from Morocco, Algeria and the Pakistan North West Frontier,* Cambridgeshire, England: Middle East & North African Studies Press Ltd, 1987.

Lane-Poole, Stanley, *Saladin and the Fall of Jerusalem,* London: Greenhill Books, 2002.

Long, Austin, *On "Other War": Lessons from Five Decades of RAND Counterinsurgency Research,* Santa Monica, CA: RAND Corporation, MG-482, 2006 (http://www.rand.org/pubs/monographs/MG482).

Lewis, Bernard, *The Assassins: A Radical Sect in Islam,* New York: Basic Books, 1968.

Peters, Rudolph, *Islam and Colonialism: The Doctrine of Jihad in Modern History,* The Hague: Mouton Publishers, 1979.

Reston, James, Jr., *Warriors of God: Richard the Lionheart and Saladin in the Third Crusade,* New York: Doubleday, 2001.

Robson, Brian, *Crisis on the Frontier: The Third Afghan War and the Campaign in Waziristan 1919–1920,* Staplehurst, England: Spellmount Ltd, 2004.

Santosuosso, Antonio, *Barbarians, Marauders, and Infidels: The Ways of Medieval Warfare*, Boulder, CO: Westview Press, 2004.

Warner, Philip, *Dervish: The Rise and Fall of an African Empire,* Ware, England: Wordsworth Editions Ltd, 2000.

Wasserman, James, *The Templars and the Assassins: The Militia of Heaven,* Rochester, VT: Inner Traditions, 2001.

The Wars in Afghanistan

Cooley, John K., *Unholy Wars: Afghanistan, America and International Terrorism*, Sterling, VA: Pluto Press, 2000.

Griffin, Michael, *Reaping the Whirlwind: Afghanistan, Al Qa'ida and the Holy War*, Sterling, VA: Pluto Press, 2003.

Jalali, Ali Ahmad, and Lester W. Grau, *Afghan Guerrilla Warfare: In the Words of the Mujahideen Fighters*, St. Paul, MN: MBI Publishing Company, 2001.

Lambeth, Benjamin S., *Air Power Against Terror: America's Conduct of Operation Enduring Freedom*, Santa Monica, CA: RAND Corporation, MG-166, 2005 (http://www.rand.org/pubs/monographs/MG166/).

Rashid, Ahmed, *Taliban: Militant Islam, Oil and Fundamentalism in Central Asia*, New Haven, CT: Yale University Press, 2001.

Roy, Olivier, *Islam and Resistance in Afghanistan*, Cambridge, England: Cambridge University Press, 1990.

Tanner, Stephen, *Afghanistan: A Military History from Alexander the Great to the Fall of the Taliban*, New York: Da Capo Press, 2002.

Yousaf, Brigadier Mohammad, and Mark Adkin, *Afghanistan—The Bear Trap: The Defeat of a Superpower*, London: Leo Cooper, 2001.

Zahab, Mariam Abou, and Olivier Roy, *Islamist Networks: The Afghan-Pakistan Connection*, London: Hurst & Company, 2004.

Osama bin Laden and al Qaeda

al-Zayyat, Montasser, *The Road to Al-Qaeda: The Story of bin Laden's Right-Hand Man*, Sterling, VA: Pluto Press, 2004.

Alexander, Yonah, and Michael S. Swetnam, *Usama bin Laden's al-Qaida: Profile of a Terrorist Network*, Ardsley, NY: Transnational Publishers, Inc., 2001.

Anonymous, *Through Our Enemies' Eyes: Osama bin laden, Radical Islam, and the Future of America*, Washington, DC: Brassey's, Inc., 2002.

Bergen, Peter L., *The Osama bin Laden I Know: An Oral History of al Qaeda's Leader*, New York: The Free Press, 2006.

_____, *Holy War, Inc.: Inside the Secret World of Osama bin Laden*, New York: The Free Press, 2001.

Bodansky, Yossef, *Bin Laden: The Man Who Declared War on America*, Rocklin, CA: Prima Publishing, 1999.

Brisard, Jean-Charles, *Zarqawi—The New Face of Al-Qaeda*, New York: Other Press, 2005.

Burke, Jason, *Al-Qaeda: Casting a Shadow of Terror*, New York: I. B. Tauris & Co Ltd, 2003.

Corbin, Jane, *Al-Qaeda: In Search of the Terror Network That Threatens the World*, New York: Thunder's Mouth Press/Nation Books, 2002.

Emerson, Steven, *American Jihad: The Terrorists Living Among Us*, New York: The Free Press, 2002.

Fouda, Yosri, and Nick Fielding, *Masterminds of Terror: The Truth Behind the Most Devastating Terrorist Attack the World Has Ever Seen*, Edinburgh and London: Mainstream Publishing, 2003.

Gray, John, *Al Qaeda and What It Means to Be Modern*, New York: The New Press, 2003.

Greenberg, Karen J. (ed.), *Al Qaeda Now: Understanding Today's Terrorists*, New York: Cambridge University Press, 2005.

Gunaratna, Rohan, *Inside Al Qaeda: Global Network of Terror*, New York: Columbia University Press, 2002.

Jacquard, Roland, *In the Name of Osama bin Laden: Global Terrorism and the Bin Laden Brotherhood*, Durham, NC, and London: Duke University Press, 2002.

_____, *Les Archives Secretes d'Al-Qaeda: Revelations sur les Heritiers de Ben Laden*, Paris: Jean Picollec, 2002.

Jenkins, Brian Michael, *Looking at al Qaeda from the Inside Out: An Annotated Briefing*, Fairfax, VA: Defense Adaptive Red Team (Hicks and Associates, Inc.), 2003.

_____, *Countering al Qaeda: An Appreciation of the Situation and Suggestions for Strategy*, Santa Monica, CA: RAND Corporation, MR-1620-RC, 2002 (http://www.rand.org/publications/MR/MR1620/).

Kiser, Stephen D., *Financing Terror: An Analysis and Simulation to Affect Al Qaeda's Financial Infrastructure*, Santa Monica, CA: RAND Corporation, RGSD-185, 2005 (http://www.rand.org/publications/RGSD/RGSD185/).

Lawrence, Bruce (ed.), *Messages to the World: The Statements of Osama bin Laden,* London and New York: Verso, 2005.

Neighbour, Sally, *In the Shadow of Swords: On the Trail of Terrorism from Afghanistan to Australia,* Australia: HarperCollins Publishers Ltd, 2004.

Randal, Jonathan, *Osama: The Making of a Terrorist,* New York: Alfred A. Knopf, 2004.

Razavi, Emmanuel, *Frères Musulmans dans l'Ombre d'Al Qaeda,* Paris: Jean-Cyrille Godefroy, 2005.

Reeve, Simon, *The New Jackals: Ramzi Yousef, Osama bin Laden and the Future of Terrorism,* Boston, MA: Northeastern University Press, 1999.

Robinson, Adam, *Bin Laden: Behind the Mask of the Terrorist,* Edinburgh and London: Mainstream Publishing, 2001.

Sageman, Marc, *Understanding Terror Networks,* Philadelphia, PA: University of Pennsylvania Press, 2004.

Schanzer, Jonathan, *Al-Qaeda's Armies: Middle East Affiliate Groups and the Next Generation of Terror,* Washington, DC: The Washington Institute for Near East Policy, 2005.

Sifaoui, Mohamed, *Inside Al Qaeda: How I Infiltrated the World's Deadliest Terrorist Organization,* London: Granta Books, 2003.

Tahiri, Amir, *Holy Terror: The Inside Story of Islamic Terrorism*, London: Sphere Books Ltd, 1987.

Thomas, Dominique, *Les Hommes d'Al-Qaida: Discours et Strategie,* Paris: Editions Michalon, 2005.

Williams, Paul L., *The Al Qaeda Connection: International Terrorism, Organized Crime, and the Coming Apocalypse,* Amherst, NY: Prometheus Books, 2005.

_____, *Al Qaeda: Brotherhood of Terror,* New York: Alpha Books, 2002.

Yusufzai, Rahimullah, et al., *Most Wanted: Profiles of Terror,* New Delhi: Lotus Collection, 2002.

The 9/11 Plot

9/11 Commission, *The 9/11 Commission Report: Final Report of the National Commission on Terrorist Attacks upon the United States*, New York: W.W. Norton & Company, 2004.

Bell, J. Bowyer, *Murders on the Nile: The World Trade Center and Global Terror*, San Francisco, CA: Encounter Books, 2003.

Der Spiegel Magazine (Reporters, Writers, and Editors), *Inside 9-11: What Really Happened*, New York: St. Martin's Press, 2001.

McDermott, Terry, *Perfect Soldiers—The Hijackers: Who They Were, Why They Did It*, New York: HarperCollins Publishers, 2005.

Miller, John, and Mitchell Stone, with Chris Mitchell, *The Cell: Inside the 9/11 Plot, and Why the FBI and CIA Failed to Stop It*, New York: Hyperion, 2002.

Connected Groups in the Jihadist Constellation

Abuza, Zachary, *Militant Islam in Southeast Asia: Crucible of Terror,* Boulder, CO, Lynne Rienner Publishers, 2003.

Barton, Greg, *Jemaah Islamiyah: Radical Islamism in Indonesia,* Singapore: Ridge Books, 2005.

Byman, Daniel, Peter Chalk, Bruce Hoffman, William Rosenau, and David Brannan, *Trends in Outside Support for Insurgent Movements*, Santa

Monica, CA: RAND Corporation, MR-1405-OTI, 2001 (http://www.rand.org/pubs/monograph_reports/MR1405/)

Daly, Sara A., John Parachini, and William Rosenau, *Aum Shinrikyo, Al Qaeda, and the Kinshasa Reactor: Implications of Three Case Studies for Combating Nuclear Terrorism*, Santa Monica, CA: RAND Corporation, DB-458-AF, 2005 (http://www.rand.org/publications/DB/DB458/).

Guendouz, Omar, *Les Soldats Perdus de l'Islam: Les Réseaux Français de Ben Laden,* Paris: Editions Ramsay, 2002.

Gunaratna, Rohan (ed.), *Terrorism in the Asia-Pacific: Threat and Response,* Singapore: Eastern Universities Press, 2003.

Gunaratna, Rohan, et al., *Conflict and Terrorism in Southern Thailand,* Singapore: Marshall Cavendish Academic, 2005.

Islam, Syed Serajul, *The Politics of Islamic Identity in Southeast Asia,* Singapore: Thomson Learning, 2005.

Jackson, Brian A., John C. Baker, Peter Chalk, Kim Cragin, John V. Parachini, and Horacio R. Trujillo, *Aptitude for Destruction*, Volume 1, *Organizational Learning in Terrorist Groups and Its Implications for Combating Terrorism*, Santa Monica, CA: RAND Corporation, MG-331-NIJ, 2005 (http://www.rand.org/publications/MG/MG331/).

_____, *Aptitude for Destruction*, Volume 2, *Case Studies of Organizational Learning in Five Terrorist Groups*, Santa Monica, CA: RAND Corporation, MG-332-NIJ, 2005 (http://www.rand.org/publications/MG/MG332/).

Kepel, Gilles, *Allah in the West: Islamic Movements in America and Europe,* Stanford, CA: Stanford University Press, 1997.

_____, *Les Banlieues de l'Islam,* Paris: Editions du Seuil, 1991.

Khosrokhavar, Farhad, *L'Islam dans les Prisons,* Paris: Editions Balland, 2004.

Kohlmann, Evan, *Al-Qaeda's Jihad in Europe: The Afghan-Bosnian Network,* New York: Berg, 2004.

Laidi, Ali, with Ahmed Salam, *Le Jihad en Europe: Les Filieres du Terrorisme Islamiste,* Paris: Editions du Seuil, 2002.

Millard, Mike, *Jihad in Paradise: Islam and Politics in Southeast Asia,* Armonk, New York: M. E. Sharpe, Inc., 2004.

Mir, Amir, *The True Face of Jehadis: Inside Pakistan's Network of Terror,* New Delhi: Roli Books, 2006.

Murphy, Paul J., *The Wolves of Islam: Russia and the Faces of Chechen Terror,* Washington, DC: Brassey's, Inc., 2004.

Neighbour, Sally, *In the Shadow of Swords: On the Trail of Terrorism from Afghanistan to Australia,* Australia: HarperCollins Publishers Ltd, 2004.

Raju, Adluri Subramanyam (ed.), *Terrorism in South Asia: Views from India,* Singapore: India Research Press, 2004.

Ramakrishna, Kumar, and See Seng Tan (eds.), *After Bali: The Threat of Terrorism in Southeast Asia,* Singapore: Institute of Defence and Strategic Studies, 2003.

Ressa, Maria A., *Seeds of Terror: An Eyewitness Account of Al-Qaeda's Newest Center of Operations in Southeast Asia*, New York: The Free Press, 2003.

Sifaoui, Mohamed, *La France, Malade de l'Islamisme: Menaces Terroristes sur l'Hexagone*, Paris: Le Cherche Midi, 2002.

Stone, Martin, *The Agony of Algeria,* New York: Columbia University Press, 1997.

Vidino, Lorenzo, *Al Qaeda in Europe: The New Battleground of International Jihad*, Amherst, NY: Prometheus Books, 2006.

Suicide Bombings

Bloom, Mia, *Dying to Kill: The Allure of Suicide Terror,* New York: Columbia University Press, 2005.

Haim, Laurence, *Les Bombes Humaines: Enquête au Coeur du Conflit Israélo-Palestinien,* Paris: Lamartinière, 2003.

Hoffman, Bruce, "The Logic of Suicide Terrorism," *Atlantic Monthly,* Vol. 291, No. 5, June 2003. Also available as RAND/RP-1187 (http://www.rand.org/pubs/reprints/RP1187/)

Khosrokhavar, Farhad, *Les Nouveaux Martyrs d'Allah,* Paris: Flammarion, 2002.

Pape, Robert A., *Dying to Win: The Strategic Logic of Suicide Terrorism,* New York: Random House, 2005.

Reuter, Christoph: *My Life Is a Weapon: A Modern History of Suicide Bombing,* Princeton, NJ: Princeton University Press, 2002.

The Counterterrorist Campaign: History and Strategy

Aaron, David (ed.), *Three Years After: Next Steps in the War on Terror,* Santa Monica, CA: RAND Corporation, CF-212-RC, 2005 (http://www.rand.org/pubs/conf_proceedings/CF212/)

Anonymous, *Imperial Hubris: Why the West Is Losing the War on Terror,* Washington, DC: Brassey's, Inc., 2004.

Artur du Plessis, Laurent, *La Troisième Guerre Mondiale a Commencé,* Paris: Jean-Cyrille Godefroy, 2002.

Baer, Robert, *See No Evil: The True Story of a Ground Soldier in the CIA's War on Terrorism,* New York: Crown Publishers, 2002.

Baud, Jacques, *Le Renseignement et la Lutte Contre le Terrorisme: Stratégies et Perspectives Internationales,* Paris: Lavauzelle, 2005.

Baxter, Jenny, and Malcolm Downing (eds.), *The BBC Reports on America, Its Allies and Enemies, and the Counterattack on Terrorism,* Woodstock, NY, and New York: The Overlook Press, 2002.

Benjamin, Daniel, and Steven Simon, *The Next Attack: The Failure of the War on Terror and a Strategy for Getting It Right,* New York: Times Books, 2005.

_____, *The Age of Sacred Terror,* New York: Random House, 2002.

Bensahel, Nora, *The Counterterror Coalitions: Cooperation with Europe, NATO, and the European Union,* Santa Monica, CA: RAND Corporation, MR-1746-AF, 2003 (http://www.rand.org/publications/MR/MR1746/).

Berman, Paul, *Terror and Liberalism,* New York: W.W. Norton & Company, 2003.

Berntsen, Gary, and Ralph Pezzullo, *Jawbreaker—The Attack on bin Laden and Al-Qaeda: A Personal Account by the CIA's Key Field Commander,* New York: Crown Publishers, 2005.

Bronson, Rachel, *Thicker Than Oil: America's Uneasy Partnership with Saudi Arabia,* New York: Oxford University Press, *2006.*

Carter, Jimmy, *Our Endangered Values: America's Moral Crisis,* New York: Simon & Schuster, 2005.

Clarke, Richard A., *Against All Enemies: Inside America's War on Terror,* New York: The Free Press, 2004.

Clarke, Richard A., et al., *Defeating the Jihadists: A Blueprint for Action,* New York: The Century Foundation Press, 2004.

Clarke, Ronald V., and Graeme R. Newman, *Outsmarting the Terrorists,* Westport, CT: Praeger, 2006 (in press).

Club de Madrid, *Series on Democracy and Terrorism, Volume I: The Causes of Terrorism, Volume II: Confronting Terrorism, and Volume III: Towards a Democratic Response,* Madrid: Club de Madrid, 2005.

Coughlin, Con, *American Ally: Tony Blair and the War on Terror,* New York: HarperCollins Publishers, 2006.

Cragin, Kim, and Peter Chalk, *Terrorism and Development: Using Social and Economic Development to Inhibit a Resurgence of Terrorism*, Santa Monica, CA: RAND Corporation, MR-1630-RC, 2003 (http://www.rand.org/publications/MR/MR1630/).

Cronin, Audrey Kurth, and James M. Ludes (eds.), *Attacking Terrorism: Elements of a Grand Strategy,* Washington, DC: Georgetown University Press, 2004.

Davis, Paul K., and Brian Michael Jenkins, *Deterrence and Influence in Counterterrorism: A Component in the War on al Qaeda*, Santa Monica, CA: RAND Corporation, MR-1619-DARPA, 2002 (http://www.rand.org/publications/MR/MR1619/).

Fair, C. Christine, *The Counterterror Coalitions: Cooperation with Pakistan and India*, Santa Monica, CA: RAND Corporation, MG-141-AF, 2004 (http://www.rand.org/publications/MG/MG141/).

Frey, Bruno S., *Dealing with Terrorism—Stick or Carrot?* Cheltenham, England: Edward Elgar Publishing Ltd, 2004.

Gaddis, John Lewis, et al., *The Age of Terror: America and the World After September 11*, New York: Basic Books, 2001.

Ganor, Boaz, *The Counter-Terrorism Puzzle: A Guide for Decision Makers*, New Brunswick, NJ: The Interdisciplinary Center Herzliya, 2005.

Harclerode, Peter, *Secret Soldiers: Special Forces in the War Against Terrorism*, London: Cassell & Co., 2000.

Hoffman, Bruce, *Inside Terrorism*, revised and expanded edition, New York: Columbia University Press, 2006.

Hoge, James F., Jr., and Gideon Rose (eds.), *How Did This Happen? Terrorism and the New War*, New York: Public Affairs, 2001.

Jenkins, Brian Michael, *Countering al Qaeda: An Appreciation of the Situation and Suggestions for Strategy*, Santa Monica, CA: RAND Corporation, 2002 (http://www.rand.org/pubs/monograph_reports/MR1620/).

Lambeth, Benjamin S., *Air Power Against Terror: America's Conduct of Operation Enduring Freedom*, Santa Monica, CA: RAND Corporation, 2005 (http://www.rand.org/pubs/monographs/MG166/).

Lance, Peter, *Cover Up: What the Government Is Still Hiding About the War on Terror*, New York: HarperCollins Publishers, 2004.

———, *1000 Years for Revenge: International Terrorism and the FBI—The Untold Story*, New York: HarperCollins Publishers, 2003.

Lesser, Ian O., Bruce Hoffman, John Arquilla, David Ronfeldt, and Michele Zanini, Foreword by Brian Michael Jenkins, *Countering the New Terrorism*, Santa Monica, CA: RAND Corporation, 1999 (http://www.rand.org/pubs/monograph_reports/MR989/).

McInerney, Lt. General Thomas, USAF (Ret.), and Maj. General Paul Vallely, US Army (Ret.), *Endgame: The Blueprint for Victory in the War on Terror*, Washington, DC: Regnery Publishing, Inc., 2004.

Mead, John Clark, *The New World War: A Behind-the-Scenes Look at Why and How Militant Muslims Plan to Destroy Western Civilization*, Fairfax, VA: Xulon Press, 2002.

Naftali, Timothy, *Blind Spot: The Secret History of American Counterterrorism*, New York: Basic Books, 2005.

Nye, Joseph S., Jr., Yukio Satoh, and Paul Wilkinson, *Addressing the New International Terrorism: Prevention, Intervention and Multilateral Cooperation*, Washington, DC: The Trilateral Commission, 2003.

Pillar, Paul R., *Terrorism and U.S. Foreign Policy*, Washington, DC: Brookings Institution Press, 2001.

Primakov, Yevgeny M., *A World Challenged: Fighting Terrorism in the Twenty-First Century,* Washington, DC: The Nixon Center and Brookings Institution Press, 2004.

Risen, James, *State of War: The Secret History of the CIA and the Bush Administration,* New York: The Free Press, 2006.

Rubin, Barry, and Judith Colp Rubin (eds.), *Anti-American Terrorism and the Middle East,* New York: Oxford University Press, 2002.

Satloff, Robert B. (ed.), *War on Terror: The Middle East Dimension,* Washington, DC: The Washington Institute for Near East Policy, 2002.

Schachter, Jonathan M., *The Eye of the Believer: Psychological Influences on Counter-Terrorism Policy-Making,* Santa Monica, CA: RAND Corporation, RGSD-166, 2002 (http://www.rand.org/publications/RGSD/RGSD166/).

Scruton, Roger, *The West and the Rest: Globalization and the Terrorist Threat,* London: Continuum/ISI Books, 2002.

Smucker, Philip, *Al Qaeda's Great Escape: The Military and the Media on Terror's Trail,* Washington, DC: Brassey's, Inc., 2004.

Tan, Andrew, and Kumar Ramakrishna (eds.), *The New Terrorism: Anatomy, Trends and Counter-Strategies,* Singapore: Eastern Universities Press, 2002.

Thompson, Paul, *The Terror Timeline: Year by Year, Day by Day, Minute by Minute: A Comprehensive Chronicle of the Road to 9/11—and America's Response,* New York: HarperCollins Publishers, 2004.

Woodward, Bob, *Bush at War,* New York: Simon & Schuster, 2005.

Intelligence

Coll, Steve, *Ghost Wars: The Secret History of the CIA, Afghanistan, and bin Laden, from the Soviet Invasion to September 10, 2001*, New York: Penguin Books, 2004.

Crelinsten, Ronald D., *Intelligence and Counter-Terrorism in a Multi-Centric World,* Stockholm: National Defence College, 2006.

Graham, Senator Bob, with Jeff Nussbaum, *Intelligence Matters: The CIA, the FBI, Saudi Arabia, and the Failure of America's War on Terror*, New York: Random House, 2004.

Kam, Ephraim, *Surprise Attack: The Victim's Perspective*, Cambridge, MA: Harvard University Press, 2004.

Keefe, Patrick Radden, *Chatter: Dispatches from the Secret World of Global Eavesdropping*, New York: Random House, 2005.

Powers, Richard Gid, *Broken: The Troubled Past and Uncertain Future of the FBI*, New York: The Free Press, 2004.

Powers, Thomas, *Intelligence Wars: American Secret History from Hitler to al-Qaeda*, New York: New York Review Books, 2004.

Riley, K. Jack, Gregory F. Treverton, Jeremy Wilson, and Lois M. Davis, *State and Local Intelligence in the War on Terrorism*, Santa Monica, CA: RAND Corporation, MG-394-RC, 2005 (http://www.rand.org/publications/MG/MG394/).

Treverton, Gregory F., *The Next Steps in Reshaping Intelligence*, Santa Monica, CA: RAND Corporation, OP-152-RC, 2005 (http://www.rand.org/publications/OP/OP152/).

_____, *Reshaping National Intelligence in an Age of Information*, New York: Cambridge University Press, 2001.

Turner, Michael A., *Why Secret Intelligence Fails*, Dulles, VA: Potomac Books, Inc., 2005.

The Conflict in Iraq

Bamford, James, *A Pretext for War: 9/11, Iraq, and the Abuse of America's Intelligence Agencies*, New York: Doubleday, 2004.

Bengio, Ofra, *Saddam's Word: Political Discourse in Iraq*, New York: Oxford University Press, 1998.

Bhatia, Shyam, and Daniel McGrory, *Brighter Than the Baghdad Sun: Saddam Hussein's Nuclear Threat to the United States*, Washington, DC: Regnery Publishing, Inc., 2000.

Blix, Hans, *Disarming Iraq*, New York: Pantheon Books, 2004.

Bremer, L. Paul, III, with Malcolm McConnell, *My Year in Iraq: The Struggle to Build a Future of Hope*, New York: Simon & Schuster, 2006.

Brisard, Jean-Charles, *Zarkaoui: Le Nouveau Visage d'Al-Qaida*, Paris: Fayard, 2005.

Chehab, Zaki, *Inside the Resistance: The Iraqi Insurgency and the Future of the Middle East*, New York: Nation Books, 2005.

Dodge, Toby, *Inventing Iraq: The Failure of Nation Building and a History Denied*, New York: Columbia University Press, 2003.

Gnesotto, Nicole, et al., *Shift or Rift: Assessing US-EU Relations After Iraq*, Paris: Institute for Security Studies, European Union, 2003.

Haldane, Sir Aylmer L., *The Insurrection in Mesopotamia, 1920*, Nashville, TN: The Battery Press (originally published 1922), 2005.

Hoffman, Bruce, *Insurgency and Counterinsurgency in Iraq*, Santa Monica, CA: RAND Corporation, OP-127-IPC/CMEPP, 2004 (http://www.rand.org/pubs/occasional_papers/op127/).

Moussaoui, Abd Samad, and Florence Bouquillat, *Zacarias Moussaoui: The Making of a Terrorist*, London: Editions Denoel, 2002.

Nakash, Yitzhak, *The Shi'is of Iraq*, Princeton, NJ, and Oxford, England: Princeton University Press, 1994.

Napoleoni, Loretta, *Insurgent Iraq: Al Zarqawi and the New Generation*, London: Constable & Robinson, Ltd, 2005.

Phillips, David L., *Losing Iraq: Inside the Postwar Reconstruction Fiasco*, Boulder, CO: Westview Press, 2005.

Polk, William R., *Understanding Iraq: The Whole Sweep of Iraqi History, from Genghis Khan's Mongols to the Ottoman Turks to the British Mandate to the American Occupation*, New York: HarperCollins Publishers, 2005.

Pollack, Kenneth M., *The Threatening Storm: The Case for Invading Iraq*, New York: Random House, 2002.

Rogers, Paul, *Iraq and the War on Terror: Twelve Months of Insurgency 2004/2005*, New York: I. B. Tauris & Co Ltd, 2006.

Shadid, Anthony, *Night Draws Near: Iraq's People in the Shadow of America's War*, New York: Henry Holt and Company, 2005.

Tripp, Charles, *A History of Iraq*, Cambridge, England: Cambridge University Press, 2000.

Woodward, Bob, *Plan of Attack,* New York: Simon & Schuster, 2004.

Psychological Operations and Political Warfare

Lennon, Alexander T. J. (ed.), *The Battle for Hearts and Minds: Using Soft Power to Undermine Terrorist Networks,* Cambridge, MA: The MIT Press, 2003.

Nicander, Lars, and Magnus Ranstorp (eds.), *Terrorism in the Information Age—New Frontiers?* Stockholm: Forsvarshogskolan, 2004.

Parfrey, Adam (ed.), *Extreme Islam: Anti-American Propaganda of Muslim Fundamentalism,* Los Angeles, CA: Feral House, 2001.

Patai, Raphael, *The Arab Mind,* New York: Hatherleigh Press, 2002.

Tuman, Joseph S., *Communicating Terror: The Rhetorical Dimensions of Terrorism,* Thousand Oaks, CA: Sage Publications, 2003.

Nightmares

Allison, Graham, *Nuclear Terrorism: The Ultimate Preventable Catastrophe,* New York: Times Books, 2004.

Flynn, Stephen, *America the Vulnerable: How Our Government Is Failing to Protect Us from Terrorism,* New York: HarperCollins Publishers, 2004.

King, Gilbert, *Dirty Bomb: Weapon of Mass Disruption,* New York: Chamberlain Bros., Inc., 2004.

Kushner, Harvey W. (ed.), *The Future of Terrorism: Violence in the New Millennium,* Thousands Oaks, CA: Sage Publications, 1998.

Lake, Anthony, *6 Nightmares: Real Threats in a Dangerous World and How America Can Meet Them,* Boston, MA: Little, Brown and Company, 2000.

Newkey-Burden, Chas, *Nuclear Paranoia,* Harpenden, England: Pocket Essentials, 2003.

Osterholm, Michael T., and John Schwartz, *Living Terrors: What America Needs to Know to Survive the Coming Bioterrorist Catastrophe,* New York: Delacorte Press, 2000.

Weldon, Curt, *Countdown to Terror: The Top-Secret Information That Could Prevent the Next Terrorist Attack on America . . . And How the CIA Has Ignored It,* Washington, DC: Regnery Publishing, Inc., 2005.

Homeland Security

Chalk, Peter, *Hitting America's Soft Underbelly: The Potential Threat of Deliberate Biological Attacks Against the U.S. Agricultural and Food Industry,* Santa Monica, CA: RAND Corporation, MG-135-OSD, 2004 (http://www.rand.org/publications/MG/MG135/).

Chalk, Peter, Bruce Hoffman, Anna-Britt Kasupski, and Robert T. Reville, *Trends in Terrorism: Threats to the United States and the Future of the Terrorism Risk Insurance Act,* Santa Monica, CA: RAND Corporation, MG-393-CTRMP, 2005 (http://www.rand.org/publications/MG/MG393/).

Chalk, Peter, and William Rosenau, *Confronting "The Enemy Within": Security Intelligence, the Police, and Counterterrorism in Four Democracies,* Santa Monica, CA: RAND Corporation, 2004, MG-100-RC (http://www.rand.org/publications/MG/MG100/).

Ervin, Clark Kent, *Open Target: Where America Is Vulnerable to Attack,* New York: Palgrave Macmillan, 2006.

Howard, Russell D., Brigadier General, U.S. Army (Ret.), James J. F. Forest, and Joanne C. Moore, *Homeland Security and Terrorism: Readings and Interpretations,* New York: The McGraw-Hill Companies, 2006.

Jenkins, Brian (Special Advisor to the International Chamber of Commerce), *Corporate Security in the Post 9-11 World,* London: ICC Commercial Crime Services, 2003.

Kamien, David G. (ed.), *The McGraw-Hill Homeland Security Handbook,* New York: McGraw-Hill, 2006.

National Research Council of the National Academies, Committee on Science and Technology for Countering Terrorism, *Making the Nation Safer: The Role of Science and Technology in Countering Terrorism,* Washington, DC: The National Academies Press, 2002.

Transportation Security

Jenkins, Brian Michael, *Protecting Public Surface Transportation Against Terrorism and Serious Crime: An Executive Overview*, San Jose, CA: Mineta Transportation Institute College of Business, 2001.

Jenkins, Brian Michael (ed.), *Protecting Surface Transportation Systems and Patrons from Terrorist Activities: Case Studies of Best Security Practices and a Chronology of Attacks*, San Jose, CA: Mineta Transportation Institute, 1997.

Jenkins, Brian Michael, and Frances Edwards-Winslow, *Saving City Lifelines: Lessons Learned in the 9-11 Terrorist Attacks*, San Jose, CA: Mineta Transportation Institute, 2003.

Jenkins, Brian Michael, and Larry N. Gersten, *Protecting Public Surface Transportation Against Terrorism and Serious Crime: Continuing Research on Best Security Practices*, San Jose, CA: Mineta Transportation Institute College of Business, 2001.

Jenkins, Brian M., and Paul Wilkinson (eds.), *Aviation Terrorism and Security*, London: Frank Cass, 1999.

Transportation Research Board of the National Academies, *Deterrence, Protection, and Preparation: The New Transportation Security Imperative*, Washington, DC: Transportation Research Board, 2002.

The Changing Shape of Conflict

Arquilla, John, and David F. Ronfeldt, *Networks and Netwars: The Future of Terror, Crime, and Militancy,* Santa Monica, CA: RAND Corporation, MR-1382-OSD, 2001 (http://www.rand.org/publications/MR/MR1382/).

Art, Robert J., and Kenneth N. Waltz (eds.), *The Use of Force: Military Power and International Politics,* Lanham, MD: Rowman & Littlefield Publishers, Inc., 2004.

Boot, Max, *The Savage Wars of Peace: Smalls Wars and the Rise of American Power,* New York: Basic Books, 2002.

Bunker, Robert J. (ed.), *Non-State Threats and Future Wars,* London: Frank Cass, 2003.

Combs, Cindy C., *Terrorism in the Twenty-First Century,* Upper Saddle River, NJ: Prentice-Hall, Inc., 2000.

Cragin, Kim, and Sara A. Daly, *The Dynamic Terrorist Threat: An Assessment of Group Motivations and Capabilities in a Changing World,* Santa Monica, CA: RAND Corporation, MR-1782-AF, 2004 (http://www.rand.org/pubs/monograph_reports/MR1782/).

de Marenches, Alexandre, and David A. Andelman, *The Fourth World War: Diplomacy and Espionage in the Age of Terrorism,* New York: William Morrow and Company, Inc., 1992.

Dunnigan, James F., *The Next War Zone: Confronting the Global Threat of Cyberterrorism,* New York: Citadel Press Books, 2002.

Gray, Colin S., *Another Bloody Century: Future Warfare,* London: Weidenfeld and Nicolson, 2005.

Khalilzad, Zalmay, and Ian O. Lesser (eds.), *Sources of Conflict in the 21st Century: Regional Futures and U.S. Strategy,* Santa Monica, CA: RAND Corporation, 1998 (http://www.rand.org/pubs/monograph_reports/MR897/).

Schilling, William R. (ed.), *Nontraditional Warfare: Twenty-First-Century Threats and Responses,* Washington, DC: Brassey's, Inc., 2002.

Smith, Rupert, *The Utility of Force: The Art of War in the Modern World,* London: Allen Lane, 2005.

Taw, Jennifer, and Bruce Hoffman, *The Urbanization of Insurgency: The Potential Challenge to U.S. Army Operations,* Santa Monica, CA: RAND Corporation, MR-398-A, 1994 (http://www.rand.org/pubs/monograph_reports/MR398/).

Related Readings on Terrorism

al-Berry, Khaled, *La Terre Est Plus Belle que le Paradis,* Paris: Editions Jean-Claude Lattes, 2002.

Braudy, Leo, *From Chivalry to Terrorism: War and the Changing Nature of Masculinity,* New York: Vintage Books, 2003.

Cragin, Kim, and Sara A. Daly, *The Dynamic Terrorist Threat: An Assessment of Group Motivations and Capabilities in a Changing World,* Santa

Monica, CA: RAND Corporation, MR-1782-AF (http://www. rand.org/ publications/MR/MR1782/).

Enders, Walter, and Todd Sandler, *The Political Economy of Terrorism,* Cambridge, England: Cambridge University Press, 2006.

Gold, Dore, *Hatred's Kingdom: How Saudi Arabia Supports the New Global Terrorism*, Washington, DC: Regnery Publishing, Inc., 2003.

Gupta, Suman, *The Replication of Violence: Thoughts on International Terrorism After September 11th, 2001*, London: Pluto Press, 2002.

Harmon, Christopher C., *Terrorism Today*, London: Frank Cass, 2000.

Jackson, Brian A., John C. Baker, Peter Chalk, Kim Cragin, John V. Parachini, and Horacio R. Trujillo, *Aptitude for Destruction, Volume 1, Organizational Learning in Terrorist Groups and Its Implications for Combating Terrorism*, Santa Monica, CA: RAND Corporation, MG-331-NIJ, 2005 (http://www.rand.org/publications/MG/MG331/).

_____, *Aptitude for Destruction, Volume 2, Case Studies of Organizational Learning in Five Terrorist Groups*, Santa Monica, CA: RAND Corporation, MG-332-NIJ, 2005 (http://www. rand.org/ publications/MG/MG332/).

Pyszczynski, Tom, Sheldon Solomon, and Jeff Greenberg, *In the Wake of 9/11: The Psychology of Terror*, Washington, DC: American Psychological Association, 2003.

Ramirez Sanchez, Ilich (Carlos), *L'Islam Revolutionnaire*, Paris: Editions du Rocher, 2003.

Reich, Walter (ed.), *Origins of Terrorism: Psychologies, Ideologies, Theologies, States of Mind*, Washington, DC: Woodrow Wilson Center Press, 1998.

Silke, Andrew (ed.), *Research on Terrorism: Trends, Achievements and Failures*, London: Frank Cass, 2004.

Notes

1. Ralph D. Sawyer, *The Seven Military Classics of Ancient China,* Boulder, CO: Westview Press, 1993, p. 163.

2. Carlos Marighella, *Mini-Manual of the Urban Guerrilla,* Chapel Hill, NC: Documentary Publications, 1985; Donald C. Hodges (ed.), *Philosophy of the Urban Guerrilla: The Revolutionary Writings of Abraham Guillen,* New York: William Morrow & Company, Inc., 1973.

3. Brian Michael Jenkins, *The Future Course of International Terrorism,* Santa Monica, CA: RAND Corporation, P-7139, 1985.

4. "TVI Survey Results," *TVI Report,* Fall 1985, Special Supplement, pp. 5–13.

5. Brian Michael Jenkins, *Will Terrorists Go Nuclear?* Los Angeles, CA: Crescent Publications, 1975.

6. Graham Allison, *Nuclear Terrorism: The Ultimate Preventable Catastrophe*, New York: Times Books, 2004, p. 15.

7. The "war on terror" is shorthand for both the war against terrorism and other military campaigns, as discussed in Chapter Four.

8. Donald Rumsfeld, "Global War on Terrorism," October 16, 2003; the text was reproduced in *USA Today,* May 20, 2005.

9. Published intercepted letter from Ayman al-Zawahiri to Abu Musab al-Zarqawi, 2005.

10. As of April 2006, there were 490 detainees held at Guantanamo. See Reuters, "Nearly 30 Percent at Guantanamo Jail Cleared to Go," April 21, 2006; approximately another 500 were being held at Kandahar, Afghanistan, and an unknown number were held at secret locations.

11. Rohan Gunaratna, "Core Al Qaeda Strength Is Under 500," interview in *Agentura,* Agentura Studies and Research Centre, Russia, November 13, 2005.

12. "Bush Details Foiled Plot: He Says United Effort to Right al-Qaida Has Thwarted 10 Attacks, Such as 2002 Plan to Hit L.A. Skyscraper," *Detroit Free Press,* February 10, 2006.

13. See Appendix B for a complete list of foiled terrorist attacks.

14. Briefing by Sundeep Waslekar, president of Strategic Foresight Group, Mumbai, India, in Washington, DC, May 5, 2006.

15. Associated Press, "Syrian Charged for Deadly Bombs in Turkey," February 10, 2006.

16. Mark Rice-Oxley, "Why Terror Funding Is Tough to Track," *Christian Science Monitor,* March 8, 2006.

17. Ibid.

18. Kim Cragin and Sara A. Daly, *The Dynamic Terrorist Threat: An Assessment of Group Motivations and Capabilities in a Changing World*, Santa Monica, CA: RAND Corporation, MR-1782-AF, 2004.

19. Initially, there were suspicions that an unidentified al Qaeda expediter may have assisted the London bombers, but intelligence officials concluded that the group planned and carried out the July 7 attack by itself. Yet, tantalizingly, the suicide tape recorded by the London group's leader, Mohammed Siddique Khan, was subsequently attached to a taped message from Ayman al-Zawahiri and broadcast on September 1, 2005, indicating that the tape was done while Khan was on an earlier trip to Pakistan or that somehow Khan's tape got from London to al Qaeda's second-in-command, indicating some link.

20. The concept of "leaderless resistance" was described in 1983 by American white supremacist Louis Beam, who said that it was first proposed by Ulius Louis Amoss in 1962. It was reprinted in Beam's "Leaderless Resistance," *The Seditionist,* Issue 12, February 1992.

21. We deduce this from the fact that target folders from a reconnaissance carried out in New York and New Jersey before 9/11 were found in the computer of Noor Khan, an al Qaeda operative, in Pakistan in 2004. The folders appeared to be part of a recently prepared proposal. The operative in Pakistan was in communication with al Qaeda operatives in the field. This discovery led to the 2004 terrorism alert in the United States.

22. Congressional testimony: "There are at least today 5,000 terrorist, insurgent, or radical web sites throughout the world."

23. Ann Scott Tyson, "Rumsfeld Urges Using Media to Fight Terror," *Washington Post*, February 18, 2006, p. A07.

24. Advisory Group on Public Diplomacy in the Arab and Muslim World, *Changing Minds, Winning Peace*, Washington, DC: U.S. Department of State, 2003.

25. Michael E. O'Hanlon and Nina Kamp, *Iraq Index: Tracking Variables of Reconstruction & Security in Post-Saddam Iraq*, Washington, DC: The Brookings Institution, published monthly.

26. Ibid.

27. Several sources provided the numbers and breakdowns by nationality of foreign militants in Iraq. These include "The Brookings Institute Iraq Index" (published monthly on the Internet); Reuven Paz, "Arab Volunteers Killed in Iraq: An Analysis," Global Research in International Affairs (GLORIA) Center, *Occasional Papers*, Vol. 3, No. 1, March 2005; and Dexter Filkins, "Foreign Fighters Captured in Iraq Came from 27 Mostly Arab Lands," *The New York Times,* October 21, 2005.

28. James Hosek, Jennifer Kavanagh, and Laura Miller, *How Deployments Affect Service Members*, Santa Monica, CA: RAND Corporation, MG-432-RC, 2006.

29. Barry R. McCaffrey, "Memorandum for Colonel Mike Meese, United States Military Academy," April 25, 2006 (http://img.slate.com/media/57/AAR%20General%20McCaffrey%20Visit%20to%20Iraq%20April%202006%20USMA.pdf).

30. Amy Belasco, *The Cost of Iraq, Afghanistan, and Other Global War on Terror Operations Since 9/11,* Washington DC: Congressional Research Service, April 24, 2006; William D. Nordhaus, *War with Iraq: Costs, Consequences and Alternatives*, The American Academy of Arts and Sciences, November 2002; Scott Wallsten and Katrina Kosec, *The Economic Costs of the War in Iraq,* Washington, DC: American Enterprise Institute—Brookings Joint Center for Regulatory Studies, September 2005. See also Ahmad Faruqui, "Cost Benefit Analysis of the Iraq War," *Daily Times,* April 24, 2006.

31. McCaffrey, op. cit.

32. Personal discussion with Ambassador L. Paul Bremer, Washington, DC, May 4, 2006.

33. Joseph R. Biden, Jr., and Leslie H. Gelb, "Unity Through Autonomy in Iraq," *The New York Times,* May 1, 2006.

34. The thoughtful work of Paul Pillar at the CIA, now at George Mason University, is an excellent example. West Point's Combating Terrorism Center, http://www.CTC.USMA.edu/, has also become a center for some very creative thinking.

35. Nathan Leites, *The Operational Code of the Politburo,* Santa Monica, CA: RAND Corporation, R-206, 1951.

36. David G. Hubbard, *The Skyjacker: His Flights of Fantasy,* New York: Macmillan Company, 1971.

37. Personal interview with Sean Holly, kidnapped in Guatemala, February 1970.

38. Maulana Masood Azhar, the chief of Jaish-e-Mohammed, quoted in Harinder Baweja (ed.), *Most Wanted: Profiles of Terror*, New Delhi: Roli Books, 2002, p. 44.

39. For a thorough discussion of psychological and sociological approaches to understanding terrorists, see Jeff Victoroff, "The Mind of the Terrorist: A Review and Critique of Psychological Approaches," *Journal of Conflict Resolution*, Vol. 49, No. 1, February 2005, pp. 3–42. See also Walter Reich (ed.), *Origins of Terrorism: Psychologies, Ideologies, Theologies, States of Mind*, Washington, DC: Woodrow Wilson Center Press, 1998.

40. There are numerous research centers that regularly track jihadist documents and publications. These include al Jazeera, www.aljazeera.net; the RAND Corporation, Voices of Jihad database, http://www.rand.org/research_areas/terrorism/database; Project for the Research of Islamist Movements (PRISM), http://www.e-prism.org, Global Research in International Affairs (GLORIA) Center, http://gloria.idc.ac.il; Middle East Research Institute (MEMRI), www.memri.org; Site Institute, http://siteinstitute.org; Terrorism Research Center, Inc., www.terrorism.com. Visual images used by the jihadists are catalogued by the Combating Terrorism Center at West Point, http://www.CTC.USMA.edu/imagery.asp.

41. Osama bin Laden, January 2004.

42. Osama bin Laden, November 12, 2002.

43. Osama bin Laden, 2006.

44. Osama bin Laden, April 15, 2004.

45. These themes recur in the recruiting of religious warriors. See Mark Juergensmeyer, *Terror in the Mind of God: The Global Rise of Religious Violence*, Oxford, England: Oxford University Press, 2000. See also Bernard Lewis, *The Assassins: A Radical Sect in Islam*, New York: Basic Books, 1968; and James Wasserman, *The Templars and the Assassins: The Militia of Heaven*, Rochester, VT: Inner Traditions, 2001.

46. Osama bin Laden, December 1998.

47. Suliman Abu Ghaith, "In the Shadow of the Lances," June 2002.

48. There is a rich literature on the process of conversion. See Peter L. Berger and Thomas Luckmann, *The Social Construction of Reality: A Treatise in the Sociology of Knowledge*, New York: Irvington, 1980; Erving Goffman, *Interaction Rituals: An Essay in Face-to-Face Behavior*, New Brunswick, NJ: Aldine Transaction, 2005; Rosabeth Moss Kanter, *Commitment and Community: Communes and Utopias in Sociological Perspective*, Cambridge, MA: Harvard University Press, 1972; John Lofland and Rodney Stark, "Becoming a World-Saver: A Theory of Conversion to a Deviant

Perspective," *American Sociological Review*, Vol. 30, 1965, pp. 862–875; Thomas Luckmann, *Life-World and Social Realities*, London: Heinemann, 1983; Marc Sageman, *Understanding Terror Networks*, Philadelphia, PA: University of Pennsylvania Press, 2004.

49. Omar Guendouz, *Les Soldats Perdus de l'Islam*, Paris: Editions Ramsay, 2002, p. 111.

50. Ibid., pp. 133–134.

51. Muhammad Muhsin Khan and Muhammad Taqi-ud-Din al-Hilall, *Interpretation of the Meanings of the Noble Qur'an in the English Language*, Riyadh: Darussalam, 1996, revised 2001.

52. Ministry of Home Affairs, Government of Singapore, *White Paper: The Jemaah Islamiyah Arrests and the Threat of Terrorism*, January 7, 2003, p. 16, cited hereinafter as *Singapore White Paper*.

53. Ibid.

54. Khaled al-Berry, *La Terre Est Plus Belle que le Paradis*, Paris: J. C. Lattes, 2002.

55. *Singapore White Paper*, p. 17.

56. Berry, op. cit.

57. *Singapore White Paper*, p. 17.

58. *The Seattle Times*, "The Terrorist Within: The Story Behind One Man's Holy War Against America," a series of articles that appeared in *The Seattle Times*, June 23–July 7, 2002; see also *Frontline*, Ahmed Ressam's Millennium Plot," www.pbs.org/wgbh.

59. Richard Engel, "Inside al Qaeda—A Window into the World of Militant Islam and the Afghan Alumni," *Jane's*, September 28, 2001, http://www.janes.com/security/international_security/news/misc/janes010928_1_n.shtml.

60. B. Raman, "Al Qaeda: The New Web," South Asia Analysis Group Paper 1100, August 27, 2004, www.saag.org; Guy Taylor, "Three Britons Indicted in Terror Plot," *Washington Post*, April 13, 2005.

61. Many of the most thorough descriptions of the 9/11 terrorists were related in Terry McDermott's book *Perfect Soldiers—The Hijackers: Who They Were, Why They Did It*, New York: HarperCollins Publishers, 2005 (see the Reading List at the end of this book).

62. Ibid.

63. Ibid.

64. Ibid.

65. Ibid.

66. Abd Samad Moussaoui and Florence Bouquillat, *Zacarias Moussaoui: The Making of a Terrorist,* London: Serpent's Tail, 2002.

67. "Jose Padilla," www.rotten.com/library/bio/crime/terrorists/jose-padilla/.

68. Jean-Charles Brisard, *Zarqawi: The New Face of al Qaeda,* New York: Other Press, 2005.

69. Josh Meyer, "Chief 9/11 Architect Critical of Bin Laden," *Los Angeles Times*, April 5, 2006.

70. "Fighting Fire with Fire," *Time*, November 5, 1984.

71. Brian Michael Jenkins, "This Time It Is Different," *San Diego Union Tribune*, September 16, 2001.

72. The author is particularly indebted to Gregory Treverton, former vice chair of the National Intelligence Council and now a senior policy analyst at the RAND Corporation, for his advice in this area.

73. Donald Rumsfeld, "War in the Information Age," *Los Angeles Times*, February 23, 2006.

74. Scott Atran, "The Genesis of Suicide Terror," *Science Magazine*, March 2003, pp. 1534–1539.

75. Sorrel Wildhorn, Brian Michael Jenkins, and Martin Lavin, *Intelligence Constraints of the 1970s and Domestic Terrorism: Volume 1, Effects on the Incidence, Investigation, and Prosecution of Terrorist Activity*, Santa Monica, CA: RAND Corporation, N-1901-DOJ, 1982.

76. The best description and assessment of the Chieu Hoi program can be found in Thomas C. Thayer, *War Without Fronts: The American Experience in Vietnam*, Boulder, CO: Westview Press, 1985.

77. His book has been translated only into French, but it deserves to be disseminated throughout the world in English and other languages.

78. James Brandon, "Koranic Duels Ease Terror," *The Christian Science Monitor,* February 4, 2005.

79. David B. Ottaway, "Saudi Effort Draws on Radical Clerics to Combat Lure of Al-Qaeda," *Washington Post*, May 7, 2006.

80. Muhammad Haniff Hassan, "Community-Based Initiatives Against JI by Singapore's Muslim Community," *IDSS Commentaries,* Institute of Defence and Strategic Studies, Nanyang Technological University, January 16, 2006.

81. Ibid; also author's personal discussion with Singaporean officials.

82. Igor Beliaev and John Marks, *Common Ground on Terrorism: Soviet-American Cooperation Against the Politics of Terror,* New York: W. W. Norton & Company, 1991.

83. Al Qaeda's advanced preparations for an "American Hiroshima" is the continuing refrain of Paul L. Williams, *Al Qaeda Connection: International Terrorism, Organized Crime, and the Coming Apocalypse,* Amherst, NY: Prometheus Books, 2005; see also Paul L. Williams' "Tangible Proof al-Qaida Deploying the Nukes," presentation at the National Press Club, Washington, DC, http://www.worldnetdaily.com, April 25, 2006.

84. See, for example, Jacques Attali, *Millennium: Winners and Losers in the Coming World Order*, New York: Random House, 1991; John Kerry, *The New War: The Web of Crime That Threatens America's Security*, New York: Simon & Schuster, 1997; Stjepan G. Mestrovic, *The Balkanization of the West: The Confluence of Postmodernism and Postcommunism,* London: Routledge, 1994; Alain Minc, *Le Nouveau Moyen Age,* Paris: Gallimard, 1993; Max Singer and Aaron Wildavsky, *The Real World Order: Zones of Peace, Zones of Turmoil,* Chatham, NJ: Chatham House Publishers, Inc., 1993.

85. Charles B. Strozier, *Apocalypse: On the Psychology of Fundamentalism in America*, Boston, MA: Beacon Press, 1994, pp. 158–159.

86. Commission to Assess the Organization of the Federal Government to Combat the Proliferation of Weapons of Mass Destruction, also known as the Deutch Commission, *Combating Proliferation of Weapons of Mass Destruction*, Report Pursuant to Public Law 293, 104th Congress, Washington, DC, 1999.

87. National Commission on Terrorism, also known as the Bremer Commission, *Countering the Changing Threat of International Terrorism*, Report of the National Commission on Terrorism Pursuant to Public Law 277, 105th Congress, Washington, DC, 2000.

88. Advisory Panel to Assess Domestic Response Capabilities for Terrorism Involving Weapons of Mass Destruction, also known as the Gilmore Panel, Annual Reports to the President and the Congress, Washington, DC, 1999–2004.

89. Steven L. Salem, Kenneth A. Solomon, and Michael S. Yesley, *Issues and Problems in Inferring a Level of Acceptable Risk*, Santa Monica, CA: RAND Corporation, R-2561-DOE, 1980; also personal conversation with Kenneth Solomon.

90. Alexis de Tocqueville, *Democracy in America,* New York: Vintage Books, 1957.

91. Lynn Davis, Tom LaTourrette, David E. Mosher, Lois M. Davis, and David R. Howell, *Individual Preparedness and Response to Chemical,*

Radiological, Nuclear, and Biological Terrorist Attacks: A Quick Guide, Santa Monica, CA: RAND Corporation, MR-1731-SF, 2003.

92. R. S. Lazarus, "From Psychological Stress to the Emotions: A History of Changing Outlooks," *American Review of Psychology*, Vol. 44, 1993, pp. 1–21.

93. James Chow, James Chiesa, Paul Dreyer, Mel Eisman, Theodore W. Karasik, Joel Kvitky, Sherrill Lingel, David Ochmanek, and Chad Shirley, *Protecting Commercial Aviation Against the Shoulder-Fired Missile,* Santa Monica, CA: RAND Corporation, OP-106, 2005.

94. Lois M. Davis, K. Jack Riley, Greg Ridgeway, Jennifer E. Pace, Sarah K. Cotton, Paul Steinberg, Kelly Damphousse, and Brent L. Smith, *When Terrorism Hits Home; How Prepared Are State and Local Law Enforcement?* Santa Monica, CA: RAND Corporation, MG-104-MIPT, 2004.

95. K. Jack Riley, Gregory F. Treverton, Jeremy Wilson, and Lois M. Davis, *State and Local Intelligence in the War on Terrorism*, Santa Monica, CA: RAND Corporation, MG-394-RC, 2005.

96. These comments benefit from the author's conversations with Deputy Police Commissioner David Cohen, NYPD; Assistant Commissioner Larry Sanchez, NYPD; John Sullivan, Los Angeles Sheriff's Office; and Los Angeles City Councilman Jack Weiss.

97. For the debate on assassination, or the currently preferred "targeted killing" as an option, see Daniel Byman, "Targeted Killing, American Style," *Los Angeles Times*, January 20, 2006; Brian Michael Jenkins, *Should Our Arsenal Against Terrorism Include Assassination?* Santa Monica, CA: RAND Corporation, P-7303, January 1987; Abraham D. Sofaer, "Responses to Terrorism: Targeted Killing Is a Necessary Option," *San Francisco Chronicle,* March 6, 2004.

98. Abraham Lincoln, "Address Before the Young Men's Lyceum of Springfield, Illinois," January 27, 1838, http://www.everything2.com/index.pl?node id=931523.

99. Comments delivered during a panel discussion at the RAND Corporation, "43 Months Since 9/11: What Should Happen Next in the War on Terrorism?" on April 14, 2005, RAND/V-500.

100. Ruth Wedgwood and R. James Woolsey, "Law and Torture," *Wall Street Journal*, June 28, 2004, p. A10.

Index

About the Author

Brian Michael Jenkins is widely considered one of the world's foremost authorities on terrorism. He has advised government agencies, international organizations, and multinational corporations on terrorism, risk management, and sophisticated crime. Currently, he serves as senior advisor to the president of the RAND Corporation.

From 1989 to 1998, Jenkins was the deputy chairman of Kroll Associates, an international investigative and consulting firm. Before that, he was chairman of RAND's Political Science Department where, in 1972, he initiated RAND's terrorism research program in the wake of the terrorist attacks at the Munich Olympic Games.

Jenkins has a bachelor's degree in fine arts and a master's degree in history, both from the University of California at Los Angeles. He studied at the University of Guanajuato in Mexico and in the Department of Humanities at the University of San Carlos in Guatemala, where he was a Fulbright fellow and recipient of a second fellowship from the Organization of American States.

Commissioned in the infantry at the age of 19, Jenkins became a paratrooper and ultimately a captain of the U.S. Army's elite Special Forces, also known as the Green Berets. He is a decorated combat veteran, having served in the Seventh Special Forces Group in the Dominican Republic during the American intervention and later as a member of the Fifth Special Forces Group in Vietnam (1966–1967). He returned to Vietnam on a special assignment in 1968 to serve as a member of the Long Range Planning Task Group; he remained with the group until the end of 1969, receiving the U.S. Department of the Army's highest award for his service. Jenkins returned to Vietnam on a third special assignment in 1971.

In 1996, President Bill Clinton appointed Jenkins to be a member of the White House Commission on Aviation Safety and Security. From 1999 to 2000, he served as an advisor to the National Commission on Terrorism, and in 2000 he was appointed as a member of the U.S. Comptroller General's Advisory Board. He is a special advisor to the International Chamber of Commerce (ICC), a member of the board of directors of the ICC's Commercial Crime Services, and director of the National Transportation Security Center at the Mineta Transportation Institute at San Jose State University.

In 2004, the Club of Madrid appointed Jenkins to lead its international working group on the role of intelligence. He has also advised numerous government agencies, foreign governments, private corporations, the Catholic Church, the Church of England, and other international organizations as an analyst, investigator, and crisis management consultant.

Jenkins is author, coauthor, or editor of numerous books and articles, including *International Terrorism: A New Mode of Conflict* (Crescent Publications, 1975), *The Fall of South Vietnam* (RAND, 1978), *Terrorism and Personal Protection* (Butterworth-Heinemann, 1984), *Countering the New Terrorism* (RAND, 1999), *Deterrence and Influence in Counterterrorism: A Component in the War on al Qaeda* (RAND, 2002), *Countering al Qaeda: An Appreciation of the Situation and Suggestions for Strategy* (RAND, 2002), and *Aviation Terrorism and Security* (Frank Cass, 2nd ed., 2006), among others.

Related Titles by the Author

Countering al Qaeda: An Appreciation of the Situation and Suggestions for Strategy

Brian Michael Jenkins

This monograph reviews the U.S. war on terrorism one year after the attacks of Sept. 11, 2001, and discusses the state of al Qaeda and the actions that can be expected of it. Because al Qaeda constitutes the most serious immediate threat to the security of the United States, it is imperative that the campaign against terrorism remain focused and pragmatic. This monograph outlines the essential, central elements that must be emphasized in this campaign, the ultimate aim of which is the destruction of a terrorist enterprise that threatens American security and, by extension, the security of the world.

42 pp. • 2002 • ISBN 0-8330-3264-X • $15 • paper

Deterrence and Influence in Counterterrorism: A Component in the War on al Qaeda

Paul K. Davis, Brian Michael Jenkins

While deterrence of terrorism may at first glance seem to be an unrealistic goal, it may be possible to influence some members of terrorist groups and to deter their supporters. The U.S. strategy should comprise not only carrying out military attacks but also engaging in political warfare, placing at risk the things that terrorists hold dear, directing a credible threat of force against any state or group that supports the terrorist acquisition of weapons of mass destruction, and maintaining cooperation with other nations. At the same time, the strategy must preserve core American values, upholding discriminate use of force and ensuring due process in the provision of speedy justice.

106 pp. • 2002 • ISBN 0-8330-3286-0 • $20 • paper